writing SKILLS

TOWARDS ACADEMIC WRITING

Contents

Writing Sentences	8
Writing Paragraphs	107
Writing Essays	211

DOROTHY E ZEMACH

writing
SENTENCES
THE BASICS OF WRITING

Contents

Introduction
    To the teacher vi
    To the student vii

1 I go to an unusual school   8
- Basic parts of speech: nouns, pronouns, and verbs
- Definition of a sentence

2 Funny stories   16
- Basic parts of speech: prepositions, adjectives, and adverbs
- Reviewing the parts of speech

3 I'm from Bangkok   23
- Vocabulary to talk about your country and city
- Subject / verb agreement with the *be* verb
- Three sentence patterns with the *be* verb
- Adding details to a sentence with adverbs of time

4 She seems lonely   31
- Vocabulary to describe people and their feelings
- Sentence pattern for stative verbs (*seems, looks*)
- New sentence pattern for the *be* verb: *There is / There are*
- Expanding sentences with adverb phrases of location (*in the corner, at the back*)

5 She has brown eyes   39
- Vocabulary to describe animals and people
- Sentence pattern for the *have* verb
- Using *a* and *an*
- Describing people with *be* and *have*

6 I like playing soccer   46
- Vocabulary to talk about hobbies and interests
- Sentence pattern for action verbs
- Combining words with *and, or,* and *but*
- Using gerunds

7 Faded jeans are cool — 54
- Vocabulary for describing clothing and fashion
- Subject and object pronouns
- Combining sentences with *and*, *but*, *or*, and *so*
- Putting two or three adjectives in the correct order

8 I'm a business major — 62
- Vocabulary for school subjects
- The simple present and present progressive tenses
- Adverbs and expressions of frequency
- Format of a paragraph

9 I'm in Barcelona — 70
- Irregular past tense verbs
- Sentences with indirect objects
- Format of a postcard and an email
- Formal and informal language
- Using questions and exclamations

10 It's a kind of French game — 77
- Vocabulary to describe popular international items
- Passive sentences
- The topic sentence, supporting sentences, and the concluding sentence

11 It has great graphics — 85
- Vocabulary to describe popular media
- Supporting sentences and concluding sentences
- Strengthening and weakening adjectives
- *Too* and *not ... enough*

12 I've never been to Australia — 93
- Vocabulary for writing about travel and experiences
- The present perfect tense
- Contrasting the present perfect and the simple past
- Using *However* in a paragraph

Additional materials — 100
- Key sentence patterns
- Verb patterns
- *Can*
- Common irregular verbs

To the Teacher

Writing is an important form of communication in day-to-day life, but it is especially important in high school and college. Indeed, almost all other subjects, from the social sciences to the hard sciences, require students to demonstrate their knowledge and opinions in writing.

Young adults who are beginning writers in a second language face the challenge of wishing to express sophisticated and relevant ideas with limited vocabulary and grammatical structures.

Writing Sentences is designed to help beginning students express their ideas clearly and accurately by teaching the most common sentence patterns and verb tenses in English. Students read sample texts to discover the target structures, which are then summarized in clear charts. Students move from tightly controlled practices to freer exercises until they can successfully write accurate sentences. As the book progresses, students learn to link words, phrases, and then sentences to create longer texts.

Units are organized around an interesting theme to engage your students. Relevant vocabulary is used both in the model writing and the students' own writing. The structures and grammar are practiced in a variety of ways, and each sentence in every exercise is linked to the unit theme. Usually the sentences in an exercise form a cohesive text, so that students are working with the content of a paragraph (with a topic sentence and supporting ideas) even when they are focusing on individual sentences. Thus even sentence-level work on grammar guides students to becoming fluent writers in English. The final three units of *Writing Sentences* specifically address paragraphs and introduce the concepts of topic sentences, supporting sentences, and concluding sentences.

Each unit ends with a writing activity that summarizes the material in the unit. Students combine the sentence patterns, vocabulary, and grammar they have learned in a creative, engaging task. The activities take students through the traditional writing process: They brainstorm ideas, organize them with the provided graphic organizers, write their texts, and then share them with other students and comment on one another's writing.

An appendix in the back of *Writing Sentences* summarizes the sentence patterns, provides additional verb charts, and lists irregular past tense verb forms and participles for easy reference. The Teacher's Guide supports the instructor by offering teaching suggestions, a discussion of marking and grading writing, suggestions for writing journals, ideas for supplemental activities for each unit, and answers to exercises in the Student's Book.

Learning to write well takes practice and patience. Students need clear guidance and support, positive feedback, and interesting ideas to write about. I hope this book provides this for your students and that you enjoy teaching from it.

To the Student

Writing is a very important part of your school and university study. You explain your ideas and show your opinions in writing in almost every class you take. Clear writing helps you communicate clearly, and even helps you think clearly.

Writing Sentences will help you write interesting, accurate sentences that express your ideas. You will study vocabulary, spelling, and grammar, and you will have many chances to practice what you learn. You will learn to write several sentences on the same topic in a unified paragraph. You can choose what to write about and what words to use, and you will even have the chance to "play" with language in a creative and enjoyable way.

As you progress though the course, you will have many chances to read example sentences and paragraphs from this book and from your classmates, and you will share your writing with them. You will learn how important the reader is to the writer, and how to express clearly and directly what you mean to communicate. I hope that what you learn in this course will help you throughout your academic studies and beyond.

You should come to your writing class every day with ideas and energy. Your instructor and classmates have much to share with you, and you have much to share with them. By asking questions, taking chances, trying new ways, and expressing your ideas in another language, you will add to your own world and the world of those around you. Good luck!

Dorothy E Zemach

1 I go to an unusual school

In this unit, you will ...
- learn and practice some basic parts of speech: nouns, pronouns, and verbs
- learn what a sentence is

This is not a grammar book; this is a writing book. However, if you know some basic grammar terms, you can learn how to write correct and interesting sentences more easily.

Nouns

A **noun** names something:
- a person or animal *(student, Ms. Clark, cats)*
- a place *(park, Taipei, classroom)*
- a thing *(chair, book, computers)*
- an idea *(love, education, friendship)*

Writers use nouns to identify what they are writing about.

1 Work with a partner. Look at the word web below. Add more nouns in the correct circles. Can you add more circles?

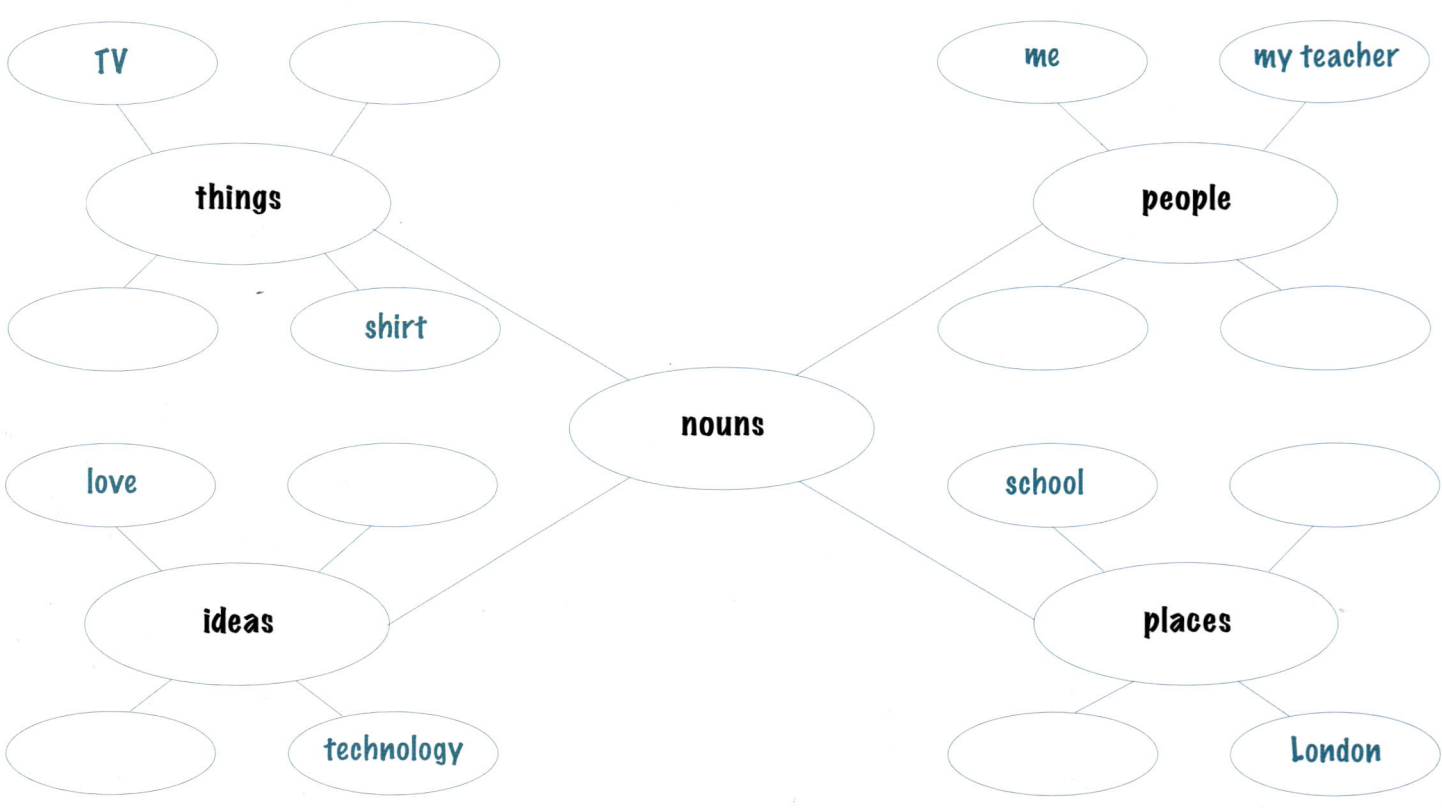

Pronouns

Pronouns *(I, you, she, it, them, there, etc.)* are words that replace nouns. They are used like nouns.

The **book** *is difficult.* (book = noun)

It *is difficult.* (it = pronoun; means the same as *book*)

Writers use pronouns so we do not need to use nouns again and again.

For example, the paragraph below is difficult to read and difficult to understand:

> *I go to an unusual high school in Vermont. The unusual high school in Vermont is for skiers. The other students and I take regular classes like math, English, and history. The other students and I also practice ski racing. The other students and I learn from our ski coaches. Our ski coaches teach the other students and me how to race faster. Our ski coaches train the other students and me hard. Studying and training at the same time is difficult, but the other students and I like studying and training at the same time.*

With pronouns, it's easier to read and understand:

> *I go to an unusual high school in Vermont.* **It** *is for skiers. The other students and I take regular classes like math, English, and history.* **We** *also practice ski racing.* **We** *learn from our ski coaches.* **They** *teach* **us** *how to race faster.* **They** *train* **us** *hard. Studying and training at the same time is difficult, but* **we** *like* **it**.

1 Writing Sentences

2 Look back at the second paragraph about the high school on page 9. What do the pronouns replace? Write the group of words.

a. **It** is for skiers.

   It = *The unusual high school in Vermont* ....

b. **We** also practice ski racing.

   We = ...

c. **They** teach **us** how to race faster.

   They = ...

   us = ...

d. Studying and training at the same time is difficult, but **we** like **it**.

   we = ...

   it = ...

3 Read the sentences. Write the second sentence again. Replace the underlined nouns with pronouns. Use the words in the box below. Each word is used once.

| her | his | ✓ it | she | them | they |

a. LaGuardia High School is in New York. <u>LaGuardia High School</u> is a special school.
   It is a special school. ....

b. Students at LaGuardia High School want to be performers. <u>Students at LaGuardia High School</u> take classes in music, art, dance, or theater.
   ....

c. English, math, history, and science classes are also required at LaGuardia. All LaGuardia students must take <u>English, math, history, and science classes</u>.
   ....

d. Jennifer Aniston went to LaGuardia High School. Now <u>Jennifer Aniston</u> is a famous actress, and many people know <u>Jennifer Aniston</u>.
   ....

e. Al Pacino is another famous actor from LaGuardia High School. Have you seen one of <u>Al Pacino's</u> movies?
   ....
   ....

 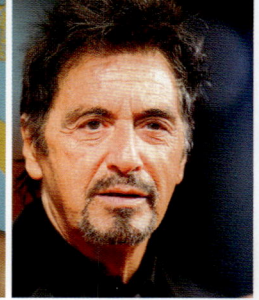

Jennifer Aniston   Al Pacino

10   I GO TO AN UNUSUAL SCHOOL

Writing Sentences

Verbs

Writers use *verbs* to tell about the action in the sentence:

He *studies*.

They *played* soccer.

She is *taking* a test.

or someone's condition or feeling:

He *seems* bored.

I *feel* happy.

She *looks* worried.

See how the verbs change to match who does the action and when the action happens:

Who	I **play** soccer. Hamid **plays** soccer. My friends and I **play** soccer.
When	I **play** soccer every day. I am **playing** soccer now. Hamid **played** soccer yesterday. Maria **has played** professional soccer for six years. My friends and I **will play** soccer tomorrow. Our team **play** soccer last week.

4 Read the story. <u>Underline</u> the verbs.

> It **was** a beautiful spring day. Two university students skipped class and went to the park instead. They missed a test in class. The next day, they spoke to their teacher. "We wanted to come to class. Unfortunately, when we were driving to class, we got a flat tire. So we couldn't come to class. We are very sorry."
>
> "That is OK," their teacher said. "You can take the test now." The boys sat down, and the teacher gave them a piece of paper. "Here is the first question," she said.
>
> "Which tire was flat?"

I GO TO AN UNUSUAL SCHOOL

1 Writing Sentences

Sentences

A sentence in English has a **subject** and a **verb**. The subject is a noun.

subject	verb
Students	learn.
The **students**	learn English.
The older **students**	learn computer science.
The **students** in our school	learn in the evening.
The best **students** in the school	usually learn quickly.

A sentence begins with a capital letter and ends with a period:
The students in our class are learning English now.
It's important to know the subject and the verb in the sentence to make sure they **agree**:

- ✗ The student learn.
- ✓ The student learns.
- ✗ The students learns.
- ✓ The students learn.
- ✗ The students go to school yesterday.
- ✓ The students went to school yesterday.
- ✗ We had a test tomorrow.
- ✓ We will have a test tomorrow.

5 Read the groups of words. Are they a sentence? Is there a subject and a verb? If yes, write the sentence again with a capital letter and a period. If no, cross them out.

a. some schools are a lot of fun *Some schools are a lot of fun.*
b. for example clown school ....
c. you learn how to make people laugh ....
d. for both children and adults ....
e. clowns take classes in acting ....
f. makeup, juggling, and making costumes ....
g. they also business classes ....
h. it isn't easy to be a clown ....
i. many clowns work in circuses ....

12 I GO TO AN UNUSUAL SCHOOL

Writing Sentences

6 Read about Hometown, USA. In each sentence, underline the subject once and the verb twice.

> **Hometown, USA** **is** a summer camp. This camp is in Minnesota. Children from many countries come there. They study English during the summer. The campers sing songs in English. They speak English to their friends. They play popular American sports. The food is American food. The campers learn a lot of English. They also learn a lot of American culture.

7 Read the sentences. Underline the subject once and the verb twice. The verbs do not agree. Write the sentences again and change the verbs.

a. American students can studies a foreign language too.

American students can study a foreign language too.

b. One language camp teach Japanese.

....

c. Its name are *Mori no Ike*.

....

d. That mean "lake of the woods."

....

e. American high school students learns Japanese language and culture.

....

f. I wanted to go to *Mori no Ike* next summer.

....

g. Students from all over the U.S. comes to study there.

....

I GO TO AN UNUSUAL SCHOOL

1 Writing Sentences

Marking nouns

Here are some words that often come before a noun:

a or an
the
this / that
these / those

- Use **an** before a vowel sound (a, e, i, o, u).
- Use **a** before words that start with consonant sounds (for example: b, d, k, m, s, t). Remember that in English, the consonant **h** is sometimes silent, so words like **hour** start with a vowel sound.
- **A**, **an**, **this**, and **that** are used before singular nouns.
- **These** and **those** are used before plural nouns.
- **The** is used before singular and plural nouns.
- An adjective can come between the noun marker and the noun:

    A large school   This unusual school.

8 Circle the correct word. Then <u>underline</u> the noun that comes after it.

a. My cousin is going to (**a** / an) <u>school</u> in Switzerland.
b. It's (**a** / an) hotel <u>school</u>.
c. (This / These) <u>school</u> teaches students about (the / those) hotel <u>business</u>.
d. It's (a / **an**) expensive <u>school</u>, but he likes it.
e. Two years ago, he went to (a / **an**) art <u>school</u>.
f. He didn't like (that / **those**) <u>classes</u>.
g. (This / **These**) <u>days</u>, he enjoys (a / **the**) <u>classes</u> at his school.

Spelling review

9 Look at these nouns and verbs about studying and learning. They are spelled incorrectly. Write them correctly.

nouns		verbs	
skool	*school*	lern	learn
clasroom	classroom	teatch	teacher
studant	student	is studing	is studying
techer	teacher	skiped	skiped
Inglish	English	sed	send
coach	Coach	trane	train

14 I GO TO AN UNUSUAL SCHOOL

Writing Sentences

Put it together: Sentence chains

a Work with a partner or small group. Look at the chart below. Add some more words.

●	★	●	★	●	★	★
The	crazy	coach	happily	kicked the ball	after school	again.
A	lazy	man	quickly	played the violin	in the classroom	all day.
This	sad	student	slowly	read a book	in the snow	at 6:00.
My	strange	teacher	carefully	sang a song	on the bus	in the morning.
Our	young	woman	loudly	told a joke	under the table	last week.

b On a separate piece of paper, each student writes a sentence with a group of words from each ■ column.

The man sang a song.

c Pass the paper to another student and read the paper passed to you. Write the sentence again, but add one group of words from a ★ column.

The man loudly sang a song.

d Repeat three more times, until the sentence has a group of words from each column.

The crazy man loudly sang a song on the bus last week.

e Share your favorite sentences with the class.

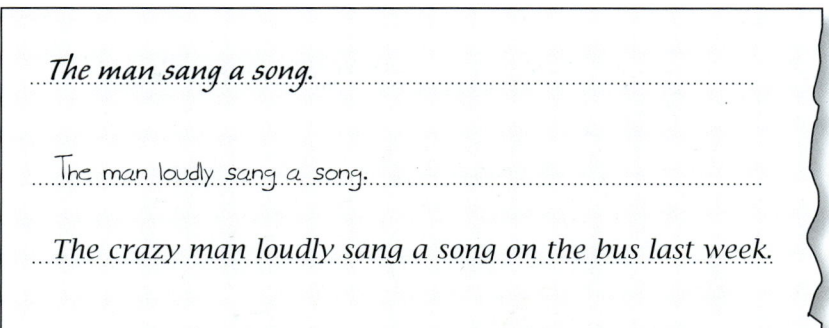

I GO TO AN UNUSUAL SCHOOL

2 Funny stories

In this unit, you will …

■ learn and practice more basic parts of speech: prepositions, adjectives, and adverbs

■ review the parts of speech

Writers use prepositions, adjectives, and adverbs to make their sentences longer. These words give more information about the subject and the verb.

Prepositions

Prepositions are short words (*at, on, for*) that connect ideas. They tell about time, location, or purpose (reason):

We eat dinner **at** seven o'clock.	time ✓
My book is **on** the desk.	location ✓
She bought a gift **for** her friend.	purpose ✓

A **prepositional phrase** includes a **preposition** and a **noun**:

We eat dinner **at** <u>seven o'clock</u>.

My book is **on** <u>the desk</u>.

She bought a gift **for** <u>her friend</u>

Writers use prepositional phrases to give more information:

16 FUNNY STORIES

Writing Sentences

1 Work with a partner. Complete the story by writing the prepositional phrase from the box in the correct place.

✓down the street	in the afternoon	to the zoo
in his car	to the movies	to the zoo
		with this kangaroo

A man was walking ...*down the street*... . Suddenly, he saw a kangaroo! He asked a police officer, "What should I do?" ....

"Take him .... ," said the police officer.

"OK," said the man.

The police officer saw the man again .... The kangaroo was ....

"I told you to take the kangaroo .... !" said the surprised police officer.

"I did," said the man. "We had a wonderful time! Now I'm taking him ...."

2 Work with a partner. Write the story in exercise 1 again. Change the prepositional phrases if you can. Practice reading your new story a few times. Then read it to another pair.

....

....

....

....

....

....

FUNNY STORIES

2 Writing Sentences

Adjectives

An **adjective** gives more information about a noun. It answers the question *What kind of?* or *Which?*

*The **red** cell phone is mine.*   [Which cell phone is yours?]

*Her jacket is **leather**.*   [What kind of jacket does she have?]

Adjectives are important to writers because they help the reader to imagine or "see" what you are describing.

3 Read the sentences. Underline the adjectives. Then draw an arrow to show which noun or pronoun they describe.

a. On a dark night, a man was looking for something in the tall grass under a streetlight.

b. A young woman saw the man. She asked him, "Did you lose something?"

c. "Yes," said the man. I lost my new watch. It's gold."

d. "Oh," said the woman. "That's terrible. Where did you lose it?"

e. "Over there by that big tree," said the man.

f. The woman was surprised. "Then why are you looking over here?" she asked.

g. "Because it's too dark over there," said the man. "The light is great here."

4 Check (✓) the pictures that go with the story in exercise 3.

18   FUNNY STORIES

Writing Sentences 2

Adverbs

An **adverb** gives more information about the verb. It can answer the questions:

Where • When • How • For how long • How often • Why?

It rained **yesterday**.	[**When** did it rain?]
She eats **slowly**.	[**How** does she eat?]
I **sometimes** play tennis.	[**How often** do you play tennis?]

Writers use adverbs to tell their stories. Adverbs help readers imagine how events happened.

5 Read the sentences from a story. Circle the verbs and <u>underline</u> the adverbs. Then draw an arrow to the verbs they describe.

a. A new mother was walking slowly down the street.
b. "You are talking calmly and gently to your baby."
c. A man was watching the woman carefully. "Good for you," he said kindly.
d. "Oh, no," replied the woman sadly. "Her name is Anne. My name is Gloria."
e. The baby inside was crying loudly.
f. She was carefully pushing a stroller.
g. He looked at the baby and asked politely, "Is the baby's name Gloria?"
h. "Please, Gloria," said the woman quietly. "Relax. Don't cry, Gloria!"

6 Now put the sentences in exercise 5 in order. Then write the story on a separate sheet of paper.

The New Mother

A new mother was walking slowly down the street. She …

FUNNY STORIES

2 Writing Sentences

Recognizing parts of speech

Some parts of speech in English have special endings. Here are some examples:

nouns	verbs	adjectives	adverbs
~er, ~or teacher, doctor	is/are + ~ing is talking, is going	~y happy, funny	~ly happily, quickly
~ist scientist, chemist	~ed used, worked	~ive active	~ward forward, backward
~tion action, nation		~ic scientific, terrific	
~ment development, government		~ful useful, careful	

7 Read the sentences. Circle the correct word.

When Americans first sent astronauts up into space, they (discovered / discovery) that ballpoint pens did not (working / work). So, American (scientific / scientists) spent ten (years / yearly) and 12 billion dollars to (develop / development) a new pen. The (new / newly) pen could write upside down, under water, on (glass / glassy), and in temperatures from -5 to 300°C. The Russians (useful / used) a pencil.

Spelling review

8 Work with a partner. Circle the correct spelling for each word. Then write the words in the correct place in the chart.

(loudly) / lowdly	replyed / replied	terrible / terible	usful / useful
offiser / officer	sceintist / scientist	their / thier	with / whith
quietly / quitely	seid / said	undre / under	youre / your

nouns	pronouns	verbs	prepositions	adjectives	adverbs
					loudly

20 FUNNY STORIES

Put it together: Grammar game pairwork

a You are going to play a grammar game! Work with a partner. Student A, stay on this page. Student B, go to page 22.

Student A

1. Look at the paragraph below. Some words are missing. Ask your partner to give you the missing words. Do NOT read the paragraph to your partner! Just ask for the words.

   For example, say *Please tell me a noun.*

2. Write the noun that your partner tells you on the line.
3. When you are finished writing every word, read the paragraph to your partner.
4. Then your partner will ask you to give some parts of speech.

Have fun!

My Favorite Sport

My favorite sport is soccer. In England, it's called

_____ (noun). It's a / an _____ (adjective) sport to learn, and

it's _____ (adjective), too. You _____ (verb) soccer with a _____ (adjective)

white and black _____ (noun). You also have to wear _____ (adjective)

shoes. You have to run _____ (adverb) and kick _____ (adverb) to be a

good soccer _____ (noun). I used to _____ (verb) soccer in high

school. I wasn't a very _____ (adjective) player at first, but later I was

the _____ (noun) of the team!

Someday I hope to play as _____ (adverb) as _____ (noun: a person's name).

He / She _____ (verb) soccer on a / an _____ (adjective) team.

---

b Share your funny stories with another pair of students.

2 Writing Sentences

Student B

(Student A, go to page 21.)

1. First, your partner will ask you for some parts of speech.

   For example, your partner will say, *Please tell me a noun*. Say any noun that you want—for example, *cat, winter, dentist*.

2. Your partner will write your answers into a paragraph. When you are finished, your partner will read the paragraph to you.

3. Now, it's your turn. Look at the paragraph below. Some words are missing. Ask your partner to give you the missing words. Do NOT read the paragraph to your partner! Just ask for the words.

   For example, say *Please tell me a noun that is a place*.

4. Write the place that your partner tells you on the line.

5. When you are finished writing every word, read the paragraph to your partner.

Have fun!

A Postcard from _____
                               (noun - a place)

Dear _____,
      (your partner's name)

Hi! How are you? I'm having a _____ time on vacation. I'm
                               (adjective)
here with my _____ and my _____. Every day we go to the
              (noun)   (noun)
_____ and _____. I'm taking _____ lessons, and now I
 (noun)   (verb)   (noun)
can _____ very _____. For lunch, we go to a local _____
     (verb)   (adverb)
and eat delicious _____. Last night, we went to
                   (noun)   (noun – plural)
a / an _____ dance show. The dancers were all _____ and
        (adjective)   (adjective)
they danced _____.
             (adverb)
I'll see you _____.
              (adverb)
Your friend,

_____
(your teacher's name)

---

b Share your funny stories with another pair of students.

22 FUNNY STORIES

3 I'm from Bangkok

In this unit, you will …
- learn some vocabulary to talk about your country and city
- learn subject/verb agreement with the *be* verb
- learn three sentence patterns with the *be* verb
- learn how to add details to a sentence with adverbs of time

1 Work with a partner. Look at the map of Thailand. Label the map with the words below.

capital	mountains	northwest	river	southwest
coast	northeast	southeast	south	west

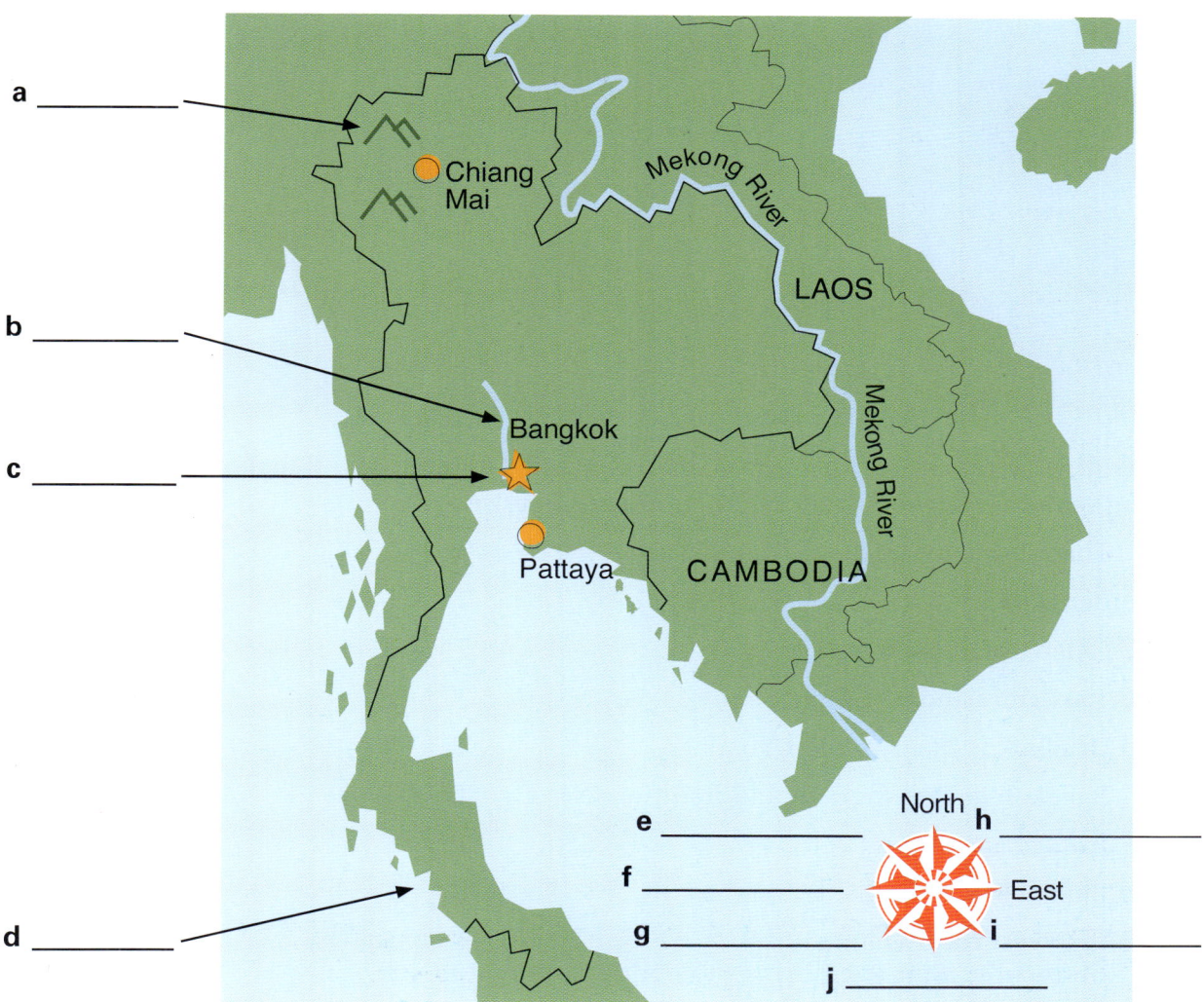

3

Writing Sentences

2 Work with a partner. Look at the pictures of Bangkok. Write a or b next to the words that describe the picture.

__ boring	__ busy	__ small
__ modern	__ international	__ crowded
__ exciting	__ rural	__ quiet
__ traditional	__ peaceful	__ colorful

3 Work with a partner. Read the sentences about Thailand and Bangkok. Circle T if the sentence is true. Circle F if the sentence is false.

a. Thailand is in Asia.   (T)   F

b. Bangkok is quiet.   T   F

c. Chiang Mai is a river.   T   F

d. Thailand is next to Cambodia.   T   F

e. Bangkok is the capital of Thailand.   T   F

f. Bangkok is both modern and traditional.   T   F

g. Pattaya is a city.   T   F

h. Chiang Mai is in the mountains.   T   F

i. The west coast is long.   T   F

j. Laos is northeast of Thailand.   T   F

Writing Sentences

The *be* verb

Look at the chart below.

subject (noun / pronoun)	verb	noun, adjective, or adverb phrase
I	am	Thai.
	am not	Chinese.
You	are	at home.
	are not	at work.
Mr. Martin / He	is	a teacher.
	is not	a doctor.
Ms. Tagawa / She	is	in Chiang Mai.
	is not	in the south.
My friends and I / We	are	at the beach.
	are not	in the mountains.
The streets / They	are	noisy.
	are not	quiet.

Note: In English, *you* can be used for one person or a group of people:
You are my teacher. (*you* = one person)
You are great students! (*you* = many people)

4 Fill in the blanks below with *am*, *is*, or *are*.

a. I .... from Chiang Mai.

b. Chiang Mai .... a city in the north of Thailand.

c. It .... not the capital, but it .... a large city.

d. It .... a modern city, and it .... popular with international tourists.

e. The weather .... nice, the people .... friendly, and the mountains .... beautiful.

f. I .... proud of my hometown, Chiang Mai.

I'M FROM BANGKOK   25

Writing Sentences

Sentence patterns with the <u>be</u> verb

Most sentences with a *be* verb include something else after the verb.

- Some have a **noun** or **noun phrase**. These give another word that means the same thing as the subject. They answer the question *Who or what is (the subject)?*

    *Sunee is **my friend**.* (Who is Sunee?)

    *The Mekong is **a river**.* (What is the Mekong?)

- Some have an **adjective** or **adjective phrase**. These tell what the person or thing is like. They answer the question *What was (the subject) like?*

    *The mountains are **high**.* (What are the mountains like?)

    *Chiang Mai is **busy** and **exciting**.*

- Some have a **prepositional phrase** that gives a **location** (place). These answer the question *Where (is the subject)?* Sentences can have more than one prepositional phrase. These are adverb phrases.

    *Phuket is **on the coast**.* (Where is Phuket?)

    Phuket is <u>on the coast</u> <u>of Thailand</u> <u>in Southeast Asia</u>.
                  1   2   3

Writing Sentences 3

5 Look back at exercise 3 on page 24. Copy the true sentences with the *be* verb into the right places here:

Followed by a noun:

a. ....

b. ....

Followed by an adjective:

c. ....

d. ....

Followed by a prepositional phrase (location):

e. ....

f. ....

6 Look at the false sentences on page 24. Change them to true sentences. Then compare your sentences with a partner.

a. *Bangkok is not quiet. Or, Bangkok is noisy.* ....

b. ....

c. ....

7 Complete the sentences about your country. Then read your sentences to a partner or small group.

a. I am from .... (*country*)

b. .... is the capital city.

c. My city is .... and ....

d. My city is not ....

e. The people are ....

I'M FROM BANGKOK 27

3 Writing Sentences

Adding more information

Look at these sentences:

The weather is beautiful.
The weather is beautiful **every day.**
The weather is beautiful **in the spring.**
The streets are quiet.
The streets are quiet **now.**
The streets are quiet **in the evening.**

The second and third sentences in each group give more information by adding an adverb or adverb phrase of time.

8 Unscramble the sentences. Add the correct form of the *be* verb. Put the adverbs and adverb phrases of time in the correct places.

a. The streets of Bangkok / in the morning / very busy

The streets of Bangkok are very busy in the morning.

b. The city / cold / in the winter

....

c. after school / The children / noisy

....

d. The restaurants / late at night / open

....

e. excited / before the holidays / Many people

....

f. in June and July / very rainy / Chiang Mai

....

9 Look back at the last three sentences of exercise 7. Write the sentences again. Add some adverbs and adverb phrases of time. Then share your new sentences with a partner or small group.

a. ....

b. ....

c. ....

Writing Sentences

Spelling review

10 Write the words that describe the pictures. Then find them in the word search below.

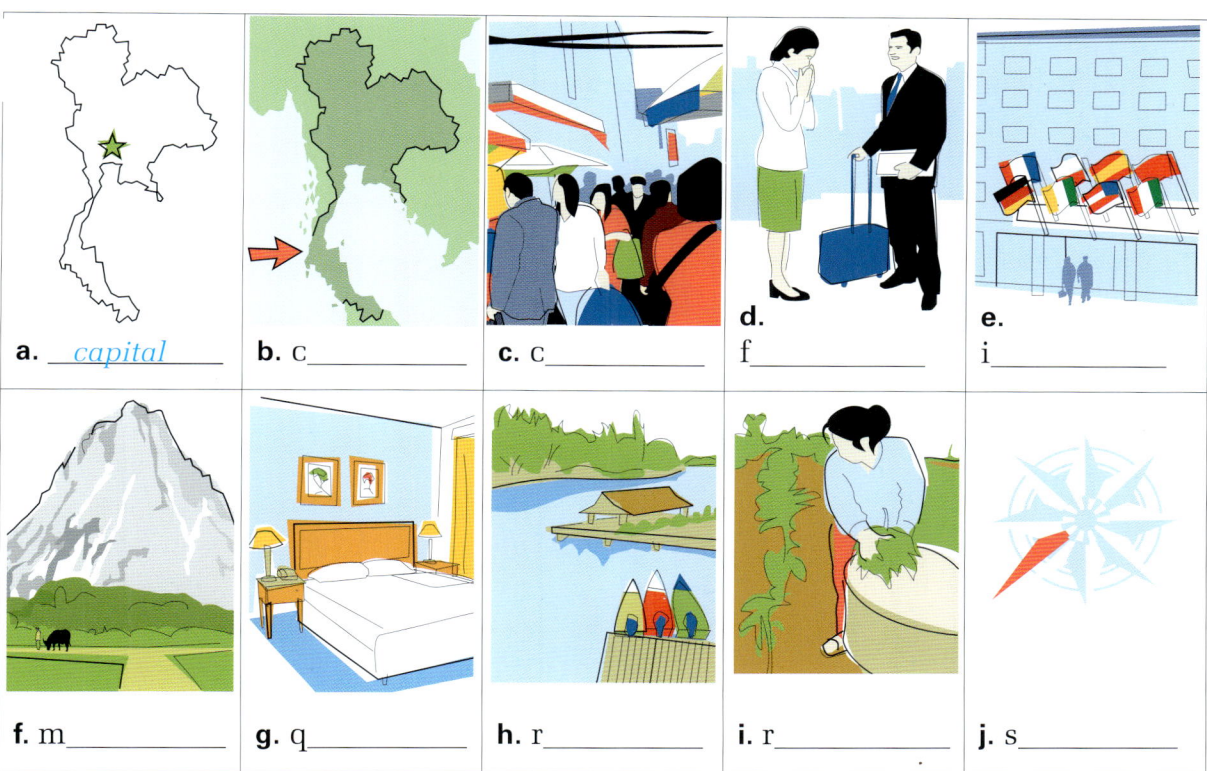

a. _capital_
b. c_____
c. c_____
d. f_____
e. i_____
f. m_____
g. q_____
h. r_____
i. r_____
j. s_____

a	h	y	i	v	c	r	o	w	d	e	d	t
m	o	u	n	t	a	i	n	b	b	k	a	e
b	u	k	a	k	e	q	w	n	g	h	k	r
x	d	s	f	b	m	m	c	v	q	t	e	u
t	c	o	a	s	t	s	f	h	v	w	h	r
j	j	u	e	z	x	c	j	h	t	k	x	a
i	n	t	e	r	n	a	t	i	o	n	a	l
q	e	h	t	u	u	p	o	t	d	f	j	v
d	r	w	t	q	u	i	e	t	x	z	q	m
g	k	e	s	t	a	t	g	b	z	x	n	v
q	x	s	v	a	n	a	j	r	i	v	e	r
l	p	t	h	e	o	l	x	r	e	c	t	m
f	r	i	e	n	d	l	y	d	l	u	o	m

I'M FROM BANGKOK 29

3

Writing Sentences

Put it together: <u>I am from</u> poem

Where are you from? Of course, you are from a city and a country. But you are also "from" your family, your childhood, your activities, your memories, and your values—the ideas that are important to you.

a Complete this chart. Write two or three nouns in each space.

hobbies or interests:	things in your house:	things or places in your neighborhood:
names of friends and relatives:	food or dishes you ate when you were a child:	family vacations, trips, or holidays:
sports, activities, or games you play:	favorite school subjects or clubs:	favorite TV shows, movies, books, or music:
your hometown or places you have lived:	special family customs:	family values (example: *love, truth, home*):

b Read this poem by a Thai student.

I am from volleyball, bicycling, and tennis,
And I am from mango and sticky rice, and my mother's green curry.
I am from temples, markets, and the river,
And I am from shopping with my friends and eating noodles late at night.
I am from my king, my parents, and my teachers,
And I am from water festivals, flowers, and smiles.
I am from pop music CDs and traditional dance lessons,
And I am from beach vacations and working in the city.
I am from Bangkok, and I am from Thailand,
But most of all, I am from love.

c Now use the ideas in the chart to write your poem. Begin every line with *I am from*. Use a separate sheet of paper.

d Share your poem with a small group or the whole class.

30 I'M FROM BANGKOK

4 She seems lonely

In this unit, you will ...
- learn vocabulary to describe people and their feelings
- learn a sentence pattern for stative verbs (*seems*, *looks*)
- learn a new sentence pattern for the be verb: *There is / There are*
- expand sentences with adverb phrases of location (*in the corner, at the back*)

1 Work with a partner. Look at the people below. Complete the sentences using adjectives from the box.

| cheerful | energetic | entertained | relaxed | ✓shy |

a. 1 She *is shy*.
   2 *She is not* .... outgoing.

b. 1 They ....
   2 .... lazy.

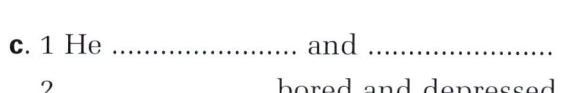

c. 1 He .... and ....
   2 .... bored and depressed.

d. 1 He .... tense.
   2 ....

4 Writing Sentences

2 Work with a partner. Look at the picture of the woman below. Talk about her and complete the chart.

Her job:	Her nationality: ....
Her age:	Her feelings now: ....

3 Now share your guesses with another pair, like this:

We think she's a student. What do you think?

4 Work with a partner. Read the sentences about the woman in exercise 2. Circle A if you agree the sentence is true. Circle D if you disagree.

a.	She seems lonely.	A	D
b.	She looks poor.	A	D
c.	I think she is unhappy.	A	D
d.	She seems healthy.	A	D
e.	She looks pretty.	A	D
f.	Maybe she is shy.	A	D

32   SHE SEEMS LONELY

Stative verbs

Stative verbs:

- describe a condition or situation that exists
- do not show actions
- are followed by adjectives

  She **seems** shy. = stative ("shy" is a condition; it is also an adjective)

  You **don't look** happy.

noun or pronoun	stative verb	adjective
I You We They	seem don't seem	friendly. shy. happy.
He She	looks doesn't look	sad.

Some common stative verbs are *be, believe, have, know, like, think*.

Note: Stative verbs do not usually take the continuous tense:
RIGHT: *She seems happy.*
WRONG: *She is seeming happy.*

Sentence patterns with stative verbs

Look at these sentences from exercise 4 on page 32:

  She **seems** lonely.

  She **looks** poor.

The verbs *look* and *seem* show that the writer is not sure about the truth, but is just guessing.

Two sentences use the verb *be*. The writer shows that he or she is just guessing by beginning the sentences with *I think* and *Maybe*:

  I think she is unhappy.

  Maybe she is shy.

4 Writing Sentences

5 Write the sentences from exercise 4 again. Change the sentences with *look* and *seem* to use the verb *be*. Begin with *I think* or *Maybe*.

a. ....

b. ....

c. ....

d. ....

Now change the sentences with *be* to use *looks* or *seems*.

e. ....

f. ....

6 Look at the photo with a partner. Talk about what you see. Then complete the sentences with your own ideas. Read your sentences to another pair of students.

a. I think this man is a ....

b. He is .... and ....

c. He looks ....

d. Maybe he is ....

e. He seems ....

f. He doesn't look ....

34 SHE SEEMS LONELY

Writing Sentences

There is / There are

	verb	noun	prepositional phrase of location
There	is	a little girl	on the bus.
	isn't	a secretary	in the office.
There	are	(some) girls	in the apartment.
	aren't	any men	in my class.

There + be shows that something exists: a thing (*a house, a cat, an elevator*) or an idea (*trouble, a thought*).

Usually we give more information by adding an adverb or prepositional phrase that shows a location:

*There is a new student **in our class**.*

*There are some people **outside the building**.*

*There aren't any people **at the park**.*

Prepositions of place

7 Work with a partner. Look at the picture of a classroom below. Then complete the paragraph on page 36 with the correct names.

4 Writing Sentences

*This is my English class. There is a whiteboard **at the front of** the classroom. _____ is **in front of** the whiteboard. She always seems energetic and happy. There is a student **next to** the window **on the left**. His name is _____. He is not interested in English. He looks bored. There is a tall student **next to** Luis **on the right**. His name is _____. I think he is from Germany. There is a boy from Italy **next to** the wall **on the right**. **He is under** the clock. _____ likes English, but he seems tired today. There is a good student **between** Rico **and** Peter. Her name is _____. She's from Korea, and she's very friendly. I think Peter likes her. Where am I? I'm **behind** Rico. My name is _____. I'm from Malaysia. This is my favorite class.*

The prepositional phrase that shows location can also come at the beginning of the sentence:

*There is a new student **in our class**.*
***In our class**, there is a new student.*
*There are some people **outside the building**.*
***Outside the building**, there are some people.*

When the prepositional phrase begins the sentence, put a comma after it.

8 Work with a partner. Write two sentences from each group of words. Remember to use a comma if necessary.

a. there is / a whiteboard / of the classroom / at the front
   There is a whiteboard at the front of the classroom.
   At the front of the classroom, there is a whiteboard.

b. a bored student / on the left / there is / next to the wall
   ....
   ....

c. on the right / a tall student / next to Luis / there is
   ....
   ....

d. next to the wall / there is / on the right / a boy from Italy
   ....
   ....

Writing Sentences

9 Circle the letter of the sentences that are correct.

a. Near my apartment, there is a park.
b. There is some young children in the park today.
c. There is a little girl on the slide.
d. There are some noisy boy on the swings.
e. Under the tree, there are two birds.
f. On the bench, there are a young woman.
g. There aren't any man in the park.
h. By the gate, there is a police officer.

10 Work with a partner. Look at the incorrect sentences in exercise 9 above. Write them again correctly on a separate sheet of paper.

11 Work with a partner. Look at the classroom. What's wrong? Talk about what you see.

12 Write sentences on a separate sheet of paper. Then compare your sentences with another pair.

Spelling review

13 Which word is spelled incorrectly? Circle the word. Then spell the word correctly.

a. left	(lonly)	whiteboard	*lonely*
b. bord	lazy	shy	....
c. frendly	happy	poor	....
d. tense	outgoing	depresed	....
e. behind	wright	between	....
f. cheerful	relaxed	pritty	....
g. outeside	front	next	....
h. unhappy	energtic	healthy	....

SHE SEEMS LONELY 37

4 Writing Sentences

Put it together: Who is in apartment 6?

a Look at the people in the apartment building and choose one apartment. On a separate sheet of paper, write a description of the person or people inside. Write about what you can see, and also what you can guess. Do NOT write the apartment number.

> *In this apartment, there is a young man.*
>
> *I think he is a student. He is tall and thin.*
>
> *He seems tense. Maybe …*

b Work in small groups. Take turns reading your descriptions to the group. Can they guess which person or people you wrote about?

I think it is the person in Apartment 5.

Yes, that's correct! / Sorry, that's incorrect.

c Who is in apartment 6? Complete the chart below from your imagination.

man or woman?	age:	nationality:
job:	description:	his/her feelings now:

d Write at least six sentences on a separate sheet of paper about the person in Apartment 6.

e 🗨 Share your favorite words and sentences about the person in Apartment 6. Read your description to the whole class or a small group and listen to your classmates. Close your eyes. Can you "see" the person in Apartment 6 in your mind?

SHE SEEMS LONELY

5 She has brown eyes

In this unit, you will …
- learn vocabulary to describe animals and people
- learn a sentence pattern for the *have* verb
- learn when to use *a* and *an*
- describe people with *be* and *have*

1 Work with a partner. Look at the pictures below. Label the parts of the animals.

beak	fin	mouth	tail
ear	fur	neck	tooth (plural: teeth)
feather	leg	nose	wing

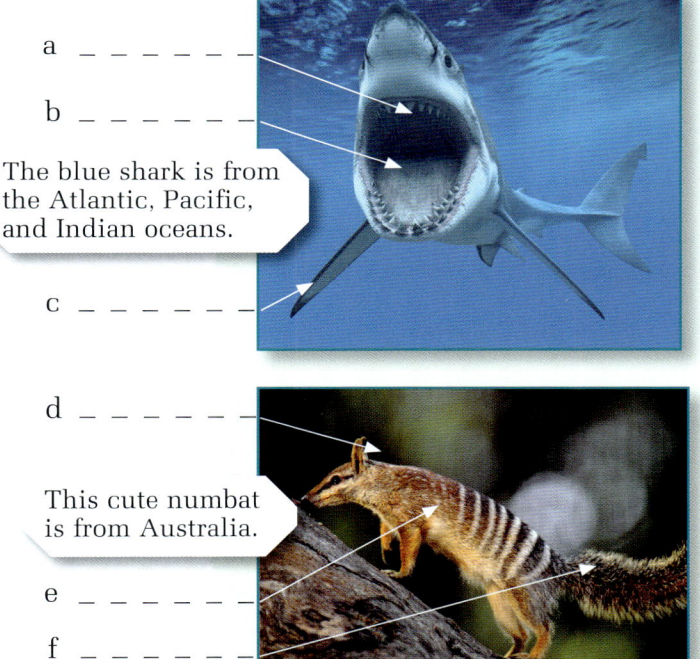

The blue shark is from the Atlantic, Pacific, and Indian oceans.

This cute numbat is from Australia.

a _ _ _ _ _ _
b _ _ _ _ _ _
c _ _ _ _ _ _
d _ _ _ _ _ _
e _ _ _ _ _ _
f _ _ _ _ _ _

The Arabian gazelle is from the desert.

g _ _ _ _ _ _
h _ _ _ _ _ _
i _ _ _ _ _ _

The quetzal is the national bird of Guatemala.

j _ _ _ _ _ _
k _ _ _ _ _ _
l _ _ _ _ _ _

MEET ENDANGERED ANIMALS FROM AROUND THE WORLD

2 Work with a partner. Complete each sentence by writing *has* or *doesn't have*.

a. The quetzal .... colorful feathers.
b. The gazelle .... long legs.
c. The numbat .... wings.
d. The shark .... sharp teeth.
e. The numbat .... striped fur.
f. The quetzal .... large eyes.
g. The gazelle .... a long tail.
h. The shark .... a blue fin.

5 Writing Sentences

The *have* verb

noun or pronoun	verb	noun
I You We They	have don't have	long legs. short legs.
He She It	has doesn't have	a tail. wings.

Sentence patterns with *have*

Look at these sentences from exercise 2 on page 39:

The quetzal has colorful feathers.
The gazelle has long legs.
The numbat has striped fur.
The shark has a blue fin.

These sentences show something (*feathers, legs, fur, a fin*) that is part of the animal. The words after *have* are nouns.

It's possible to write:

The numbat has a tail.
The gazelle has legs.

However, we usually use an adjective before the noun:

*The numbat has a **beautiful** tail.*
*The gazelle has **long** legs.*

3 Complete the sentences about the animals on page 39 by writing an adjective. Then share your sentences with a partner.

a. The quetzal doesn't have .... legs.

b. The numbat has .... ears.

c. The shark has .... teeth.

d. The gazelle has a(n) .... neck.

e. The shark doesn't have a(n) .... tail.

f. The quetzal has a(n) .... beak.

g. The gazelle doesn't have .... fur.

Using *a* and *an*

- Remember to use *a* or *an* in front of a singular noun—even if there is an adjective in front of it.

  The gazelle has **a nose**.

  It has **a long nose**.

- Don't use *a* or *an* in front of plural words (look for the ~s ending!).

  The quetzal has **wings**.

  It has black **eyes**.

- Some words in English can't be singular or plural. Don't use *a* or *an* in front of these words:

  The cat has nice **fur**.

  A shark doesn't have **hair**.

4 Read the sentences below and correct the mistake in each one.
   a. The shark doesn't have a hair.
   b. The quetzal has soft wing.
   c. The gazelle has strong neck.
   d. The numbat has a brown ears.
   e. The shark has a many teeth.
   f. The quetzal doesn't have a fur.
   g. The numbat has cute nose.

5 Look at the photos below. With a partner, write sentences with your own ideas on a separate sheet of paper. Then read your sentences to another pair. Were any of your sentences the same?

ostrich

wolf

Writing Sentences

6 Think of an animal. Write at least five sentences about it. Then read your sentences to a partner. Can your partner guess the animal?

....

....

....

....

....

> It has four legs and a short tail. It has a long gray nose.

> Is it an elephant?

Vocabulary for describing people

7 Look at the picture on the right. Then complete the paragraph about people with *have* or *don't have*.

> People are animals, but they are different too. For example, people don't have fur. They _____ hair. They _____ skin, not feathers.
> People _____ wings or fins.
> They _____ arms and legs.
> People _____ hands, too, with fingers.
> People and animals _____ eyes, ears, a nose, and a mouth.

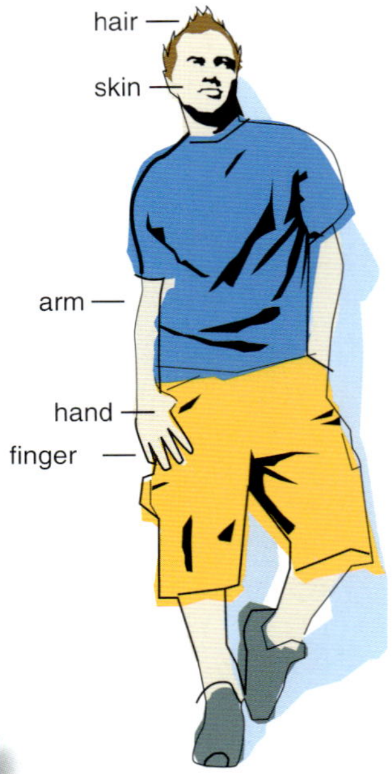

8 Complete the paragraph with *a*, *an*, or ∅ (nothing).

> I have _____ new sister! She's very pretty. She has _____ small body and _____ big head. She has _____ big brown eyes, but she doesn't have _____ much hair. She has _____ tiny hands and _____ cute little fingers. She has _____ soft skin and _____ nice smile. I love my baby sister.

42 SHE HAS BROWN EYES

Writing Sentences

Have and *be*

In Units 3 and 4, you described people using *be*. In this unit, you described people using *have*:

My father **is** an engineer. She **has** big brown eyes.

He **is** tall. My baby sister **has** soft skin.

I think he **is** friendly. She **has** a nice smile.

> **Remember:** Use **be** with a noun that:
> • means the same thing as the subject:
> She **is** a baby.
> • describes the subject:
> She **is** cute.
> • tells where the subject is:
> She **is** in the living room.
> Use **have** with parts of the body that belong to the subject:
> She **has** large eyes.

9 Look at the photo album. Complete the descriptions by writing the correct form of *be* or *have*.

Friends at my school

This is Maya. She _____ in my math class. In this picture, she _____ long hair, but now she _____ short hair. I think the short hair _____ cute. She seems shy, but she _____ friendly. She _____ very smart, and she _____ a good friend.

This _____ Ian. He _____ an exchange student from New Zealand. He _____ big hands, and he _____ long fingers. He _____ a very good guitar player. He _____ short brown hair and a kind face. He _____ tall and thin.

Who _____ pretty hair? Greta! I think she _____ beautiful. She _____ long red hair and green eyes. She _____ nice skin, a small nose, and small ears. She _____ tall, too. But she _____ not very nice. I don't know why.

5

Writing Sentences

10 A UFO landed last night! What do the aliens look like?

  a Work with a partner. What words can you use to describe the aliens?

  b Write sentences about them. Check to see that you used *have* and *be* correctly.

……………………………………………………………   ……………………………………………………………

……………………………………………………………   ……………………………………………………………

……………………………………………………………   ……………………………………………………………

……………………………………………………………   ……………………………………………………………

  c Share your sentences with another pair. Did you write any similar sentences?

Spelling review

11 One <u>underlined</u> word in each sentence is spelled incorrectly. Circle it, and then write the correct spelling above.

  a. The model has a small (noze) and <u>beautiful</u> hair. *nose*

  b. My cat has <u>soft</u> gray <u>furr</u>.

  c. The condor has black <u>feithers</u> and a long <u>beak</u>.

  d. My <u>friend</u> is short, and she has <u>tiney</u> feet.

  e. That man <u>dosen't</u> have any <u>hair</u>.

  f. The baby has small <u>handes</u> and nice <u>skin</u>.

  g. The numbat is <u>stripied</u>, and it has sharp <u>teeth</u>.

Writing Sentences

5

Put it together: A photo album

Imagine you are making a photo album. You can use real photos, draw pictures, or just write descriptions.

a Choose a theme for your album. For example, *My Classmates, My Family, My Friends, Interesting Animals, Celebrities, Alien Visitors*.

Write it here: _____

b Write descriptions of at least four people or animals. First write your ideas in the word web below. Use the correct forms of *have* and *be* in your notes. Use *a* or *an* if necessary.

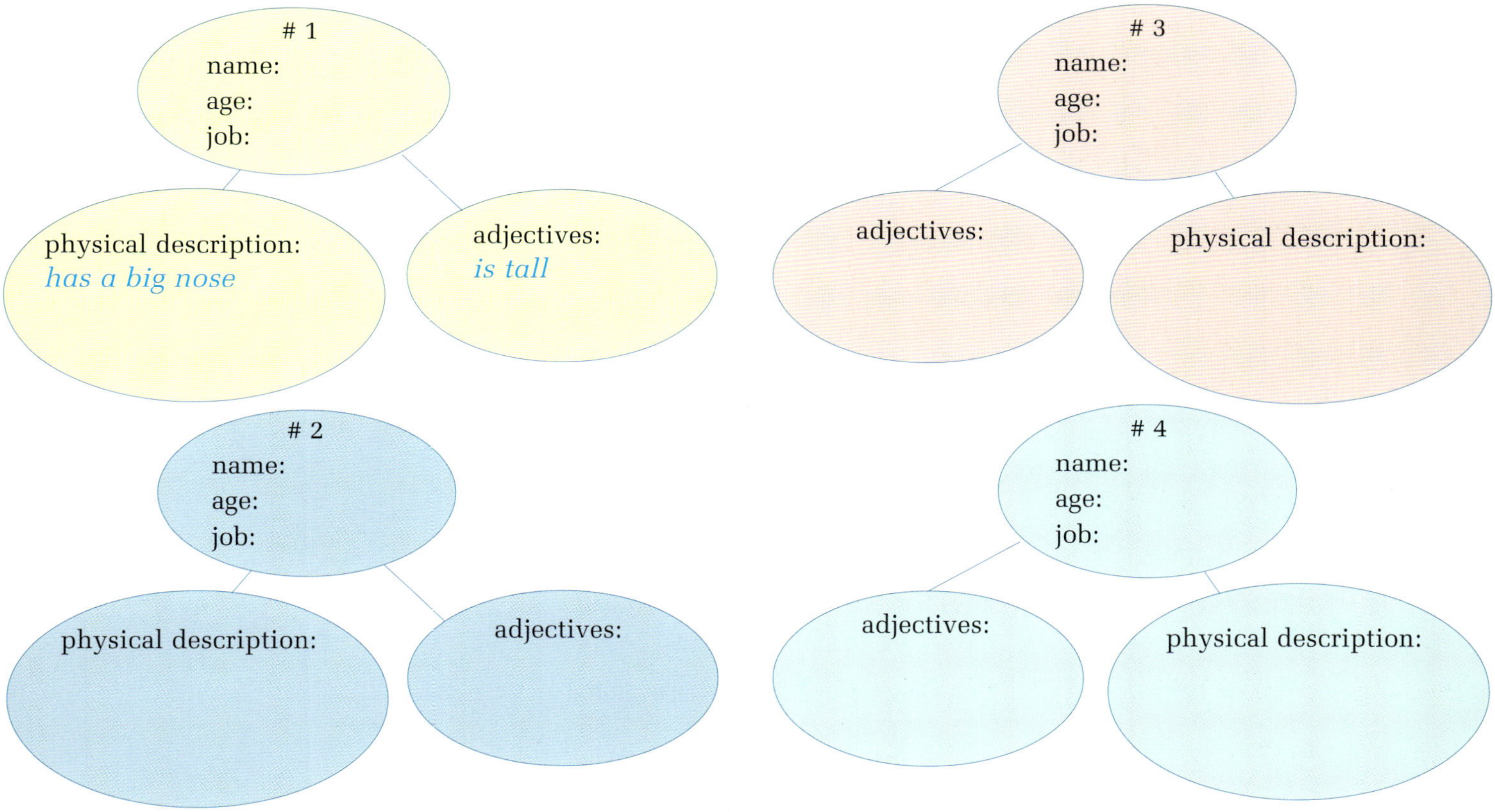

#1
name:
age:
job:

physical description:
has a big nose

adjectives:
is tall

#3
name:
age:
job:

adjectives:

physical description:

#2
name:
age:
job:

physical description:

adjectives:

#4
name:
age:
job:

adjectives:

physical description:

c Now write descriptions of each person or animal. Use a separate sheet of paper.

d Share your ideas with a small group. Take turns reading your descriptions. If you have pictures, show them to your group. Make one comment about each description you hear.

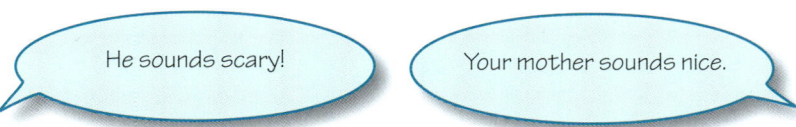

He sounds scary!

Your mother sounds nice.

SHE HAS BROWN EYES 45

6 I like playing soccer

In this unit, you will …
- learn vocabulary to talk about hobbies and interests
- learn a sentence pattern for action verbs
- learn to combine words with *and*, *but*, and *or*
- learn to use gerunds

1 Work with a partner. Look at the website below. Write the verbs from the box in the correct place.

| go   have   like (x 2)   live   read   speak   watch |

About Me: Sung-woo.

Nationality/hometown: I'm Korean. I _____ in Pusan. Pusan is a large city on the coast.

School or work: I _____ to Pusan University of Foreign Studies. I'm a first-year student. I'm studying English and Japanese.

Favorites:

Activities: I _____ playing and watching soccer. Playing soccer is good exercise.

TV Shows: I don't _____ TV. I watch DVDs and movies sometimes.

Movies: I like science fiction and action movies. I don't like sad or scary movies.

Books: I don't _____ books or magazines. I like anime. I _____ many Japanese comic books!

Music: I like listening to rock and pop music. My favorite singer is BoA. Her full name is BoA Kwon. She's Korean. She is popular in Japan too. She speaks Japanese very well!

Food: My favorite food is kimchi. My favorite dessert is ice cream. I also _____ making sushi.

Friends: My best friend's name is Hiro. He's Japanese. I play soccer with him. I _____ Japanese with him too.

Photos

Sung-woo

46 I LIKE PLAYING SOCCER

Writing Sentences

6

2 Work with a partner. Complete the sentences with information from page 46.
  a. Sung-woo lives in ......*Pusan*............................ .
  b. He's studying ....
  c. He likes playing .... and ....
     soccer.
  d. He doesn't like ....
  e. He likes reading ....
  f. BoA speaks .... very well.

Action verbs with objects

Action verbs show what the subject is doing.

Subject	verb	noun (direct object)	prepositional phrase
I You We They	play	the piano	on Saturday.
He She	is reading	a book	in the library.

Sentence patterns with action verbs

It's possible in English to write a sentence with just a subject and an action verb:
He reads.
I play.

Usually, though, something comes after the action verb, such as

- a phrase that shows a place:
    *He reads **on the train**.*
- a phrase that shows a time:
    *He reads **on the weekends**.*
- a noun that receives the action of the verb, called a *direct object*:
    *I play **soccer**.*
- a combination of a direct object and a phrase that shows a place or time (or both):
    *I play **soccer in the park**.*
    *I play **soccer after school**.*
    *I play **soccer in the park after school**.*

I LIKE PLAYING SOCCER 47

6 Writing Sentences

3 Work with a partner. Add the words and phrases to the chart. Then add two of your own ideas to each column.

✓ at college	in the supermarket	French	teach
practice	tennis	at 6:30	in the morning
study	✓ the men	my friends and I	the guitar
you	my teacher	sing	✓ play
in the kitchen	on Sunday	✓ chess	songs

subject	verb	direct object (noun)	prepositional phrase of time or place
The men	play	chess	at college.

4 Make sentences from the chart above. Make sure your subjects and verbs agree! Then compare your sentences with a partner.

a. ....

b. ....

c. ....

d. ....

e. ....

f. ....

g. ....

h. ....

Writing Sentences

Combining words with <u>and</u> and <u>or</u>

Combining words in one sentence makes your sentences sound more fluent. Here are two ways to do this:

- Use *and* to combine two words that are similar:
    I like cake. I like ice cream.
    *I like cake **and** ice cream.*

- Use *or* to combine two similar words after a negative verb:
    I don't play baseball. I don't play basketball.
    *I don't play baseball **or** soccer.*

> **Note:** Combine the same kind of words (for example, two nouns or two adjectives).

5 **Write the correct form of the verb.**
  a. Kendra ...*plays*........................ basketball and tennis. (play)
  b. I .... cats or dogs. (like)
  c. My teacher .... French and Arabic. (know)
  d. My sister .... the piano and the violin. (play)
  e. We .... in a small or quiet town. (live)
  f. My best friend .... Chinese or Thai. (speak)

Combining words with <u>but</u>

- Use *but* to combine two words that don't usually go together. *But* shows that the information is surprising. *But* is often used in this way with adjectives:
    She is small. She is strong.
    *She is small **but** strong.*

6 **Complete the sentences by circling the best word.**
  a. This book is long but *tall / interesting*.
  b. Our teacher was surprised but *happy / angry*.
  c. My phone was cheap but *good / new*.
  d. I feel happy but *sad / tired*.
  e. Today is sunny but *cold / warm*.
  f. The pizza was simple but *delicious / cheap*.

I LIKE PLAYING SOCCER

Writing Sentences

7 Complete the following sentences with *and*, *or*, or *but*.

a. I'm not a high school student .... a university student.

b. I'm an office worker .... an artist.

c. During the week, I work in an office in the center of the city. My work is hard .... interesting.

d. I'm an artist on Saturday .... Sunday.

e. I don't paint .... draw.

f. I take photographs of people .... animals.

g. I give my photos to friends .... family.

h. I'm very busy .... happy.

8 Write true sentences about yourself with *and*, *or*, and *but*. Then share your sentences with a partner.

a. (and) ....

b. (but) ....

c. (or) ....

Gerunds

Gerunds are nouns made from verbs. They end with ~*ing*.

Look at these examples. Notice how the gerunds are in the same position in the sentence as a regular noun:

I like sports.
I like baseball and tennis.
*I like **playing** soccer.*
*I like **swimming** and **skiing**.*

Gerunds are common after these verbs: *like, enjoy, can't stand, hate*.
Because they are nouns, gerunds can also be sentence subjects:

***Playing** baseball is fun.*
***Swimming** is good exercise.*
***Making** movies is an interesting hobby.*

> **Note:** Don't confuse a gerund with the present continuous.
> A gerund is a noun:
>   I like **swimming**. (*swimming* is a noun. You could also say, I like **sports**.)
> The present continuous is a verb tense. It is made with the be verb:
>   I am **swimming**. (*swimming* is a verb. You could also say, I am **walking**.)

50   I LIKE PLAYING SOCCER

Writing Sentences

Spelling and gerunds

Look at these rules for spelling gerunds:

v = vowel (a, e, i, o, u)

c = consonant (b, c, d, f, g, h, j, k, l, m, n, p, q, r, s, t, v, w, x, y, z)

If the word ends with

- c + c (wa**lk**, thi**nk**)

then add ~ing (wa**lking**, thi**nking**)

- v + v + c (sp**eak**, r**ead**)

then add ~ing (sp**eaking**, r**eading**)

- c + v + c, and the word is one syllable (r**un**, st**op**)

then double the last consonant and add (~ing) (ru**nning**, sto**pping**)

- v + c + the letter e (m**ake**, wr**ite**)

then drop the e and add ~ing (m**aking**, wr**iting**)

> **Remember:** These rules are *usually* true. They are not *always* true.

9 Write the gerund form of the following words.

a. live ....   f. cook ....
b. eat ....   g. drive ....
c. shop ....   h. swim ....
d. sing ....   i. take ....
e. study ....   j. watch ....

10 Look back at the website on page 46. Copy the four sentences with gerunds.

a. ....

b. ....

c. ....

d. ....

One sentence uses the present continuous. Write it here:

e. ....

I LIKE PLAYING SOCCER

Writing Sentences

11 Complete these sentences that begin with gerunds. You can use an adjective or a noun. Then share your sentences with a partner.

a. Cooking is ....

b. Reading novels is ....

c. Swimming is ....

d. Studying English is ....

e. Listening to music is ....

f. Exercising is ....

12 Complete the following sentences with gerunds. Then share your sentences with a classmate.

a. I can't stand ....

b. My favorite sport is ....

c. On weekends I hate ....

d. On rainy days I like ....

e. I enjoy ....

f. My parents don't like ....

g. .... is boring.

h. .... is my friend's hobby.

i. .... is fun.

j. .... is difficult.

Spelling review

13 Write the missing letters.

a. bas ___ b ___ ll

b. exer ___ ___ ___ e

c. fav ___ ___ ___ te

d. int ___ ___ ___ sting

e. Kor ___ ___ n

f. lis ___ ___ ning

g. p ___ pul ___ r

h. delic ___ ___ ___ s

i. stud ___ ___ ng

j. wri ___ ___ ___ g

52   I LIKE PLAYING SOCCER

Writing Sentences

6

Put it together: Your personal website

You are going to make a personal website. You can make more than one page if you want.

a What do you want to write about? Make notes in the chart below. You can also use your own ideas.

About you (name, home, school)	activities & interests	likes / dislikes
family:	friends:	favorite music / food:

b On a separate sheet of paper, design your website and write your information. Start like this:

> Hello! Welcome to _____'s website. Here you can learn a little about me. I hope you enjoy this site.

Try to use *and*, *or*, *but*, and gerunds.

c Share your web page. Move around the classroom speaking to one person at a time. If your classmate has a similar interest or hobby, "link" to his or her web page by writing his or her name and underlining it. See how many classmates you can link to!

I LIKE PLAYING SOCCER

7 Faded jeans are cool

In this unit, you will …
- learn vocabulary for describing clothing and fashion
- write sentences with subject and object pronouns
- combine sentences with *and*, *but*, *or*, and *so*
- put two or three adjectives in the correct order

1 Work with a partner. Read the fashion blog. Write the <u>underlined</u> expressions next to the correct pictures.

Miki's Fashion Blog

Hi! I'm Miki, and I'm a junior college student in Tokyo. Here are some popular fashions in my neighborhood. What do you think of them?

Many guys wear <u>baggy pants</u> but I don't like them. I think they're ugly! My brother wears <u>faded jeans</u> and <u>athletic shoes</u> like these. He says they're comfortable.

For girls, <u>short skirts</u> and <u>striped leggings</u> are very popular. They also like colorful accessories like <u>hats</u> and bags. I like this style. I think it's cute!

Black is always a fashionable color, but now some people mix it with other <u>bright colors</u>. These days, girls wear <u>knee-high boots</u> and <u>platform shoes</u>. They hurt my feet, so I don't wear them very often.

What do you like to wear?

a. *baggy pants*
b. ....
c. ....

d. ....
e. ....
f. ....

g. ....
h. ....
i. ....

54 FADED JEANS ARE COOL

Writing Sentences

7

2 Do you like these fashions? Write true sentences with *I like* or *I don't like*. Then share your sentences with a partner.

a. .... striped pants.   d. .... faded clothing.

b. .... baggy jeans.   e. .... platform boots.

c. .... athletic pants.   f. .... black leggings.

3 Work with a partner. Are these adjectives positive or negative? Write them in the correct column.

| ✓ comfortable | silly | cool | ugly |
| cute | unattractive | fashionable | uncomfortable |

positive	negative
....	....
....	....
....	....
....	....

4 Write one adjective from exercise 3 (or use your own ideas, such as a color) for each piece of clothing.

.... cap
.... scarf
.... T-shirt
.... belt
.... bag
.... shorts
.... socks

5 Work with a partner. What other types of clothing are the people in your class wearing today? Make a list. Use a dictionary if necessary.

....
....
....
....

FADED JEANS ARE COOL 55

Writing Sentences

Subject and object pronouns

subject	*be* verb	adjective
My scarf } It	is	old.
Platform shoes } They	are	uncomfortable.

subject	verb	object
My brother	likes	{ his faded T-shirt. / it.
I	want	{ knee-high boots. / them.

- Use *it* for singular nouns (both subjects and objects).
- Use *they* for plural subject nouns.
- Use *them* for plural object nouns.

6 Draw a line to connect the sentences that go together. Use the pronouns as clues.

a. My blue jeans are very old.
b. I like that scarf.
c. I like my new boots.
d. I don't like that short skirt.
e. I have new white socks.
f. This bag is cute.

1. They are black.
2. I keep my cell phone in it.
3. I can't wear them.
4. I wear them with my athletic shoes.
5. It's not fashionable.
6. It's very long.

7 Write about the clothing below. Use:

- I wear / I don't wear
- an adverb of frequency
- subject and object pronouns
- adjectives

a. leggings — *I never wear them. They're silly.*
b. my jacket — *I often wear it. It's comfortable.*
c. platform shoes ....
d. baggy pants ....
e. my outfit today ....
f. my favorite T-shirt ....
g. brand-name jeans ....
h. my watch ....

Combining sentences with <u>and,</u> <u>but,</u> <u>or,</u> and <u>so</u>

Use *and*, *but*, *or*, and *so* to join two complete sentences.

- *and* shows similar activities or feelings:

  I like my hat, **and** I often wear it.

  I like bright yellow, **and** I like bright pink.

- *but* shows a contrast or difference:

  I wear a uniform to school, **but** I wear fashionable clothing at home.

  I have some pink socks, **but** I never wear them.

- *or* shows two choices or alternatives:

  You can buy the boots, **or** you can buy the shoes.

  On weekends, I wear baggy pants, **or** I wear my faded jeans.

- *so* shows that the second sentence is a result of the first one:

  Brand-name clothing is expensive, **so** I rarely buy it.

  I don't like my hat, **so** I never wear it.

Note: Use a comma before **and**, **but**, **or**, and **so** when you combine two complete sentences.

8 Look back at the blog on page 54. Write the sentences that show two complete sentences combined with these words:

a. (and) ....

b. (but) ....

c. (but) ....

d. (and) ....

e. (so) ....

FADED JEANS ARE COOL

7 Writing Sentences

9 Work with a partner. Combine the two sentences with *and*, *but*, *or*, or *so*. Write a comma in the correct place.

a. I like long skirts. I often wear them.
....

b. My jeans are very faded. I want new jeans.
....

c. I'm very busy. I'm not going shopping.
....

d. I can wear my old jacket. I can buy a new one.
....

e. I have a lot of fashionable clothes. I never wear them.
....

10 Complete the sentences. Then share your sentences with a partner.

a. I don't like this shirt, so ....

b. I wear a uniform to school, but ....

c. I'm wearing socks today, and ....

d. You can buy the pink leggings, or ....

e. I like baggy pants, but ....

f. This dress is uncomfortable, so ....

Writing Sentences

7

Combining adjectives

Often English writers use two adjectives to describe a noun, and sometimes even three adjectives. The chart shows which adjectives come first.

opinion	size	age	color	material	noun
	large		white		shirt
		new		leather	watch
strange	little				hat
ugly		old	black		jacket
			pink	cotton	dress

11 Work with a partner. Write the words in the box into the chart above. Can you add any other words?

big	cute	pretty	silk	sweater	wool
brown	mini	purple	small	unusual	yellow

Note: We usually say *little old* and not *small old*.

12 Complete the sentences with an adjective from the chart or your own idea.

a. I don't like ……………………………… leather shoes.

b. I'm wearing a large ……………………………… cotton shirt.

c. That's an ugly ……………………………… dress.

d. Do you have a long ……………………………… scarf?

e. I have a / an ……………………………… black jacket.

f. She likes ……………………………… purple boots.

13 Write at least five true sentences about what you are wearing today. Then share your sentences with a partner. Use a separate sheet of paper.

Writing Sentences

Spelling review

14 **Complete the crossword puzzle.**

across

5. Many people think colorful accessories are c... .
6. These boots are very small. They're u... .
7. I play sports in my a... shoes.
8. I like b... colors like pink and yellow.
10. She usually wears l... with her skirt.
12. Do you like p... shoes?

down

1. I don't often wear brand-name c... .
3. I wear a wool s... in the winter.
4. This is a l... belt.
6. Don't buy that jacket. It's u... now.
9. Baggy pants are s... . I don't like them.
11. My favorite color is p... .

Put it together: A fashion blog

a What do people in your neighborhood or school wear? Write notes.

clothing	like or don't like?	opinion
faded jeans	*like*	*they're cool*

b Choose three or more fashions. Write blog entries. Follow the examples on page 54. If you like, you can draw pictures or cut out photographs of the fashions.

c Share your work in small groups. Read your blog entries to your group. Do they have the same opinions or different opinions? Are there any fashions that everyone likes? Are there any fashions that everyone dislikes?

> I agree! I think faded clothing is fashionable.

> I don't agree. I think faded clothing is ugly.

8 I'm a business major

In this unit, you will …
- learn vocabulary for school subjects
- use the simple present and present progressive tenses
- learn adverbs and expressions of frequency
- learn the format of a paragraph

1. Work with a partner. Read about the students. Then use the underlined words to label the pictures on page 63. Can you do it without a dictionary?

I'm a business major. I like my business classes. I'm also taking a math class, but I'm not getting good grades now. I rarely study. I don't like numbers very much.
— Samira

I'm studying art. I love drawing and painting. I usually paint in my studio, but sometimes I paint outside. I like playing the piano too, so next term I'm taking a music class.
— Paulo

I'm good at foreign languages. My favorite subject is English, and I'm also studying Spanish and French. I'm an international studies major.
— Jee-hyun

I'm in high school, so I don't have a major. My father is a doctor, and I think that's interesting. I also enjoy playing baseball all the time, so I'm thinking about studying sports medicine.
— Takeshi

I play video games all the time—every morning, every evening, and every weekend! I enjoy designing video games too. I'm a computer science major, of course!
— Tyler

Writing Sentences

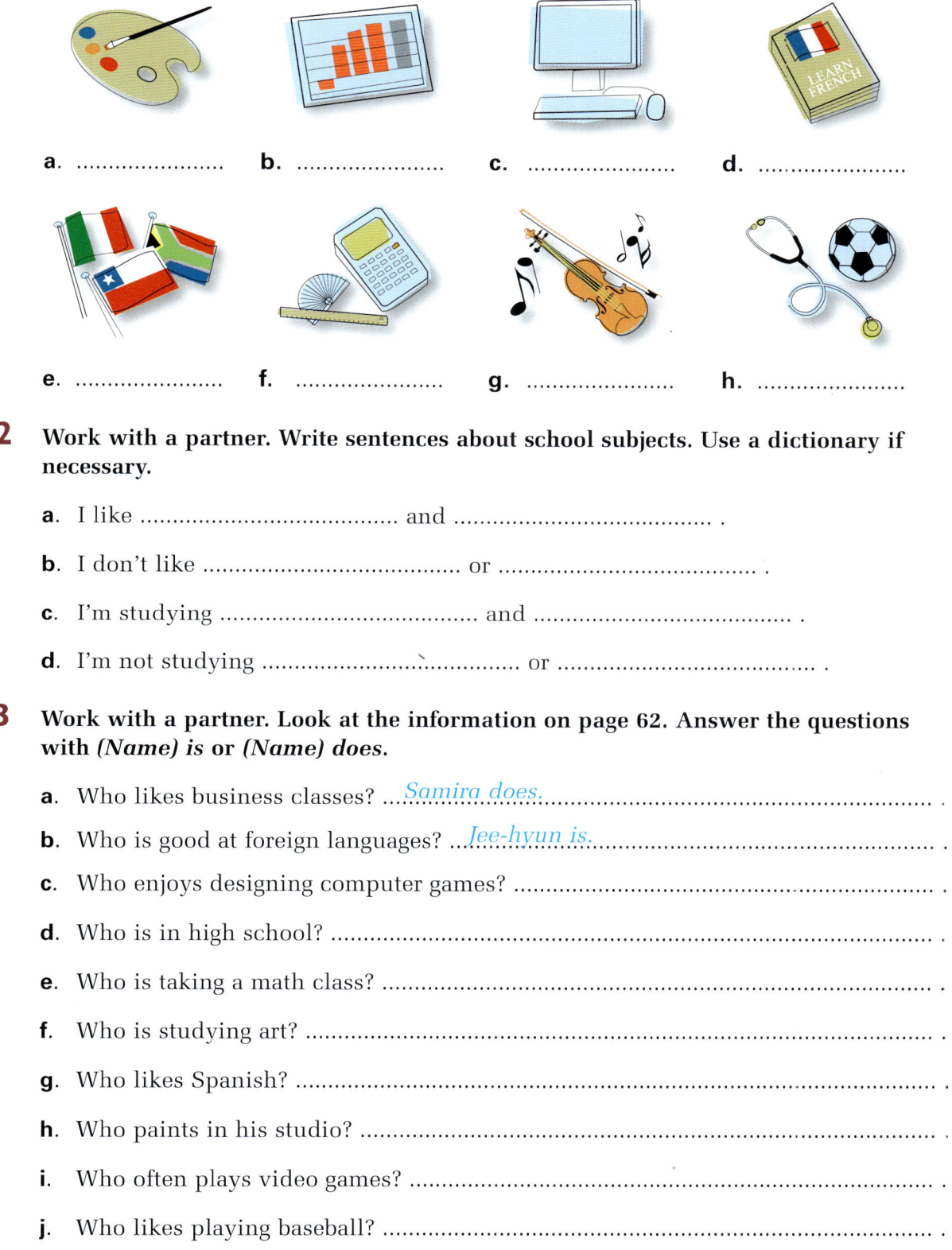

a. .... b. .... c. .... d. ....

e. .... f. .... g. .... h. ....

2 Work with a partner. Write sentences about school subjects. Use a dictionary if necessary.

a. I like .... and ....

b. I don't like .... or ....

c. I'm studying .... and ....

d. I'm not studying .... or ....

3 Work with a partner. Look at the information on page 62. Answer the questions with *(Name) is* or *(Name) does*.

a. Who likes business classes? *Samira does.* ....

b. Who is good at foreign languages? *Jee-hyun is.* ....

c. Who enjoys designing computer games? ....

d. Who is in high school? ....

e. Who is taking a math class? ....

f. Who is studying art? ....

g. Who likes Spanish? ....

h. Who paints in his studio? ....

i. Who often plays video games? ....

j. Who likes playing baseball? ....

I'M A BUSINESS MAJOR   63

8 Writing Sentences

Verb tense: The simple present

Use the simple present

- for actions that you do regularly:
  I **play** the piano.
  I **drive** to work.

- to describe something that's always true about you:
  I **like** chocolate.
  I**'m** a French major.

- with expressions like *always, usually, sometimes, never*:
  I <u>often</u> **sleep** late.
  I <u>never</u> **watch** TV.

- with expressions like *on Saturdays, every week, in the afternoon*:
  I **play** soccer <u>every weekend</u>.
  I **have** a math class <u>on Tuesdays</u>.

> **Note:** Remember to use *do / does* to make questions and negative statements with action verbs.
>
> *Do you play the piano?*   No, I don't.
> *Does she like chocolate?*   No, she doesn't.

4 Complete the questions with *Do*, *Does*, *Are*, or *Is*. Then match them to the answers.

a. <u>Do</u> you have a major?
b. .... your friend like foreign languages?
c. .... you good at math?
d. .... you usually get good grades?
e. .... your business class in the morning?
f. .... your sister play sports?
g. .... you like playing music?
h. .... your friend in college?

1. Yes, he does. He's a Chinese major.
2. Yes, I am. I love math!
3. Yes, I do. I'm a science major.
4. No, she doesn't. She doesn't like exercising.
5. No, I don't. I'm not good at music.
6. Yes, she is. She's a computer science major.
7. Yes, I do. I study hard!
8. No, it isn't. It's in the afternoon.

5 Work with a partner. Write three questions for your partner. Then ask the questions and write a short answer. Then write a complete sentence about your partner.

a. Do <u>you like English?</u>   <u>Yes, he does.</u>   <u>Hassan likes English.</u>
b. Do .... ? ....
c. Does .... ? ....
d. Are .... ? ....

64   I'M A BUSINESS MAJOR

Adverbs of frequency

Look at the chart of adverbs and examples of expressions we use to write about how often something happens.

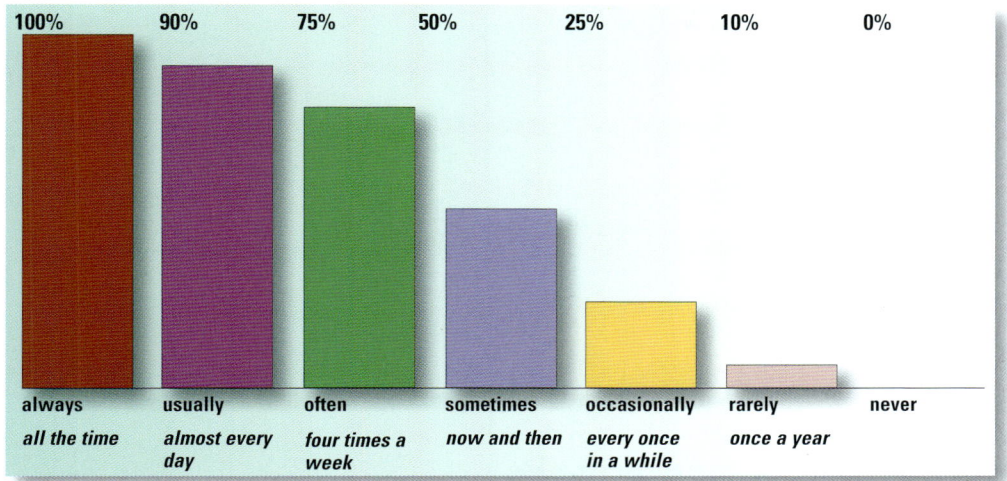

- **Adverbs of frequency** go between the subject and an action verb:

    I **always** do my work.
    I **occasionally** ride by bike to school.

- However, they come after the *be* verb:

    I am **sometimes** lonely.
    I am **never** late.

- *Usually, often, sometimes,* and *occasionally* can also go before the subject:

    Usually I study with a friend.
    Sometimes I play games online.

- **Expressions of frequency** go after the verb at the end of the sentence, or before the subject at the beginning of the sentence. However, they are most common at the end of the sentence:

    I go to the movies **now and then**.
    Once a year, I take a vacation.

6 Look back at the student profiles on page 62. Copy the sentences ...

- that have an adverb of frequency after the subject:

a. ....

b. ....

- that have an adverb of frequency before the subject:

c. ....

- that have an expression of frequency after the verb:

d. ....

Writing Sentences

7 Complete the following sentences with true information about yourself. Then compare your sentences with a partner.

a. I usually ....

b. I am rarely ....

c. I .... every once in a while.

d. I never ....

e. I .... almost every week.

f. I .... once or twice a year.

g. Usually I .... , but sometimes I ....

h. Often I ....

Verb tense: The present progressive

Use the present progressive

- for an action that's happening right now:
  I'm typing my paper.
  I'm having lunch.

- to describe a temporary action; something that you're doing now, and will continue in the future, but will end:
  I'm taking a dance class.
  I'm studying science.

- to talk about something you plan to do soon:
  I'm having dinner in a restaurant tonight.
  I'm traveling to Europe this summer.

Note: Remember that the present progressive is almost never used with stative verbs, such as **be**, **have**, **think**, **feel**, **know**, etc. (see Unit 4, page 33).

8 Complete the sentences from page 62 with the correct form of the verb. Don't look until you're finished. Then check your answers.

a. Samira (not / get) .... good grades now.

b. Sometimes Paulo (paint) .... outside.

c. Jee-hyun (take) .... Spanish and French.

d. Takeshi (be) .... in high school.

e. Tyler (play) .... computer games all the time.

Writing Sentences

9 Answer the questions with true information about yourself. Write a short answer and a complete sentence. Then compare your sentences with a partner.

a. Do you have a major? *Yes, I do. I'm a business major.*
   No, I don't. But I like computer science.

b. Are you a business major? ....

c. Are you taking music lessons? ....

d. Do you often play baseball? ....

e. Do you like math? ....

f. Are you usually good at foreign languages? ....

g. Are you studying science? ....

Paragraph format

In English writing, sentences are often arranged in paragraphs. Paragraphs have a special shape. Each paragraph is about one topic or idea. Every sentence in the paragraph gives some information about that topic. When you want to write about another topic, begin a new paragraph.

10 Work with a partner. Look at the examples below. Check (✓) the one that has the right shape for a paragraph in English. How can you describe that shape?

WHAT'S YOUR ZODIAC SIGN?

March 21 – April 19
You're an Aries.
You're active and outgoing.
You like being the leader and you like organizing things.
You always have a lot of ideas, and you like telling people what to do.
You're good at sports.
Sometimes you are too pushy! ☐

April 20 – May 20
You're a Taurus. You're calm and patient. Usually you like being alone, but you're lonely every once in a while. Sometimes other people don't understand you very well. You like animals and nature. Maybe you have a pet. ☐

May 21 – June 20
You're a Gemini.
You love people, and you talk all the time. You're usually good at making money, and you're always good at spending it.
Maybe you're an economics or a business major. A Gemini loves adventure and travel. ☐

I'M A BUSINESS MAJOR 67

8 Writing Sentences

11 Unscramble the sentences. Then copy them in correct paragraph format in the box below.

a / Cancer / you're

romantic / you're / interesting and

a lot of / you / friends / have

feel / you / every day / different almost

you / understand / your friends don't / always /

quiet and / sometimes you're / shy

June 21 – July 20

Spelling review

12 Write the missing letters to form common expressions.

a. business m ___ ___ ___ r

b. art s ___ ___ ___ ___ o

c. c ___ ___ ___ ___ ___ ___ r science

d. foreign l ___ ___ ___ ___ ___ ___ ___ s

e. high s ___ ___ ___ ___ l

f. international s ___ ___ ___ ___ ___ s

g. sports m ___ ___ ___ ___ ___ ___ e

h. v ___ ___ ___ o games

Writing Sentences

8

Put it together: A new zodiac

a Create a new zodiac! Use the animals below or your own ideas.

Tiger	Shark	Hawk
 • play sports every day • are on many teams • are good at games • like winning • rarely study •	 • • • • • •	 • • • • • •
Squirrel	**Mermaid**	**Butterfly**
 • • • • • •	 • • • • • •	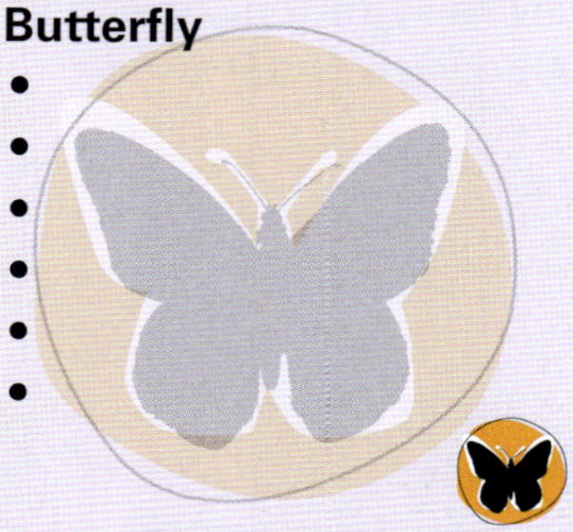 • • • • • •
your idea: • • • • • • •	**our idea:** • • • • • • •	**your idea:** • • • • • • •

b Choose three "new zodiac" signs. On a separate sheet of paper, write a short paragraph about each one. Use good paragraph format! Follow the example.

> *Tiger: You're an athlete. You play sports every day. You play baseball every spring and basketball every fall. You're also on the tennis team. You're good at games, and you like winning. You don't like school, and you rarely study.*

c Share your new zodiac with a small group. Read your three paragraphs to the group. Can they think of any students who match your descriptions?

I think Jill is a Tiger.

I'M A BUSINESS MAJOR 69

9 I'm in Barcelona

In this unit, you will …
- learn some irregular past tense verbs
- learn to write sentences with indirect objects
- learn how to format a postcard and an email
- learn the difference between formal and informal language
- use questions and exclamations

1 Work with a partner. Complete the postcard below with verbs from the box. One verb is not used.

| ate | bought | got | had | sent | took | was | went |

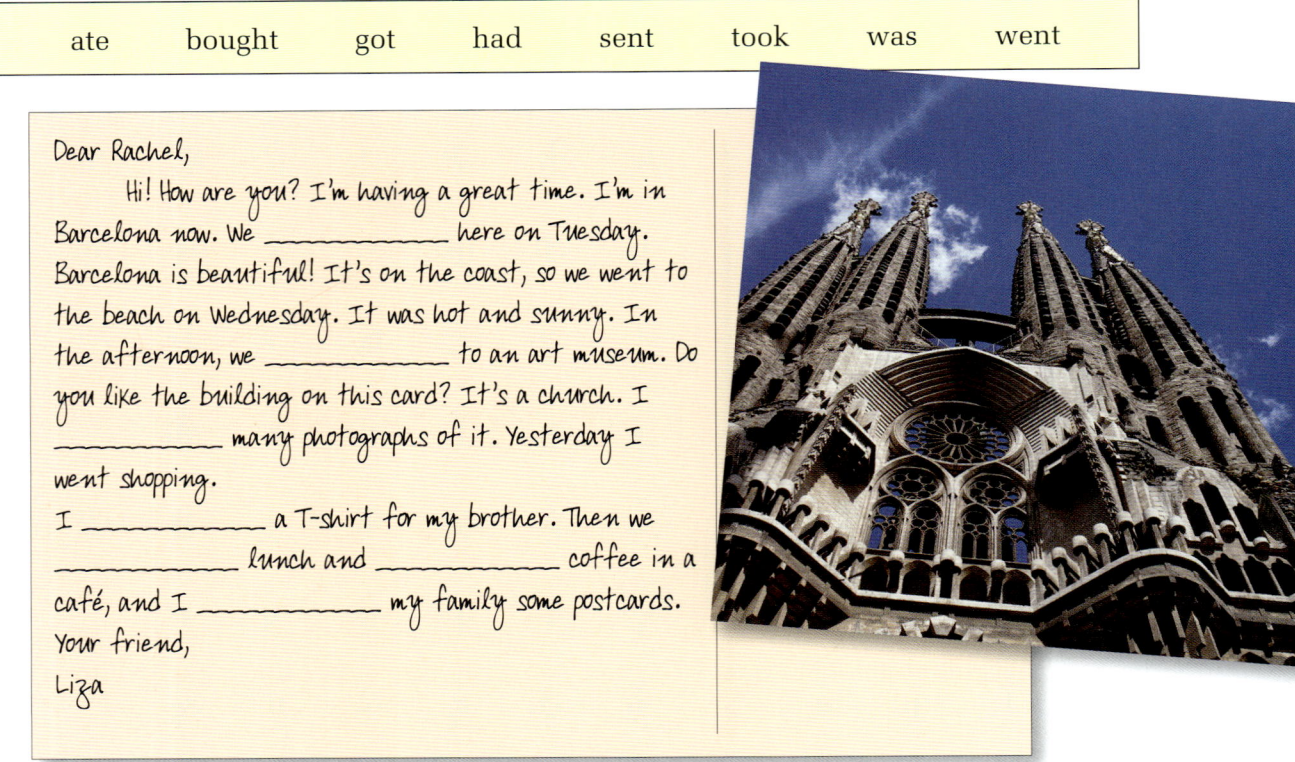

Dear Rachel,
   Hi! How are you? I'm having a great time. I'm in Barcelona now. We _____ here on Tuesday. Barcelona is beautiful! It's on the coast, so we went to the beach on Wednesday. It was hot and sunny. In the afternoon, we _____ to an art museum. Do you like the building on this card? It's a church. I _____ many photographs of it. Yesterday I went shopping.
I _____ a T-shirt for my brother. Then we _____ lunch and _____ coffee in a café, and I _____ my family some postcards.
Your friend,
Liza

2 Next, Liza sent an email from an Internet café. Use the notes below to write complete sentences in the past tense. Write the sentences in correct paragraph form on page 71.

Guess what? I (meet) a Spanish man.

He (be) very handsome and friendly.

He (give) me a tour of Barcelona.

I (have) a good time.

He also (give) me his phone number and email address.

I (not call) him, but I (email) him my home address in Canada.

Writing Sentences

> Hi Rachel,
>
> ....
>
> ....
>
> ....
>
> ....
>
> ....
>
> See you soon,
> Liza

Indirect objects

Noun	verb	noun (direct object)	preposition + noun (indirect object)
I	wrote	a letter	to Charlie.
You	gave	some money	to me.

Noun	verb	noun (indirect object)	noun (direct object)
I	wrote	Charlie	a letter.
You	gave	me	some money.

You know that direct objects receive the action of the verb (see page 47):

*I wrote **a letter**.*
*You gave **some money**.*

- Indirect objects receive the direct object. They can come after the direct object, with a preposition such as *to* or *for*:

  *I wrote a letter **to Charlie**.*
  *You gave some money **to me**.*

- Or they can come before the direct object, without a preposition:

  *I wrote **Charlie** a letter.*
  *You gave **me** some money.*

I'M IN BARCELONA   71

9 Writing Sentences

3 Look back at the postcard on page 70. Copy the sentences with indirect objects …

- that come after the direct object:

  ....

- that come before the direct object:

  ....

  ....

4 Unscramble the sentences. Then write them again and move the indirect object.

a. me / wrote / a poem / Carlos *Carlos wrote me a poem.*
   Carlos wrote a poem for me.

b. made / for / a scarf / I / my sister *I made a scarf for my sister.*
   I made my sister a scarf.

c. us / Min-hee / a letter / sent ....
   ....

d. I / a cake / you / for / baked ....
   ....

e. to / our teacher / any homework / didn't give / us ....
   ....

f. emailed / her / a photo / Rashad ....
   ....

5 Answer the questions. Use an indirect object in your answer.

a. Did you send an email to someone? *Yes. I sent my parents an email.*

b. Did you cook dinner for someone? ....

c. Did you buy someone a gift? ....

d. Did you do someone a favor? ....

e. Did you write a letter to someone? ....

f. Did you give someone a message? ....

Writing Sentences

Format of a postcard or email

Look at the postcard on page 70. Who wrote the postcard? Who will read it? How do you know?

Begin an email or postcard with the name of the person you are writing to:

Dear Rachel,   /   Hi Rachel,

End it with your name:

Your friend,   /   See you soon,
Liza   Liza

The first line of an email or postcard is usually a greeting. What greeting did Liza use in her postcard?

Informal and formal language

When you write to someone you know well, like a friend or a family member, you use **informal language**. Use **very informal language** only with a close friend of about your same age.
When you write to someone you don't know well, or someone older or more important than you, you use **formal language**.

6 Write the words and expressions into the correct place in the chart.

Greetings	Questions	Closings
Hello.	Whassup?	Sincerely,
Yo!	How are you?	Catch ya later!
Hi.	How are you doing?	Your friend,

formal	informal	very informal
....	....	....
....	....	....
....	....	....

7 Work with a partner or group. Discuss these questions.
- What other informal or very informal words or writing styles do you know?
- In your own language, do you usually write with formal or informal language?
- List some people you know that you would use these styles with:

formal: ....

informal: ....

very informal: ....

9 Writing Sentences

8 Look at this email from Mike Smith, a student, to his professor, Dr. Brown. It is too informal. Write it again, in correct format, with more formal language. Then compare your email with a partner.

> Yo, Brownie! Whassup? I hope U R fine. Sorry I wuz late 2 class. ☹
> Didja give NE homework 2 us? I hope not! Ha ha! I will C U in class 2morrow. Catch ya l8r.
>
> ....
> ....
> ....
> ....

Using questions and exclamations

Most sentences in English end with a period [.]. However, sentences can also end with a question mark [?] or an exclamation mark [!].

You know that a question mark is used with a question. When do you use an exclamation mark? Is it formal or informal? Look at the postcard and email on page 70 and find the sentences that end with a question mark or an exclamation mark.

> **Note:** Don't use too many exclamations in one paragraph. In formal writing, don't use more than one question mark or exclamation point at the end of one sentence.
>
> Very informal: That was a difficult test!!!

9 End the sentences in the postcard below with a period, a question mark, or an exclamation point. Then discuss your choices with a partner.

Dear Chen,
 I went to Marrakech on vacation _____ Do you know where Marrakech is _____ It's in Morocco _____ It's a famous city, but it isn't the capital _____ We went shopping, and we ate at some great Moroccan restaurants _____ I bought a beautiful leather belt and some gold earrings _____ Later, we took a trip to the desert _____ I rode a camel _____ It wasn't very comfortable, but it was interesting _____
Your friend,
Mike

Writing Sentences

Spelling review

10 Write the past tense of the verbs into the puzzle. Then read down to answer this question:

What city is this?

1. make: *made*
2. go: ....
3. email: ....
4. bake: ....
5. write: ....
6. buy: ....
7. ride: ....
8. send: ....
9. give: ....

9 Writing Sentences

Put it together: A vacation postcard

a You're on vacation! Choose one of the postcards below, find your own postcard, or draw your own picture.

b Write some ideas for your postcard.

Who I'm writing to: ....

Will it be formal or informal? ....

Where I am: ....

What I'm doing: ....

What I did: ....

A question or exclamation: ....

c Write your postcard on a separate sheet of paper. Include the name of the person you are writing to and your own name.

d Share your postcards. Put them on the walls of your classroom, or spread them on a desk or table. Cover your name, or fold the paper so that no one can read your name. Then read your classmates' postcards. Can you guess who wrote each one?

I think that one's from Luisa!

That postcard sounds like it's from Ken.

I'M IN BARCELONA

10 It's a kind of French game

In this unit, you will …
- learn vocabulary to describe popular international items
- learn when and how to use passive sentences
- learn about the topic sentence, supporting sentences, and the concluding sentence

1 Work with a partner. Look at the vocabulary categories on the left. Then cross out the example that does not belong.

a. clothing	dress	suit	~~cheese~~	hat
b. game	chess	tiger	ping-pong	sudoku
c. dessert	jazz	ice cream	cheesecake	chocolate
d. food	curry	dumplings	salad	necklace
e. toy	kite	yo-yo	rose	doll
f. musical instrument	TV	piano	guitar	drum

2 Keep the same partner. What is the word that you crossed out? Take turns explaining.

Cheese is a kind of food.

3 Read the paragraphs below. Complete the description with a category word from exercise 1.

pétanque, France   hanbok, Korea   mochi, Japan   poi balls, New Zealand

Pétanque is a kind of French _____. Sometimes it is called *boules*. It is played in the park with metal balls. It's usually played by older people, but I like playing pétanque too!

The *hanbok* is a kind of Korean _____. It is worn on special occasions. *Hanbok* are very colorful. My *hanbok* has a blue skirt and a red blouse.

Mochi is a kind of Japanese _____. It is made from rice. It is used in many dishes. My favorite kind of mochi is sweet, and it is eaten for dessert.

Poi balls look like they are used for sports or games, but they are actually a kind of traditional _____. They make a sound when they are used. These days, they are used in dances and for exercise.

IT'S A KIND OF FRENCH GAME

10

Writing Sentences

The passive

Active voice

subject	verb	object	prepositional phrase
My mother	made	cookies	with flour, eggs, butter, and sugar

Passive voice

subject (the object from an active sentence)	be + verb (participle)	prepositional phrase
Mochi	is made	from rice.
Varenyky	are eaten	in Ukraine and Russia.

You know that the most common pattern of an English sentence is
subject + verb + object
My mother made cookies.

In English, the first noun of the sentence is usually the most important. In the sentence above, we pay attention to the words "My mother."

However, sometimes you don't know the subject (who made the cookies), or you don't care. Then the passive is useful. The object is moved to the front of the sentence to become a new subject:

Cookies are made with flour, eggs, butter, and sugar.

The object of the first sentence (*cookies*) is now the subject. The original subject (*mother*) is not in the sentence. A prepositional phrase follows the verb.

It's also possible to use the passive to emphasize the object:

The best cookies are made by my mother.

Again, the object of the first sentence (*cookies*) is now the subject. The original subject (*my mother*) is part of a prepositional phrase that comes after the verb.

4 Work with a partner. Read the paragraphs on page 77 again. <u>Underline</u> the passive sentences.

Forming the passive

The passive is formed with a form of the *be* verb plus the participle of the main verb. (For a list of common participles, see page 105). Remember that the *be* verb will agree with the new subject in front of it:

Present   Tigers **are found** in India.
             Jazz **is played** in that club.

Past   That dress **was worn** on special occasions.
             Traditional music **was played** at my wedding.

Writing Sentences

5 Write the missing verb forms in the chart.

present	past	participle
a. eat	_____	eaten
b. _____	found	_____
c. _____	_____	made
d. play	_____	_____
e. _____	threw	thrown
f. use	_____	_____
g. wear	wore	_____

6 Complete the sentences with the correct form of the passive. Pay attention to singular, plural, present, and past.

a. Dominoes are a kind of tile. Many different games .... played with dominoes.

b. Dominoes .... made from plastic now.

c. Many years ago, dominoes .... made from animal bone.

d. A domino tile .... painted with black spots. Each side of the domino has a different number of spots.

e. The spots .... matched together when you play a game.

f. For example, a domino with three spots on one side .... matched with another domino with three spots on one side.

g. This kind of simple matching game .... played in my kindergarten. My classmates and I learned to count with this game.

h. Today, it .... enjoyed by many people in my country.

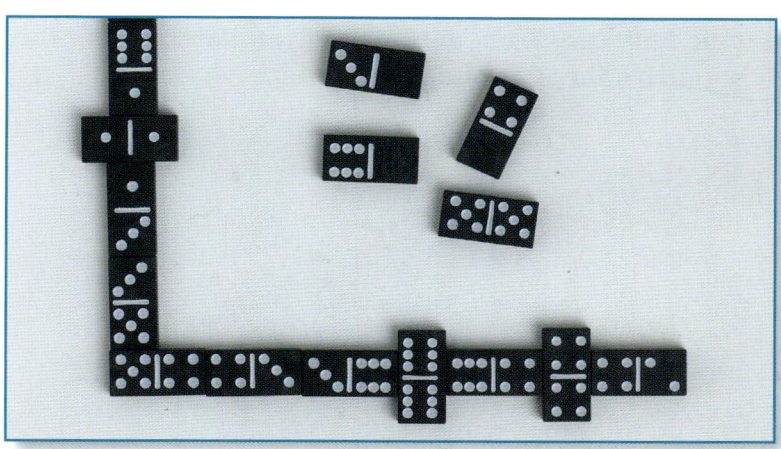

IT'S A KIND OF FRENCH GAME

10 Writing Sentences

7 Read the paragraph. Write the correct form of the verb (active or passive). Then compare your choices with a partner.

A boomerang is a kind of Australian toy. However, long ago, it was not a toy. It (use) _____ for hunting. The hunter (throw) _____ the boomerang at an animal, and it _____ (kill) the animal. Boomerangs (make) _____ of wood, and sometimes they (paint) _____ with colorful designs. Now, boomerangs are popular with tourists. If you visit Australia, why don't you buy a boomerang as a souvenir?

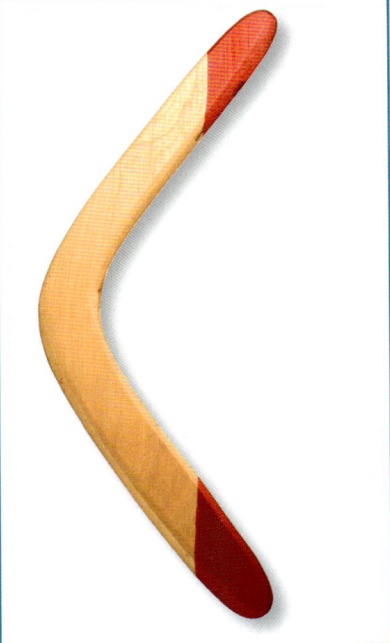

The topic sentence

You already know that a paragraph is a group of sentences about one topic or idea. Many English paragraphs—and all of the ones that you will write for school assignments—include a *topic sentence*. This sentence tells the reader:

- your topic
- your idea or opinion about that topic, or an explanation of the topic

<u>My friend and I</u> <u>have had many similar experiences</u>.
    topic   idea

<u>Mochi</u> <u>is a kind of Japanese food</u>.
topic   explanation

The topic sentence is usually, but not always, the first sentence in the paragraph.

8 Look at these topic sentences from paragraphs you have read in this book. Circle the topic, and <u>underline</u> the idea about the topic.

a. <u>I'm studying</u> (art).

b. I go to an unusual high school in Vermont.

c. I have a new sister!

d. You're an Aries.

e. I went to Marrakech on vacation.

f. Pétanque is a kind of French game.

80   IT'S A KIND OF FRENCH GAME

Writing Sentences

10

Supporting sentences

After the topic sentence come the supporting sentences. These sentences can:

- explain the idea in the topic sentence
- give examples
- give reasons to prove your opinion
- tell a story

However, the supporting sentences must all be about the topic and the idea in the topic sentence.

9 Work with a partner. Read the paragraph. Cross out any sentences that do not support the topic sentence.

Varenyky are a kind of Ukrainian food. I went to Ukraine a few years ago. They are made from flour. Inside, they are stuffed with potatoes, cheese, and onions. I really like potatoes. They are seasoned with a little salt and pepper. Sometimes people make sweet *varenyky*. These are filled with fruit or berries and sugar. *Borchst* is a kind of Ukrainian soup. *Varenyky* are also eaten in Russia. You should try *varenyky*. They're really delicious.

10 Work with a partner. Check (✓) the sentences that you could add to the paragraph in exercise 9 as support. Where would you add them?

- ☐ Potatoes are not expensive in Ukraine.
- ☐ They look like dumplings.
- ☐ Many Ukrainian dishes taste good to me.
- ☐ They are served for dessert.
- ☐ I never cooked varenyky.

10 Writing Sentences

The concluding sentence

The last sentence in a paragraph is often a concluding sentence. This sentence can:

- repeat the idea of the topic sentence
- offer a final comment on the topic

Not all paragraphs have concluding sentences. The writer chooses whether to finish with a concluding sentence or not.

11 Work with a partner. Read some paragraphs from previous units again. Do they have a concluding sentence?

a. Unit 1, exercise 6, page 13 ☐ yes ☐ no
b. Unit 4, exercise 7, page 36 ☐ yes ☐ no
c. Unit 5, exercise 7, page 42 ☐ yes ☐ no
d. Unit 5, exercise 8, page 42 ☐ yes ☐ no
e. Unit 8, exercise 1, page 62 ☐ yes ☐ no
f. Unit 9, exercise 9, page 74 ☐ yes ☐ no

12 Read the paragraph. Then check (✓) the best concluding sentence. Discuss your choice with a partner.

> Mah jongg is a kind of Chinese game. It's played with tiles and dice. It's usually played by four people. It's not difficult to learn, but you need skill to win. You also need luck! These days, you can even play mah jongg on the computer.

a. ☐ It's more difficult than chess.
b. ☐ Mah jongg is popular all over the world now.
c. ☐ I usually lose.

82   IT'S A KIND OF FRENCH GAME

Writing Sentences

13 Work with a partner. Below are sentences from a paragraph.

a Number them in the correct order. Write 1 by the first sentence, 2 by the second sentence, etc.

b Then write them into a paragraph. Use good paragraph form.

> .... First, the beef, cheese, and vegetables are put inside taco shells.
> .... Salsa is a spicy tomato sauce.
> .... Tacos are a kind of Mexican food.
> .... Then they are served with salsa.
> .... They are delicious!
> .... They are made with beef, cheese, and vegetables.
> .... They look a little like a sandwich.

....
....
....
....
....

c Now compare your paragraph with another pair. Did you choose the same order?

Spelling review

14 Write the missing letters.

a. ___ ___ ss ___ ___ ___	This is eaten after dinner.
b. ___ ___ zz	A kind of music
c. ___ ___ rr ___	A spicy sauce
d. ___ ___ ee ___ ___	It's made from milk.
e. ___ oo ___ ___ ___ ___	A kind of sweet snack
f. ___ ___ ___ ss	A kind of clothing for women
g. ___ ___ ff ___ ___ ___ ___ ___	Not easy
h. ___ ___ pp ___ ___	A black spice
i. ___ oo ___ ___ ___ ___ ___ ___	An Australian toy
j. ___ ___ ___ ll	You need this to win at chess.

10 *Writing Sentences*

Put it together: International fair

a Choose something from your own country or a country that interests you. Write your ideas about it in the word map.

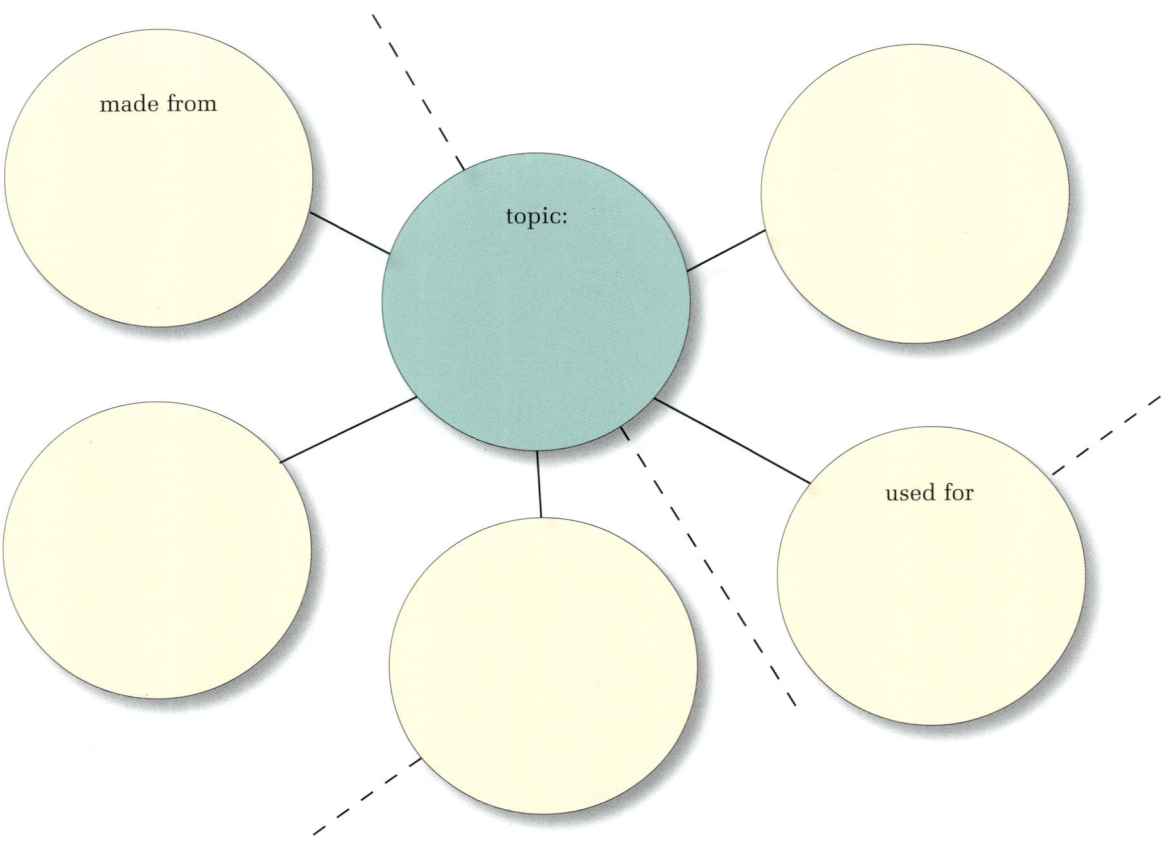

b What do you want to say about your topic? Write your topic sentence here:

....

c Write a concluding sentence here:

....

d Write your paragraph on a separate sheet of paper.

e Share your ideas. Post your paragraphs on the walls of your classroom or spread them on a table or desk. Read your classmates' paragraphs. Then tell the class about something you want to see, do, or try.

> I want to throw a boomerang. It sounds difficult but fun.

> I want to try dumplings. They sound delicious!

11 It has great graphics

In this unit, you will …
- learn vocabulary to describe popular media
- add supporting sentences and concluding sentences
- learn to strengthen and weaken adjectives
- learn to use *too* and *not … enough*

1 Read the different reviews of a video game. Who liked the game? Who didn't like it?

★★★★☆ AAAGamer	I think Omega Chronicles is a wonderful game. It's an action-adventure game for teens and adults. It has great graphics and really interesting gameplay. The characters are realistic. I recommend this game.
★★★★★ Dark Lord	I didn't like this game. It's too difficult, and the directions aren't clear enough. The soundtrack was quite good, but it was too loud.
★★★★★ Angelady	This game is cool! I love the special effects. You can play by yourself or with a friend. The puzzles are very challenging, but they aren't too difficult. Buy or rent this game! You will enjoy it.
★★★★★ Time Knight	Omega Chronicles is really fun. The action is fast, the plot is amazing, and the gameplay is realistic. It's kind of expensive, but I recommend it. It's a great game.

2 Work with a partner. Read the sentences. Circle T if the sentence is true. Circle F if the sentence is false.

a. *AAAGamer* thinks the game is for children.   T   F

b. *Dark Lord* thinks the game isn't easy enough.   T   F

c. *Dark Lord* didn't like the soundtrack.   T   F

d. *Angelady* thinks the puzzles are difficult.   T   F

e. *Time Knight* likes the game.   T   F

f. *Time Knight* thinks the game is expensive.   T   F

Writing Sentences

3 Work with a partner. Write these adjectives into the correct place in the chart below. Can you think of other positive and negative adjectives to describe a video game?

> ✓amazing   challenging   childish   clear   difficult   disappointing
> expensive   fun   great   interesting   realistic   wonderful

positive	negative
amazing	

4 Work with a partner. Complete the word map below with words from the box and your own ideas. Some words can be used for more than one category.

> actor   beat   character   gameplay   graphics   lyrics
> plot   sound effects   soundtrack   special effects   vocals   writing

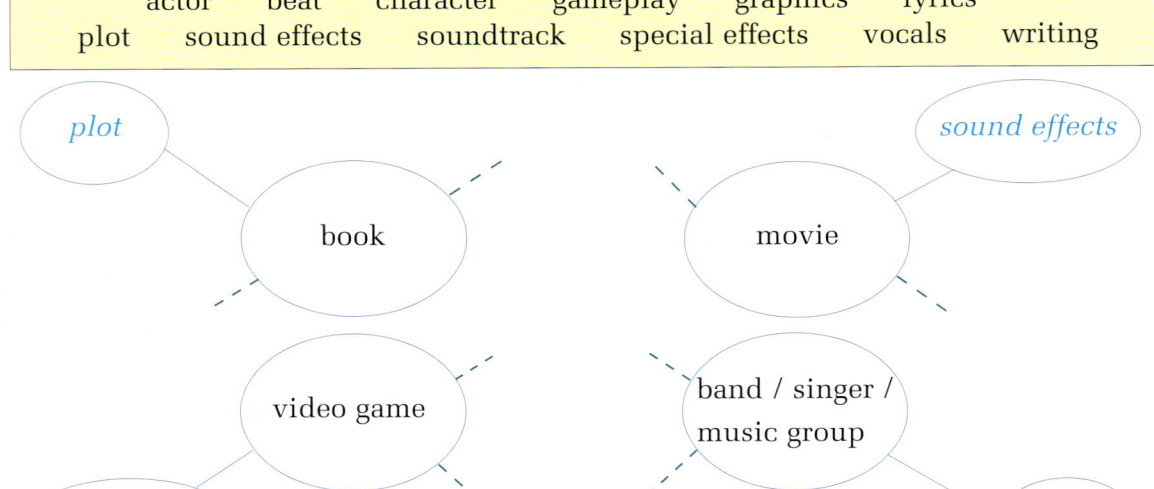

5 Complete the sentences with the name of a book, movie, video game, group or singer. Then share your sentences with a partner. Were any of your sentences about the same thing?

a. ………………………………… has a boring plot.

b. I liked the special effects in ………………………………… .

c. ………………………………… has/have great vocals.

d. I didn't notice the sound effects in ………………………………… .

e. My favorite character in ………………………………… is ………………………………… .

6a Work with a partner. Choose a movie, book, singer or musical group, or video game. Write sentences about it, but do not write its name.

....

....

....

....

....

....

....

....

....

b Now join another pair and read your sentences. Can they guess its name?

There are four movies in this series. The actors are very famous.

Is it Lord of the Rings?

No, I'm sorry.

The special effects are amazing. The main character is a pirate.

Is it Pirates of the Caribbean?

Yes, that's right!.

11 Writing Sentences

Adding support

The paragraphs in this unit describe what something is like—what it looks like, what it sounds like, what the experience is like.

The topic sentence names what you are describing (a book; a movie) and your opinion about it (you liked it; you think it's terrible).

The supporting sentences add details and examples about your topic that explain your opinion.

7 Read the topic sentences. Then check (✓) the sentences you think support the topic sentence. Discuss your choices with a partner.

a *Pirates of the Caribbean* is an excellent movie series.
- [ ] The movies are based on a ride at Disneyland.
- [ ] The actors are terrific. I especially like Johnny Depp.
- [ ] I have the first movie on DVD.
- [ ] The stories are not realistic, but they are interesting.
- [ ] The costumes and soundtrack are great, too.
- [ ] Some of Johnny Depp's other movies are a little strange.
- [ ] They are action movies, but there is humor and romance, too.

b I think *Moby Dick* is a boring book.
- [ ] It is too long.
- [ ] I can't understand all of the old-fashioned language.
- [ ] I'm not interested in the sea or fishing.
- [ ] I never saw the movie of *Moby Dick*.
- [ ] The plot moves really slowly.
- [ ] I don't like the characters.
- [ ] Actually, I'm not very interested in reading.
- [ ] There is too much description and not enough action.

8 Write a concluding sentence for each paragraph in exercise 7. Then compare your sentences with a partner or group.

....

....

Writing Sentences

Strengthening and weakening adjectives

Here are some words and phrases to make your adjectives stronger or weaker:

stronger	weaker
very	a little
really	a bit
quite	kind of
extremely	somewhat

Use these expressions before the adjective:

The plot was strange.
*The plot was **quite** strange.* = more strange
*The plot was **somewhat** strange.* = less strange

These expressions are common after the verbs *be* and *have*.

9 Underline the expressions from the chart that are used in the reviews on page 87.

10 Rewrite the sentences with the expressions in parentheses.
   a. I think animated movies are interesting, so I like *Princess Mononoke*. (very)
      I think animated movies are very interesting, so I like "Princess Mononoke."
   b. The movie is old. (kind of) ....
   c. It is still good. (quite) ....
   d. The plot is confusing. (somewhat) ....
   e. The animation is amazing. (really) ....

Stand-alone adjectives

Some adjectives are not usually strengthened or weakened because they are already very strong or weak: *best, worst, unique, favorite, only*

11 Work with a partner. Read the sentences. Strengthen, weaken, or add nothing to the underlined adjective. Then compare your ideas with another pair.
   a. I like this book, but the vocabulary is *very* difficult.
   b. *Harry Potter* is the top children's book.
   c. The words to this song are childish, but I still like it.
   d. *Shadow of the Colossus* is my favorite video game.
   e. A-mei has a beautiful voice.

IT HAS GREAT GRAPHICS

Writing Sentences

12 Work with a partner. Rewrite the following paragraph. Add four expressions to strengthen and weaken some of the adjectives. Then share your new paragraph with another pair.

> Krazy 4 English is my favorite new group. Their songs have funny lyrics and a strong beat. Their guitar player is amazing, too. Their best single, "Luv 2 Take Tests," has a nice melody. I like to sing it. I'm shy, so I sing it alone in my room. Krazy 4 English are popular now, but I think they will be more popular in the future.

....
....
....
....
....

too and **not ... enough**

Here is another way to strengthen or weaken an adjective that means you are criticizing something:

The gameplay is difficult.

*The gampelay is **too** difficult.*   = more difficult

*The gameplay **isn't** difficult **enough**.*   = less difficult

13 Rewrite the sentences below. Add *too* for the sentences marked ↗. And *not ... enough* to the sentences marked ↘.

I don't like Krazy 4 English.

a. ↗ I think they're popular. *I think they're too popular.*

b. ↗ Their songs are short. ....

c. ↗ The lead singer is strange. ....

d. ↘ The words are clear. ....

e. ↗ Their top song is childish. ....

f. ↘ The vocals are loud. ....

g. ↘ The beat is clear. ....

h. ↗ Their concert tickets are expensive. ....

Writing Sentences

14 Unscramble the sentences.

a. is / movie / that / long / too

....

b. interesting / enough / the / effects / special / aren't

....

c. too / the gameplay / challenging / is / a little bit

....

d. extremely / the / is / exciting / soundtrack

....

e. enough / the / realistic / isn't / plot

....

f. somewhat / is / beat / slow / the

....

g. long and / is too / boring / the book / too

....

h. effects / really / are / the / cool / sound

....

Spelling review

15 One word in each sentence is spelled incorrectly. Cross it out and correct the spelling.

a. *Stormbreaker* is an ~~extremly~~ *extremely* good book.

b. The main caracter is a high school boy. His name is Alex Rider.

c. It's an action-adventere book, and it's for teens and adults.

d. The plot is somwhat unrealistic, but it's exciting.

e. The writing is quiet good, and it's funny too.

f. A movie was made from this book, but it wasn't good enouff.

g. It was kind of disapointing, but it had good special effects.

h. I didn't enjoy the movie, but I reccomend the book.

11 Writing Sentences

Put it together: A media review

a Choose a book, movie, band, video game, or something similar to review. You can choose something you recommend–or something you *don't* recommend! Complete the word map below with your ideas.

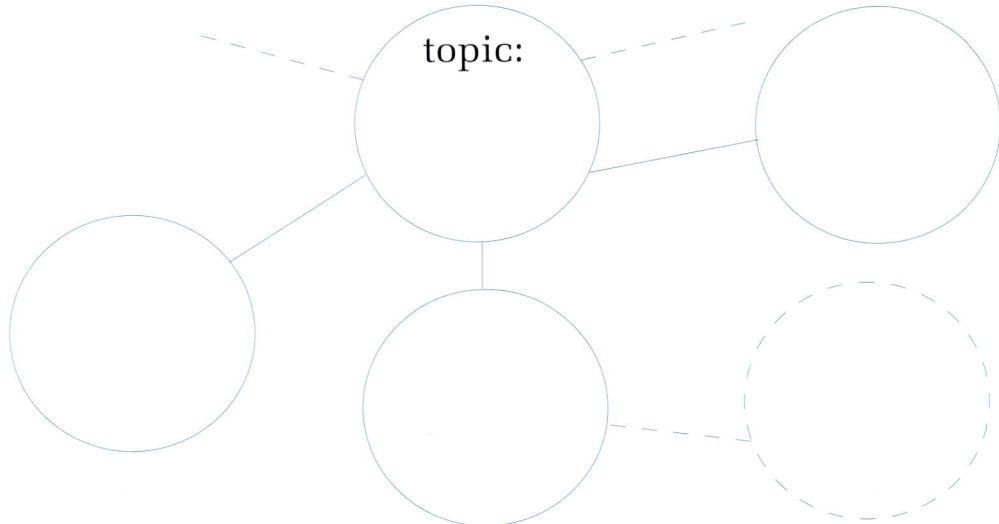

b What do you want to say about your topic? Write your topic sentence here:

....

c Do you want to have a concluding sentence? If so, write it here:

....

d Write your paragraph on a separate sheet of paper.

e Share your reviews. Post your paragraphs on the walls of your classroom or spread them on a table or desk. Read your classmates' reviews. Then tell the class about one or two things you learned about that you'd like to experience, and why.

> I want to see Howl's Moving Castle. It sounds really interesting.

> I want to read Twilight. My best friend also likes it.

12 I've never been to Australia

In this unit, you will …
- learn vocabulary for writing about travel and experiences
- learn and practice the present perfect tense
- contrast the present perfect and the simple past
- use *However* in a paragraph

1 Write the verbs under the correct pictures.

✓ fly   go   hold   see   travel   visit

a. _fly_ in an airplane Sam ☐ Writer ☐
b. _____ to a foreign country Sam ☐ Writer ☐
c. _____ Australia Sam ☐ Writer ☐
d. _____ kangaroos Sam ☐ Writer ☐
e. _____ a koala Sam ☐ Writer ☐
f. _____ surfing Sam ☐ Writer ☐

2 Read the paragraph below. Check (✓) the activities in exercise 1 that Sam did and then check (✓) the activities that the writer has done.

> I envy my friend Sam. He's traveled to many foreign countries. Last year, he flew to Australia. He saw kangaroos, and he held a koala. He went to the beach and went surfing. I've never been to a foreign country. I've never flown in an airplane. I've seen kangaroos and koalas, but I saw them in a zoo. I've been to the beach, but I've never gone surfing. Sam has had more interesting experiences than I have.

12 Writing Sentences

The present perfect

This tense is called the "present" perfect, but we use it to talk about things that happened in the past. It is one of the most common tenses in written English.

Noun	verb: have + past participle	noun (direct object)	preposition + noun (adverb phrase)
Sam He	has hasn't has never	seen been	kangaroos. to Australia.
We	have haven't have never	flown	in an airplane.

Use the *present perfect*:

- to describe a life experience:
  Sam **has seen** a kangaroo.
  I've never **been** to Australia.

- to describe something you've done in the past more than once:
  I've seen "Star Wars" eleven times.
  I've played that game a lot.

- to talk about something that started in the past, and is still true now:
  I've lived here for three years.
  Nina **has played** the piano for a long time.

Form the present perfect with the present tense of *have* + the past participle.

Remember: *have* must agree with the subject.

(See page 105 for a list of common irregular past participles).

3 **Write the past participle of the following verbs.**

a. have: I have ...*had*............... many interesting experiences.

b. travel: I have .... to several countries.

c. take: I have .... many photographs.

d. eat: On vacation, I have .... a lot of delicious food.

e. see: I haven't .... every country.

f. be: For example, I've never .... to Kenya.

Writing Sentences

4 Write the verb in the present perfect. Make sure that *has* and *have* agree with the subject.

   a. My parents .... (be) to many interesting places.

   b. My father .... (travel) to Switzerland and Austria.

   c. He loves mountains, so he .... (see) the Alps many times.

   d. My mother likes swimming. She .... (take) diving trips to Guam and Saipan.

   e. I .... never .... (visit) a foreign country, but my parents .... (tell) me about their travels many times.

Contrast with the simple past

Use the *simple past*:

- to describe an action that happened once in the past:
   Sam **saw** a kangaroo last year.
   I **went** to China.

- to describe an action that had a clear start and finish, and is finished now:
   I **drove** to school.
   I **ate** lunch at 12:00.

Use the **simple past** with expressions such as *at 3:00, yesterday, on Monday, last year, this morning*:
   I **got up** at 6:00.
   I **had** a piano lesson on Tuesday.

Use the **present perfect** with adverbs such as *already, never, ever, yet, for, since*:
   Have you ever **gone** surfing?
   I've never **traveled**.
   I've **known** my best friend since elementary school.

5 Work with a partner. <u>Underline</u> the sentences on page 93 that use the present perfect. <u>Double</u> <u>underline</u> the sentences that use the simple past. For each sentence, explain why the present perfect or simple past was used with one of the reasons below:

present perfect	simple past
• It's talking about his life experience. • It's talking about something he did more than one time in the past.	• It's talking about something he did only one time in the past.

12 Writing Sentences

6 Answer the questions with information from exercise 2 on page 93. Use short answers (*Yes, he has; Yes, they have; No, he hasn't; No, they haven't*).

a. Has Sam flown in an airplane? ....

b. Has Sam held a koala? ....

c. Has the writer visited Australia? ....

d. Have Sam and the writer seen kangaroos? ....

e. Has the writer been to the beach? ....

f. Has the writer gone surfing? ....

7 Look at the activities in exercise 6. Have you done those activities once, many times, or never? Write sentences. Follow the example.

I flew in an airplane last year. Or, *I've flown in an airplane many times.*

a. ....

b. ....

c. ....

d. ....

e. ....

f. ....

8 Read the following paragraph. Write the correct form of the verb in parentheses.

My friend Amy and I (have) _____ many similar experiences. We both (live) _____ in this town all our lives. We (go) _____ to the same elementary school and middle school, and now we're in the same high school. Amy and I (study) _____ musical instruments for several years. She plays the piano and I play the violin. Amy (travel) _____ to Kaohsiung, and I (visit) _____ Hong Kong. We (not / be) _____ to Europe or South America, but we both want to go. We are different people, but we (have) _____ similar lives so far.

9 Write five questions for a partner using the present perfect and, in case your partner answers "yes," the past tense. Use a separate sheet of paper and follow the example.

Have you ever been to New York? When did you go?

Writing Sentences

10 Interview your partner. Then use your partner's answers to write a paragraph about you and your partner like the one on page 96. Use a separate sheet of paper, and begin with one of these sentences:

My classmate (_____) and I have had many similar experiences.
My classmate (_____) and I haven't had many similar experiences.

However

You already know how to use *but* in a sentence to show contrasting information:

I've been to Australia, **but** *I haven't been to New Zealand.*

However has a similar meaning. It is used at the beginning of a sentence to show that the next sentence, or even the next section of the paragraph, is different from what came before:

I've been to Australia, New Zealand, and Tahiti. **However,** *I haven't been to many cities in my own country.*

11 Draw a line to match the sentences on the left with the sentences on the right.

a. I've eaten Mexican food.
b. I haven't ridden a camel.
c. I've been to France.
d. I've never been to India.
e. I've gone skiing.
f. I've never gone surfing.

1. However, I've never been to Paris.
2. However, I've tried windsurfing.
3. However, I've ridden a horse several times.
4. However, I've never tried snowboarding.
5. However, I've never cooked it.
6. However, I've eaten Indian food.

12 Read the following paragraph. Where would you put the word *However*? Discuss your choice with a partner.

I'm still in high school, but I think I've done many interesting things. I haven't traveled much, and I haven't been to a foreign country.
a) _____ I haven't ridden a horse or a camel, and I haven't seen many famous places.
b) _____ I've ridden my bicycle all around my city. I've taken a lot of interesting photos, and I've met a lot of people. I've played a lot of sports, like basketball, soccer, and tennis. I've had several part-time jobs, and I learned a lot about working. c) _____ I want to do many more things in my life, but I think I've already done a lot.

Writing Sentences

13 Read the following sentences. Check (✓) the sentences that tell about the foods the person has tried. Write an (✗) by the foods the person hasn't tried.

✓   I've tried Indian food.
_____ I can cook some Chinese dishes, too.
_____ I've never eaten French food.
_____ I've cooked a lot of Italian food.
_____ I made spaghetti last week.
_____ I haven't tried Korean food.
_____ I've eaten a lot of Chinese dishes.
_____ I'm interested in Spanish food, but I haven't tried any yet.

14 Work with a partner. Use the information in exercise 13 to write about the foods the person has tried. Then use *However* and write about the foods the person hasn't tried.

> I'm very interested in international food. I've tried a lot of different kinds of food, but there are some kinds I haven't tried yet. ....
> ....
> ....
> ....
> ....
> There are still many kinds of food I want to try.

Spelling review

15 Look at the chart with examples of how participles are spelled. Then write the verbs below into the correct column.

regular: add ~ed/d	double the last letter and add ~ed	drop the ~y and add ~ied	irregular
visit → visited	stop → stopped	hurry → hurried	go → gone

eat	live	shop	try	wear
do	plan	stay	want	worry

98   I'VE NEVER BEEN TO AUSTRALIA

Writing Sentences

12

Put it together: My story so far

a What have you done in your life so far? What haven't you done yet? Make a list. Follow the examples.

places	activities	foods	sights	subjects
I've been to (Dubai).	I've (gone surfing).	I've tried (coconut).	I've seen …	I've studied …
I haven't / I've never been to (Brazil).	I haven't …	I've never eaten (snake).	I've never seen …	I've never learned …

b Choose one of these topic sentences to begin your paragraph.

> I've lived for _____ years, but I haven't experienced many things yet.

(Write first about the things you have done. Then use *However* and write about the things you haven't done.)

> I've lived for _____ years, and I've already experienced many things.

(Write first about the things you haven't done. Then use *However* and write about the things you have done.)

c Write your paragraph on a separate sheet of paper.

d Share your story with a small group. Read your paragraph to the group. Talk about experiences you've all had that are similar, and what experiences only one of you has had.

Writing Sentences

Key sentence patterns

The verb *be* (Unit 3)

Subject (noun / pronoun)	verb *be*	noun, adjective, or prepositional phrase (adverb)
I	am	Thai.
My friends and I	are	hungry.
My hometown	is	in the mountains.

Stative verbs (Unit 4)

Subject	stative verb	adjective
You	seem	friendly.
My teacher	looks	happy.

Action verbs with objects (Unit 6)

Subject	verb	noun (direct object)	prepositional phrase
I	play	soccer	in the park.
Kiyo	takes	piano lessons	

Action verbs with direct and indirect objects (Unit 9)

Subject	verb	noun (direct object)	(preposition) + noun (indirect object)
I	wrote	a letter	to Charlie.
You	gave	some money	to me.

Subject	verb	noun (indirect object)	noun (direct object)
I	wrote	Charlie	a letter.
You	gave	me	some money.

The passive (Unit 10)

Subject (the object from an active sentence)	*be* + verb (participle)	prepositional phrase
Mochi	is made	from rice.
Tigers	are found	in India.

Regular verbs

PRESENT TENSE
Affirmative Statements

I like You like He likes She likes It likes We like They like	school.

Negative Statements

I do You do He does She does It does We do They do	not like	school.

Yes / No **Questions**

Do I Do you Does he Does she Does it Do we Do they	like	school?

Short Answers

affirmative	negative
Yes, I do.	No, I don't.
Yes, you do.	No, you don't.
Yes, he does.	No, he doesn't.
Yes, she does.	No, she doesn't.
Yes, it does.	No, it doesn't.
Yes, we do.	No, we don't.
Yes, they do.	No, they don't.

Writing Sentences

PAST TENSE
Affirmative Statements

I You He She It We They	liked	school.

Negative Statements

I You He She It We They	did not like	school.

Yes / No **Questions**

Did	I you he she it we they	like	school?

Short Answers

affirmative	negative
Yes, I did.	No, I didn't.
Yes, you did.	No, you didn't.
Yes, he did.	No, he didn't.
Yes, she did.	No, she didn't.
Yes, it did.	No, it didn't.
Yes, we did.	No, we didn't.
Yes, they did.	No, they didn't.

Can

PRESENT TENSE

Affirmative Statements

| I
You
He
She
It
We
They | can | speak | English. |

Negative Statements

| I
You
He
She
It
We
They | can not | speak | English. |

Yes / No **Questions**

| Can | I
you
he
she
it
we
they | speak | Swedish? |

Short Answers

affirmative			negative		
Yes,	I you he she it we they	can.	No,	I you he she it we they	can't.

Writing Sentences

PAST TENSE
Affirmative Statements

I You He She It We They	could	play	the piano.

Negative Statements

I You He She It We They	could not	play	the piano.

Yes / No **Questions**

Could	I you he she it we they	play	the piano?

Short Answers

affirmative			negative		
Yes,	I you he she it we they	could.	No,	I you he she it we they	couldn't.

Common irregular verbs

Here is a list of common irregular verbs in English with their past tense (*I took* the test) and past participle (*I have taken* three tests this month).

Infinitive	Simple past	Past participle	Infinitive	Simple past	Past participle
be	was/were	been	make	made	made
become	became	become	meet	met	met
begin	began	begun	pay	paid	paid
break	broke	broken	put	put	put
bring	brought	brought	read	read	read
buy	bought	bought	ride	rode	ridden
catch	caught	caught	run	ran	run
choose	chose	chosen	say	said	said
come	came	come	see	saw	seen
cost	cost	cost	sell	sold	sold
cut	cut	cut	send	sent	sent
do	did	done	show	showed	shown
draw	drew	drawn	sing	sang	sung
drink	drank	drunk	sit	sat	sat
drive	drove	driven	sleep	slept	slept
eat	ate	eaten	speak	spoke	spoken
fall	fell	fallen	spend	spent	spent
feel	felt	felt	stand	stood	stood
find	found	found	swim	swam	swum
fly	flew	flown	take	took	taken
forget	forgot	forgotten	teach	taught	taught
get	got	gotten	tell	told	told
give	gave	given	think	thought	thought
go	went	gone	throw	threw	thrown
have	had	had	understand	understood	understood
hear	heard	heard	wear	wore	worn
know	knew	known	win	won	won
leave	left	left	write	wrote	written
lose	lost	lost			

DOROTHY E ZEMACH
& CARLOS ISLAM

writing
PARAGRAPHS
FROM SENTENCE TO PARAGRAPH

Contents

To the Teacher cx
To the Student cxi

Introduction — 112
- Formatting assignments and writing headings
- Process writing

1 Beginning to Work — 115
- Recognizing and writing complete sentences
- Beginning and ending a sentence
- Common paragraph features
- Identifying the topic of a paragraph
- Identifying strong and weak paragraphs

2 Giving and Receiving Gifts — 123
- Identifying topics and main ideas
- Identifying strong and weak topic sentences
- Writing topic sentences
- Combining sentences using *and* and *but*
- Using commas in sentences with *and* and *but*

3 A Favorite Place — 130
- Developing paragraphs with descriptive details
- Using lists to brainstorm
- Learning to edit lists
- Combining sentences containing adjectives
- Writing about places

4 An Exceptional Person — 136
- Using word maps to brainstorm
- Using adjectives in sentences
- Writing concluding sentences
- Using capital letters
- Writing about people

5 Trends and Fads — 144
- Review of descriptive vocabulary
- Using freewriting to brainstorm
- Review of paragraph contents
- Developing peer feedback skills
- Writing about a trend

6 White Lies — 152
- Opinions and examples in supporting sentences
- Using discussion to brainstorm
- Writing about your opinions

7 Explanations and Excuses — 158
- Paragraphs explaining cause and effect / result
- Combining sentences with *so* and *because*
- Practicing word maps and freewriting
- Writing about explanations and excuses

8 Problems and Challenges — 165
- Expressing personal feelings about problems
- Using *would like to*, *want to*, and *have to*
- Logical order of supporting sentences
- Editing lists by ordering ideas logically
- Writing about problems or difficulties

9 Strange Stories — 172
- Using time expressions: *after*, *before*, and *when*
- Identifying the main parts of a narrative
- Ordering events in a narrative logically
- Writing about interesting or unusual experiences

10 Differences — 179
- Using double lists to brainstorm
- Using *whereas* and *however* to make comparisons
- Organizing a comparison paragraph
- Comparing different situations / events
- Writing about life changes

11 Difficult Decisions — 185
- Writing about cause and effect relationships
- Using pair interviews to brainstorm
- Beginning paragraphs with a question
- Writing about a difficult decision

12 Fate or Choice? — 190
- Writing about hopes and plans for the future
- Review of brainstorming techniques
- Review of transition expressions
- Writing about the future

Additional Materials — 195
- Useful grammar for writers
- Useful punctuation for academic paragraphs
- Sample brainstorming, 1st draft, peer review notes, and final draft paragraph
- Peer Review Forms

To the Teacher

Writing is an important form of communication in day-to-day life, but it is especially important in high school and university. Writing is also one of the most difficult skills to master in both a first language and a second language. Students can find it challenging to find ideas to include in their writing, and each culture has its own style for organizing academic writing. However, with the help of this book and your guidance, your students will learn to recognize good academic paragraphs and develop their own paragraph writing skills.

Writing Paragraphs is designed to help low-intermediate students analyze model paragraphs, find ideas for their writing, put their ideas into sentences, organize their sentences into paragraphs, review their paragraphs, and revise their paragraphs so that they become even stronger. This process approach to writing will not only develop your students' paragraph writing skills, but will also encourage them to become independent and creative writers.

Each main unit provides an interesting theme to engage your students and motivate them to read and analyze the model paragraphs. The unit themes also inspire your students to create their own writing. An introductory unit shows students how to format their writing and introduces the idea of process writing.

The activities in each unit help students with a particular aspect of paragraph writing, such as brainstorming, writing topic sentences, and developing paragraphs with supporting sentences. A unit's activities might also teach correct punctuation for academic writing and useful grammatical functions for writing, such as conjunctions and connecting words and expressions. The units also show students how to review their own and their classmates' writing in order to make revisions.

Each unit ends with a structured writing assignment that provides an opportunity for students to use everything presented in the unit. Included in *Writing Paragraphs* are samples of a paragraph from brainstorming to final draft, with a completed Peer Review Form. There is also a guide to common grammatical terms and concepts useful for writers, and a guide to punctuation for easy reference.

The Teacher's Guide supports the instructor by offering teaching suggestions, a discussion of marking and grading writing and ideas for supplemental activities for each unit.

Learning to write well takes a lot of practice and patience. Students need clear guidance, positive feedback, and interesting ideas to write about. We hope this book provides this for you and you enjoy using it.

To the Student

Writing is a very important part of your school and university study. You will write assignments that may be one paragraph or several paragraphs, and you will write answers for tests and exams that may be a few sentences, a paragraph or two, or a complete essay.

Academic writing in English may be different not only from academic writing in your own language, but even from other writing in English. The purpose of *Writing Paragraphs* is to help you recognize and produce the sort of paragraph writing that will be expected of you in academic situations.

During this course, you will have many opportunities to study and discuss examples of English academic paragraph writing. You will also have many opportunities to discuss your own paragraphs and the paragraphs of your classmates. You will learn how important the reader is to the writer, and how to express clearly and directly what you mean to communicate. We hope that what you learn in this course will help you throughout your academic studies and beyond.

You should come to your writing class every day with energy and a willingness to work and learn. Your instructor and your classmates have much to share with you, and you have much to share with them. By coming to class with your questions, taking chances and trying new ways, and expressing your ideas in another language, you will add not only to your own world, but to the world of those around you.

Good luck!

Dorothy E Zemach
Carlos Islam

Introduction

In this unit, you will learn ...
- formatting for handwritten and word-processed assignments.
- how to write headings.
- about process writing.

Formatting

1. Look at these student papers. Check (✓) the ones that have the correct form for an academic assignment.

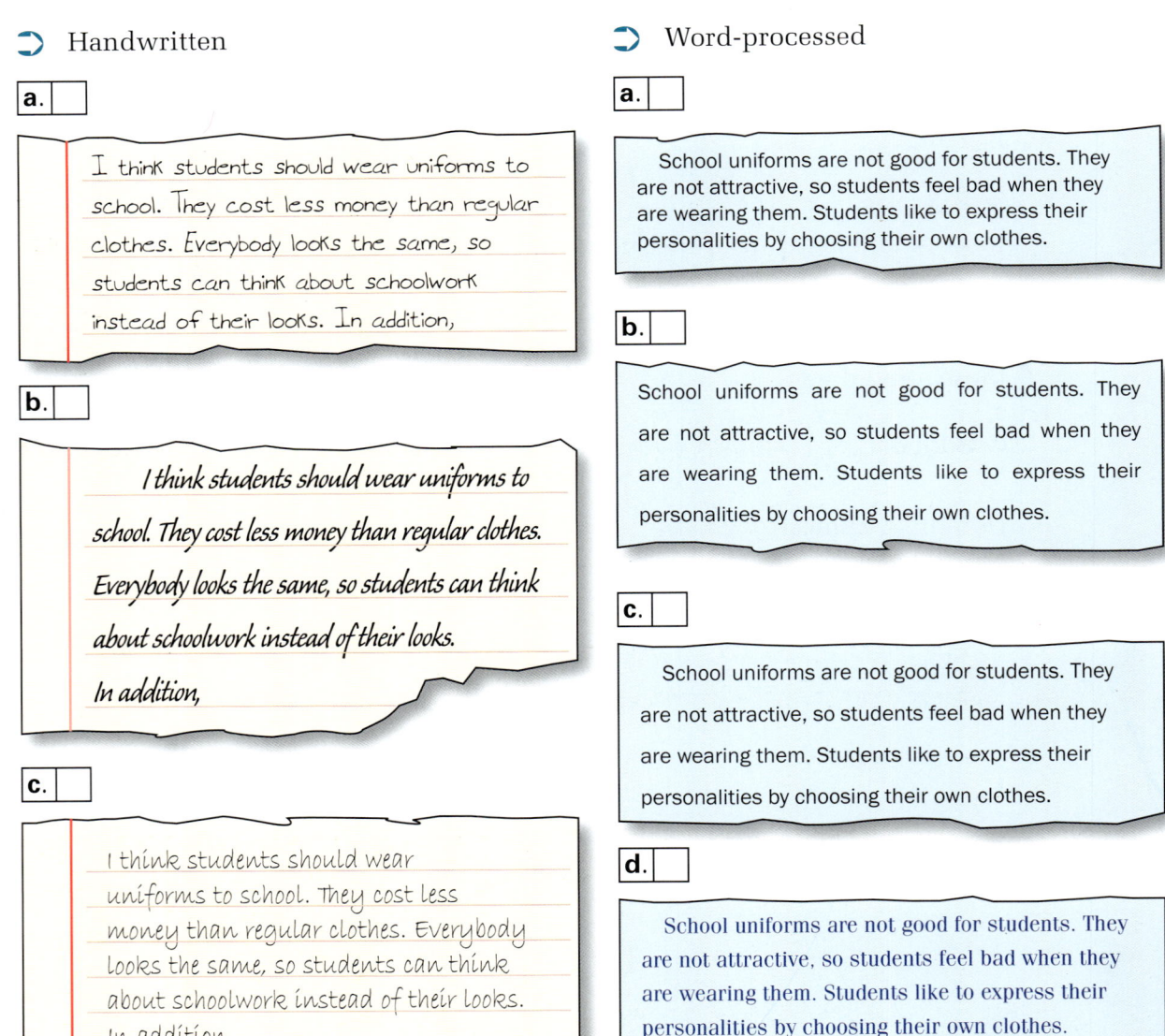

Writing Paragraphs

2 Look at these different ways of writing headings for student papers. Answer the questions below.

a.

> Karen Chou
> Professor Miller
> English Writing 1
> April 12, 2011
>
> School Uniforms Are Good

1. What is the writer's name?
2. What is the name of the class?
3. Who is teaching the class?
4. What is the title of the assignment?

b.

> Sebastian Mitchell
> School uniforms
> 2nd draft
> September 5, 2011
>
> Students Should Choose Their Own Clothes

1. What is the writer's name?
2. What is the title of the assignment?
3. What is the assignment about?
4. What does "2nd draft" mean?
5. When did the writer write the assignment?

How does your teacher want you to write headings in this class?
Write an example here:

INTRODUCTION 113

Writing Paragraphs

Process writing

3 Take a quiz! First guess the correct answers. Then read the paragraphs below to check your guesses.

a. "Process writing" means
- ☐ writing in English.
- ☐ writing with a word processor.
- ☐ writing in several stages (steps).

b. Before you begin to write, you should
- ☐ finish the homework for your other classes.
- ☐ get some ideas.
- ☐ ask your friends for help.

c. Your teacher may ask you to read a classmate's paper and answer some questions about it. This is because
- ☐ you can learn a lot by reading your classmate's assignment.
- ☐ your teacher is too busy to read all the students' papers.
- ☐ you are a better writer than your classmate.

d. Your teacher may ask you to write another draft. This is because
- ☐ your teacher can't think of any new assignments.
- ☐ the first time, your paper was bad.
- ☐ you can make your paper better by making some changes.

e. Before you hand in your paper for a grade, you should
- ☐ ask your teacher to give you a good grade.
- ☐ check it carefully.
- ☐ put some pretty stickers on it.

a. Musicians practice their pieces many times before a concert. Athletes work out before a competition. In the same way, good writers go through several stages when they write. "Process writing" will guide you through these stages so your final paper is really your effort.

b. The first stage of process writing is getting ideas. In this course, you will learn and practice several different ways to get ideas. Try them all and see which way works best for you.

c. An important stage in process writing is sharing your writing. You can see how other writers like you handled the same assignment, and you can get some good ideas from them. You can also see how well someone else understands your ideas.

d. After you finish your assignment, put it away for some time. When you look at it again, you may have new ideas. Your classmates may help you find new ideas, too. Writing your paper again (called "revising") gives you the chance to improve your paper.

e. Before you give your teacher your paper, check it carefully. Read it out loud. Does it sound natural? Did you forget any words? Did you remember to write the heading correctly? Does your paper look neat? Remember to give your teacher your best effort!

Beginning to Work

In this unit, you will ...
- recognize and write complete sentences.
- learn how to begin and end a sentence.
- learn the common features of a paragraph.
- identify the topic of a paragraph.
- identify strong and weak paragraphs.

1 Look at this chart. Check (✓) the answers for your country.

	It's common.	It's not common.	I'm not sure. / It depends.
a. High school students have part-time jobs.	☐	☐	☐
b. University students have part-time jobs.	☐	☐	☐
c. University students have volunteer jobs (jobs that don't pay a salary).	☐	☐	☐
d. Part-time jobs pay a good salary.	☐	☐	☐
e. After graduation, both men and women want to find a full-time job.	☐	☐	☐

2 Share your information with a group of your classmates. Ask and answer these questions about part-time jobs.

- What are common part-time jobs?
- Have you ever had a job? What was your first job?
- What kind of job do you think is best for a high school / university student?
- (your idea)

BEGINNING TO WORK 115

Writing Paragraphs

3 You are going to read a paragraph called *Part-time Jobs and High School*. What do you think the paragraph is about? Circle the answer.

    a. Useful high school subjects

    b. Working and studying at the same time

    c. How much money a part-time job pays

4 Read the paragraph. Did you choose the right answer in exercise 3 above?

> Part-time Jobs and High School
>
> 1. High school students should not have part-time jobs. 2. High school is a very important time for a student, and students are very busy. 3. Students have to study hard to enter a good university. 4. Many high school students also play sports, and they practice before and after school. 5. High school students also spend time with friends of the same age. 6. Those friendships can be important for the rest of their lives. 7. A part-time job takes time away from studying, playing sports, and making friends. 8. People work for most of their adult lives. 9. When they are in high school, it's important for them to just be high school students.

5 Which sentence tells the writer's most important idea?

    1 ☐   2 ☐   3 ☐   8 ☐

6 What do sentences 3, 4, and 5 do?

    a. They show new ideas.

    b. They give examples.

    c. They show different opinions.

7 Do you agree with the writer? Why / Why not?

Writing Paragraphs

Writing focus: What is a sentence?

How many words are in the shortest English sentence? Except for one-word commands (*Sit!*), a complete sentence in English needs two words: a subject (a noun or pronoun) and a predicate (a verb) (*She sits*).

Of course, most English sentences are longer than just two words, but every sentence tells a complete thought. Groups of words that do not make complete sentences are called *phrases*.

If you need more information on complete sentences and phrases, see pages 195–197.

8 Work with a partner. Look at the following. Some of them could be sentences with the correct punctuation. Check (✓) the ones that could be sentences.

a. ☐ housewives and young parents
b. ☐ some retired people want to work
c. ☐ earn some extra money
d. ☐ meet new people
e. ☐ volunteer jobs don't pay a salary
f. ☐ an opportunity to learn new skills
g. ☐ several part-time jobs

Language focus: Capital letters and final punctuation

Sentences in a paragraph ...

- start with a capital letter
  Part-time jobs can be stressful.

- end with a period (.) question mark (?) or exclamation point (!)
  Many students work as tutors**.**
  How old were you when you got your first job**?**
  I will never work in a restaurant again**!**

> **Note:** Exclamation points are not as common in academic writing as they are in casual writing. Don't use them too often. Never use more than one exclamation point at the end of a sentence in academic writing.
>
> *The company offered me a part-time job!!* = when writing to friends
>
> *The company offered me a part-time job.* = when writing in school

BEGINNING TO WORK 117

1

Writing Paragraphs

9 Unscramble the sentences and write them on the lines below. Begin and end each sentence correctly.

a. in a shop / my sister / works

   My sister works in a shop.

b. is / a useful subject / computer science

   ....

c. don't / I / like / working with people

   ....

d. can't find / many students / a job / easily

   ....

e. more women / are / after college / working ?

   ....

f. first job / was / my / wonderful / a / experience

   ....

10 Look again at exercise 8 on page 117. Write the complete sentences with correct punctuation. Add to the phrases to make complete sentences. Then share your sentences with a partner. How are they different?

a. ....

b. ....

c. ....

d. ....

e. ....

f. ....

g. ....

Writing Paragraphs

Writing focus: What is a paragraph?

A paragraph is a group of about 6–12 sentences about one *topic*. Every sentence in a strong paragraph is about the same topic. All of the sentences explain the writer's *main idea* (most important idea) about that topic. When the writer wants to write about a new main idea, he / she begins a new paragraph.

A paragraph can give information, tell an opinion, explain something, or even tell a short story. The sentences are arranged logically, so the reader can easily understand what the writer wants to say.

In academic writing, a paragraph has a *topic sentence* that directly tells the reader the main idea. The other sentences in the paragraph, called **supporting sentences**, give more information about the topic. They add specific details and explanations. In academic English, the topic sentence is usually (but not always!) first or last.

1 Work with a partner. Read the groups of sentences below and on page 120. Circle the letters of the strong paragraphs. If you think the sentences make a weak paragraph, say why. Choose one or more of these reasons:

- The sentences are not all about the same topic.
- There are not enough sentences.
- There is no topic sentence.
- Some sentences say the same thing.

> When I need a good place to study, I go to the library. It's always quiet there, so I can concentrate. It's easy to find the books I need, and I can search for information on the Internet because there are several computers. The other people in the library are also reading or working, so the mood is good for studying. I study better and faster in the library than in any other place.

a. ....

> I need to buy a motorcycle. With a motorcycle, I could get to my job more quickly. It takes two hours to get to work by train. That's very slow. A motorcycle is much faster. If I had a motorcycle, I could save a lot of time. Taking the train is not fast enough for me.

b. ....

Writing Paragraphs

> First, insert a blank CD into the computer. Then, select the song list that you want to copy. You will see a button that says, "Click here to burn." Click on that button. Then just wait a few minutes. That's all!

c. ....

> *I will never forget my first day of high school. I was very nervous because I didn't know any of the other students. In my first class, I looked around for someone friendly. I saw a girl at the front of the room who also looked nervous, so I decided to make friends with her. Even though I was shy about talking to her, I went up to her and said, "Don't be nervous. I will help you. Do you want to sit with me?" She looked a little surprised and said, "Actually, I am the new teacher."*

d. ....

> Smart phones are very popular. They're convenient. They have a lot of applications.

e. ....

> *Sports instructor is a good part-time job. You can enjoy your favorite activity and earn money at the same time. Some other jobs pay better. You can also volunteer as an instructor. I had a difficult time learning to swim, because my instructor wasn't very good. My tennis instructor was much better. If you get a lot of experience as a sports instructor, you can get a job at a gym or as a coach in the future.*

f. ....

Writing Paragraphs

12 Read this paragraph about a student's first job. What is the topic?
   a. Working in a laboratory
   b. Getting my first job
   c. What my first job taught me

> ### Learning Responsibility
>
> 1. My first job was as a sales clerk in a small clothing store. 2. It wasn't a difficult job, and it wasn't really a very interesting job. 3. My best friend had a more exciting job. 4. Every weekend I had to open the store at 10:00 a.m. 5. I couldn't be late. 6. Now on weekends I like to sleep late. 7. I helped customers find clothes, and I kept the store neat and clean. 8. My parents' house was very clean, too. 9. I used the cash register and handled credit cards, so I had to be very careful. 10. These things all taught me responsibility. 11. Now I work in a research laboratory. 12. I don't work with clothing anymore, but I still use that important skill I learned in my first job.

13 Cross out the sentences that are not connected to the topic.

14 Which additional sentences could be connected to the paragraph? Write C (connected) or U (unconnected).
   a. .... I answered the phone and opened the mail.
   b. .... On weekdays I did my homework for school.
   c. .... I once worked delivering pizza, too.
   d. .... I learned how to choose and order new clothing.
   e. .... Dressing neatly and professionally was an important part of the job.
   f. .... A lab assistant is a good job for me.
   g. .... In the future, I would like to take some business trips.

1 Writing Paragraphs

Put it together

a Look at these sentences for a paragraph about having a part-time job in high school. Cross out the ones that are not connected. On a separate sheet of paper, write a paragraph using the connected sentences. They are already in the right order but are not yet correctly punctuated.

> having a part-time job is a valuable experience for American high school students
>
> they can learn many things that are not usually taught in a classroom
>
> for example, they can learn how to work with older people
>
> I was the youngest person in my high school class
>
> they also get experience with the business world
>
> I took a business class in college that was very good
>
> having a part-time job gives students a sense of independence
>
> they can also earn money to use for college
>
> college tuition in the U.S. is more expensive than in many other countries
>
> education is more than just school subjects
>
> learning about the real world is also important
>
> some colleges help their graduates find jobs after graduation

b Check your writing.
Did you ...
- [ ] include a heading on your paper?
- [ ] format the paragraph properly (see page 2)?
- [ ] start and end each sentence correctly?
- [ ] give the paragraph a title?

c Hand in your paragraph to your teacher.

122 BEGINNING TO WORK

2 Giving and Receiving Gifts

In this unit, you will ...
- identify topics and main ideas.
- identify strong and weak topic sentences.
- practice writing topic sentences.
- combine sentences using *and* and *but*.
- learn how to use commas in sentences with *and* and *but*.

1 Tell a partner about the last gift you received.
- Who gave you the gift?
- When did they give you the gift?
- What was the gift? Did you like it?

2 Read the paragraph and answer the questions.
   a. What is the topic of the paragraph?
   1. celebrating birthdays
   2. the writer's family
   3. choosing gifts

   b. What is the writer's most important opinion about the topic?
   1. Gifts should be old.
   2. Gifts should be chosen carefully.
   3. A photograph is a good birthday gift.

   c. Why does the writer like the photograph?
   1. It helps him think about his father.
   2. It wasn't expensive.
   3. It was a birthday gift.

A Birthday Gift

1. Choosing a birthday gift for a friend or family member is fun, but it can be difficult. 2. The gift should be personal and has to be thoughtful. 3. For example, the best birthday gift I ever got wasn't fancy or expensive. 4. Last year my mother gave me a photograph of my father when he was my age. 5. He is standing with his mother and father (my grandparents) in front of their house, and he looks happy. 6. I think of my father every time I see that photo. 7. It was a perfect birthday gift.

2 Writing Paragraphs

Writing focus: Topic sentences

A good topic sentence should include either of the following:

- one clear topic
  weak: *It's important to have friends, and also to do well in school.*
  strong: *I don't think I will ever have a better friend than Heather.*

- an opinion or idea about the topic
  weak: *I have been studying karate.*
  strong: *Studying karate has given me strength and self-confidence.*

A good topic sentence should **not** be:

- too *broad* (too much to write about)
  weak: *Australia is an interesting country.*
  strong: *On my visit to Australia, I saw many unusual animals.*

- too *narrow* (not enough to write about / is just a fact)
  weak: *School starts at 8:30 a.m.*
  strong: *Getting ready for school in the morning is more difficult than any of my classes.*

Remember: The topic sentence is *usually* the first or last sentence, but it can be any sentence in the paragraph.

3 Look at these topic sentences. Circle the topic of the sentence. Underline the main idea.

a. This (soccer ball) was the gift I liked best.
b. Shopping for gifts online takes a lot of time.
c. The last CD I received changed my life.
d. There are three reasons why I want a new laptop.
e. Reading novels, such as the *Twilight* series, can help students improve their English.
f. A present tells you a lot about the person who bought it.
g. An amusement park was the perfect place to hold our graduation party.

4 Look again at the paragraph on page 123, *A Birthday Gift*. Which sentence is the topic sentence? Circle the topic and underline the main idea.

Writing Paragraphs 2

5 In the following pairs, circle the number of the best topic sentence. Then explain your choice to a partner. Say why the sentence you didn't choose is weak. Use one or more of these reasons:

- It's too broad.
- It's too narrow.
- There is no main idea or opinion.
- There is more than one main idea.

a. 1. Gifts can cost a lot of money, and then you also have to wrap them.
   2. (Wrapping a gift in a special way can make your gift seem even more special.)
   There are two main ideas.

b. 1. Receiving gifts can make some people feel uncomfortable.
   2. I really like gifts.
   ....

c. 1. Parents spend too much money on birthday gifts for babies.
   2. For my last birthday, I got a gold watch with a leather band from my father.
   ....

d. 1. Different countries all over the world have interesting gift-giving customs.
   2. Several gift-giving customs in China surprised me when I lived there.
   ....

e. 1. The best gift I ever gave didn't cost me anything.
   2. I spent €130 on a gift for my parents.
   ....

f. 1. Shopping online makes it easier to find an appropriate gift.
   2. Buying gifts online can be a good way to save money, but then sometimes you spend more money that way.
   ....

g. 1. There are many proverbs in English.
   2. There are several proverbs in English about gift-giving.
   ....

GIVING AND RECEIVING GIFTS

2 Writing Paragraphs

6 Improve these topic sentences. Circle the topic. Choose a main idea for each topic and write a topic sentence. Then share your new sentences with a partner or small group.

a. I have a (photo of my girlfriend.)
   idea: *The photo reminds me of her.*
   topic sentence: *I carry a photo of my girlfriend to remind me of her.*

b. I have a new jacket.
   idea: ....
   topic sentence: ....

c. The Internet is good.
   idea: ....
   topic sentence: ....

d. My friend is nice.
   idea: ....
   topic sentence: ....

e. I learn English at school.
   idea: ....
   topic sentence: ....

Language focus: Using *and* and *but* to join sentences

7 Work with a partner. Look at these pairs of sentences. How are they similar? How are they different? Which do you like better, and why?

a. 1. I sent my mother a birthday card. I called her.
   2. I sent my mother a birthday card and called her.

b. 1. I like getting flowers. I don't like getting candy.
   2. I like getting flowers, but I don't like getting candy.

c. 1. I didn't send my brother a birthday gift. He didn't send me one.
   2. I didn't send my brother a birthday gift, and he didn't send me one.

- In each case, the sentences in 2 *flow* better—that is, they sound more fluent and natural.
- Sentences about the same topic can often be combined with words like *and* and *but*.
- Use *and* to join *similar* ideas. In 7a, the writer did two things for her mother's birthday (sent a card; called her). How are the actions in 7c similar?
- Use *but* to show *contrasting* ideas: good / bad, easy / difficult, positive / negative. What is the contrast in 7b?

8 Look again at the paragraph on page 123, *A Birthday Gift*. Underline the sentences joined by *and* and *but*.

9 Complete this paragraph with *and* or *but*.

Same Holiday, Different Customs

People in the United States and Japan celebrate Valentine's Day on February 14. However, the holiday is celebrated in different ways in each country. In the U.S., Valentine's Day is enjoyed by friends and romantic partners, a. .... in Japan usually only romantic partners celebrate this day. Chocolate is the most popular gift in Japan, b. .... it is common in the U.S. too. However, in the U.S., other kinds of gifts are also given, c. .... many people exchange cards. The biggest difference is that in Japan, girls and women give chocolate to boys and men, d. .... in the U.S., boys and girls give cards or small gifts to all of their friends. American men and women give gifts and cards to each other. In fact, women usually get more expensive gifts than men. I would like to be a man in Japan, e. .... a woman in the U.S.!

Note: Don't begin sentences with *And* or *But* in academic writing. Use *In addition* or *However* instead.

2 Writing Paragraphs

Language focus: Punctuation

When you join two complete sentences with *but*, you must always use a comma before *but*:

I didn't want to send her a gift. I sent her one anyway.

I didn't want to send her a gift, but I sent her one anyway.

When you join two complete sentences with *and* and the subjects of the sentences are both written, use a comma before *and*:

Shopping at the mall is expensive. Parking is hard to find.

Shopping at the mall is expensive, and parking is hard to find.

(*Shopping* and *parking* are both written.)

When you join two complete sentences and remove the subject of the second sentence, don't use a comma before *and*:

These days people mail paper cards. People e-mail electronic cards.

These days people mail paper cards and e-mail electronic cards.

These days people send paper and electronic cards.

(The subject *people* is not written a second time.)

10 Join these sentences with *and* or *but*. Use a comma if you need one. Then share your sentences with a partner. Did you make the same choices? Talk about any differences.

a. I got a camera for my birthday. I got clothes for Christmas.

I got a camera for my birthday, and I got clothes for Christmas.

I got a camera for my birthday and clothes for Christmas.

b. Ahmed speaks English very well. He enjoys his classes.

....

c. Yoshi studies hard. He doesn't get good grades.

....

d. In Asia, most people eat rice for breakfast. In Canada, most people have cereal.

....

e. Morocco has lovely mountains. Morocco has beautiful beaches.

....

f. Spanish is spoken in most of South America. Portuguese is spoken in Brazil.

....

g. Gifts are difficult to choose. Gifts are fun to give.

....

h. Noodles are easy to cook. Noodles are popular in many countries.

....

Writing Paragraphs

Put it together

a Make a quick list of gifts you have given and received.

Gifts given	Gifts received
....	....
....	....
....	....
....	....

b Choose one gift. Tell your partner about it. Ask and answer questions like these.

Gifts given
- Who gave it to you?
- When did you receive it?
- Why did someone choose that gift for you?
- What did you think of the gift?
- (your ideas)

Gifts received
- Who did you give it to?
- When did you give it?
- Why did you choose this gift?
- What did your friend or family member think of the gift you gave?
- (your ideas)

c On a separate sheet of paper, write a topic sentence about your gift, and then write sentences with *and* and *but*.

d Exchange papers with a partner.
- Circle your partner's topic and underline the main idea.
- Circle the commas your partner used.
- Talk with your partner and decide if your commas are in the right places.

e Hand in your sentences to your teacher.

GIVING AND RECEIVING GIFTS

3 A Favorite Place

In this unit, you will ...
- develop paragraphs with descriptive details.
- use lists to brainstorm.
- learn to edit lists.
- combine sentences containing adjectives.
- write about places.

1 Describe this picture to a partner. Have you been to the beach before? Tell your partner what it was like.

2 Read the paragraph and answer the questions on page 131 with a partner.

Relaxing at the Beach

[1.] Where is your favorite summer vacation place? [2.] The beach is the perfect place for me. [3.] The air is hot, but the water is cool, wet, and fresh. [4.] First, I enjoy swimming and surfing in the ocean. [5.] When I am tired, I come out and lie on the beach. [6.] The sand is soft and white. [7.] The beach is noisy with seagulls and children laughing, but it's a pleasant noise. [8.] I even like the beach smells. [9.] The air smells salty from the sea and sweet from everybody's suntan lotion. [10.] I feel peaceful and relaxed. [11.] When I want to relax in summer, I go to the beach!

a. Which sentence is the topic sentence?

1 ☐ 2 ☐ 10 ☐

b. What do sentences 3, 4, 6, 7, and 9 do?

1. Say the same information in a different way.

2. Tell a story about the topic.

3. Explain the topic sentence by giving more information.

Language focus: Descriptive vocabulary

You know that a topic sentence tells the main idea of a paragraph. *Supporting sentences* develop the paragraph by adding more information. When you describe a place, you can develop your paragraph by adding descriptive details—information that tells how a place looks, sounds, or smells, or feels.

3 With a partner, put these adjectives that can describe places into the chart below. Some words can be used in more than one place. Check a dictionary or ask your teacher to explain any new words.

dark	friendly	musical	soft
dry	green	quiet	spicy
exciting	humid	relaxed	sweet
fragrant	loud	sharp	warm

look	sound	smell	feel
....	....	....	....
....	....	....	....
....	....	....	....
....	....	....	....
....	....	....	....
....	....	....	....
....	....	....	....
....	....	....	....

4 Look again at the paragraph on page 130, *Relaxing at the Beach*. Circle the descriptive adjectives, and then put them into the chart in exercise 3 above.

Writing Paragraphs

Brainstorming: Lists

You cannot write if you don't have something to write about. So, before they start to write, good writers *brainstorm* ideas (they think of and write down ideas that they can use).

In this book, you will practice several different ways of brainstorming. Try them all, and then choose the way that works best for you.

⊃ How to make a list

- Use a separate, whole sheet of paper.
- Write your topic at the top.
- Write down as many ideas as you can about your topic.
- Write single words or short phrases, but don't write long sentences.
- Write down every idea that comes to you, and don't worry about whether the ideas are "good" or "bad."

⊃ Editing your list

After you brainstorm, you need to go back and see which ideas you can use. This is called *editing*.

- Underline or highlight the good ideas.
- Cross out ideas that are not related to your topic or that you don't want to use.

5 This example shows a list for the paragraph on page 130, *Relaxing at the Beach*. Cross out the ideas that the writer didn't use. Compare your list with a partner, and say why you think the writer didn't use the crossed out ideas.

6 Choose one of the topics below. In five minutes, make a list of ideas. Share your list with a partner. How many descriptive adjectives did your partner use?

a. My favorite place to relax

b. An interesting city

7 Edit your list by crossing out unrelated ideas or ones you don't like. Show your partner what you crossed out, and explain your decisions.

Beach

vacation
relax
air—hot, dry, windy?
water—cold, cool, fresh, wet
swim, surf
can't windsurf
seagulls
good snack food
beach umbrellas / expensive to rent
too far away
smell—salt, suntan lotion
feel—sandsounds—birds, children, ocean waves
taste—salt water tastes bad

Writing focus: Combining sentences containing adjectives

8 Look at the picture. With a partner, brainstorm a list of adjectives to describe the scene.

9 Read the following paragraphs. How are they the same? How are they different? Which paragraph seems better to you? Explain your choice to a partner. Then check your ideas below.

My Mother's Kitchen

1. My mother's kitchen is not big. 2. It is comfortable. 3. It is warm. 4. My mother cooks a lot. 5. Her kitchen smells spicy. 6. It smells sweet. 7. Sometimes she taught my brother and me how to cook. 8. We liked learning new things. 9. We liked working together. 10. We liked making delicious foods. 11. Now I live far away. 12. I often think about my mother's kitchen.

My Mother's Kitchen

1. My mother's kitchen is not big, but it is warm and comfortable. 2. My mother cooks a lot, and her kitchen smells spicy and sweet. 3. Sometimes she taught my brother and me how to cook. 4. We liked learning new things, working together, and making delicious foods. 5. Now I live far away, but I often think about my mother's kitchen.

The first paragraph is less interesting because many sentences are all the same type: noun + verb + adjective.

You remember from Unit 2 that sentences about similar topics can often be combined. One effective way to do this is by combining sentences with adjectives.

3 Writing Paragraphs

To make more varied and interesting sentences, you can:

- combine the adjectives in two sentences with *and* or *but*. Remove the subject and verb from the second sentence.

    Example: *The movie was long. The movie was boring.*

                                   and
    The movie was long. ~~The movie was~~ boring.
    The movie was long and boring.

    Example: *Our homework is difficult. Our homework is fun to do.*

                               ,   but
    Our homework is difficult. ~~Our homework is~~ fun to do.
    Our homework is difficult, but fun to do.

- combine three sentences. Notice how commas are used after the first two adjectives. Remove the subjects and verbs from the second and third sentences.

    Example: *Her skirt was short. It was black. It was fashionable.*

                         ,   , and
    Her skirt was short. ~~It was~~ black. ~~It was~~ fashionable.
    Her skirt was short, black, and fashionable.

10 Find and underline three examples of combined sentences in the paragraph on page 130, ***Relaxing at the Beach***.

11 Combine these sentences. Then compare with a partner. Which sentences did you combine the same way? Which were different?

    a. Charles is interesting. He is a little strange.

    ....

    b. The river was deep. The river was wide. It was cold.

    ....

    c. Our teacher is strict. He is fair.

    ....

    d. July was hot. It was humid.

    ....

    e. Kim is my best friend because she is kind. She is smart. She is funny.

    ....

    f. The food in that restaurant is delicious. It is expensive.

    ....

Writing Paragraphs 3

Put it together

a Work with a partner to complete the paragraph below and make it better. First, make a list of details you could add to the paragraph. This is an imaginary place, so use your imagination!

A Horrible Hotel

....

The rooms are small. The rooms are dark. The rooms are dirty. There is no air-conditioning. The rooms are hot in summer. There is no heating. The rooms are cold in winter. There are big windows. The view is terrible. ....

....

....

....

....

That is why I want to warn you never to stay in that hotel.

b On a separate sheet of paper, write your completed paragraph.
- Combine sentences to make it more interesting.
- Write a topic sentence.

c Check your writing.
Did you ...
- ☐ include a heading on your paper?
- ☐ format the paragraph properly (see page 112)?
- ☐ start and end each sentence correctly?

d Exchange papers with another pair. Compare your paragraphs. What is the same? What is different?

e Hand in your paragraph to your teacher.

A FAVORITE PLACE 135

4 An Exceptional Person

In this unit you will ...
- use word maps to brainstorm.
- practice using adjectives in sentences.
- learn to write concluding sentences.
- learn when to use capital letters.
- write about people.

1 Look at the people and describe them to a partner.

2 Read this paragraph about Jack Collins. Decide which person is most like Jack. Then answer the questions on page 137.

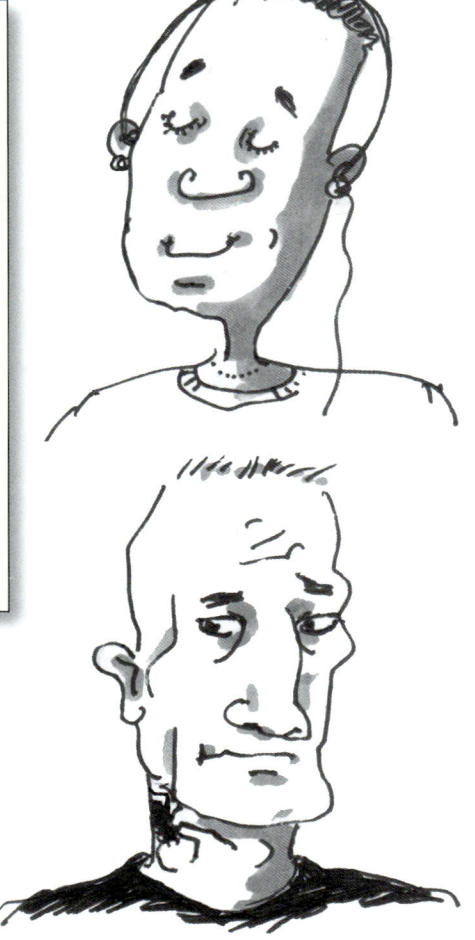

Jack Collins

1. Jack Collins is the most amazing person I have ever met. 2. He came to my school and talked about his difficult life in prison. 3. He was in prison for 15 years. 4. He made a lot of mistakes when he was young, but now he has changed his life. 5. He saw a lot of violence in prison, so he uses his experience to help high school students. 6. Jack is tall and strong. 7. He also looks a little scary because he has some spider tattoos. 8. The thing I remember most is his sensitive personality. 9. He really wants to help young people. 10. I've never met anyone like Jack before.

a. Which sentence is the topic sentence?

   Circle the topic and underline the main idea.

b. Which sentences tell about Jack's personality?

c. Which sentences tell about Jack's physical appearance?

3 Find the nouns these adjectives describe:

a. amazing .....*person*..........   d. tall, strong ....

b. difficult ....   e. scary ....

c. young ....   f. sensitive ....

> **Note:** Nouns can be used as adjectives; for example, **spider** tattoos in the paragraph on page 26 about Jack Collins.

4 Look again at the paragraph on page 136, *Jack Collins*, and underline the other noun that has been used as an adjective.

Brainstorming: Word maps

> **Remember**: In Unit 3, you learned that brainstorming was used ...
> - to think of many ideas for your writing.
> - to help you see the connections between ideas.
>
> and you learned how to brainstorm using lists.

A word map is another kind of brainstorming. Word maps can help you think of many ideas for your writing and see the connections between the ideas.

- Use a separate, whole sheet of paper.
- Write your topic in the middle, and draw a circle around it.
- Write an idea about the topic nearby, and circle it.
- Draw a line to connect the circles. This shows that the idea and the topic are related.
- Add more ideas and circle the ideas.
- Draw lines to connect any circles with related ideas.
- Write down as many ideas as you can. Don't worry about whether they are "good" or "bad."
- After you finish, cross out any ideas you don't want to use.

4 Writing Paragraphs

This example shows a word map for the paragraph on page 136, *Jack Collins*. Notice which ideas the writer kept and which ones he / she crossed out.

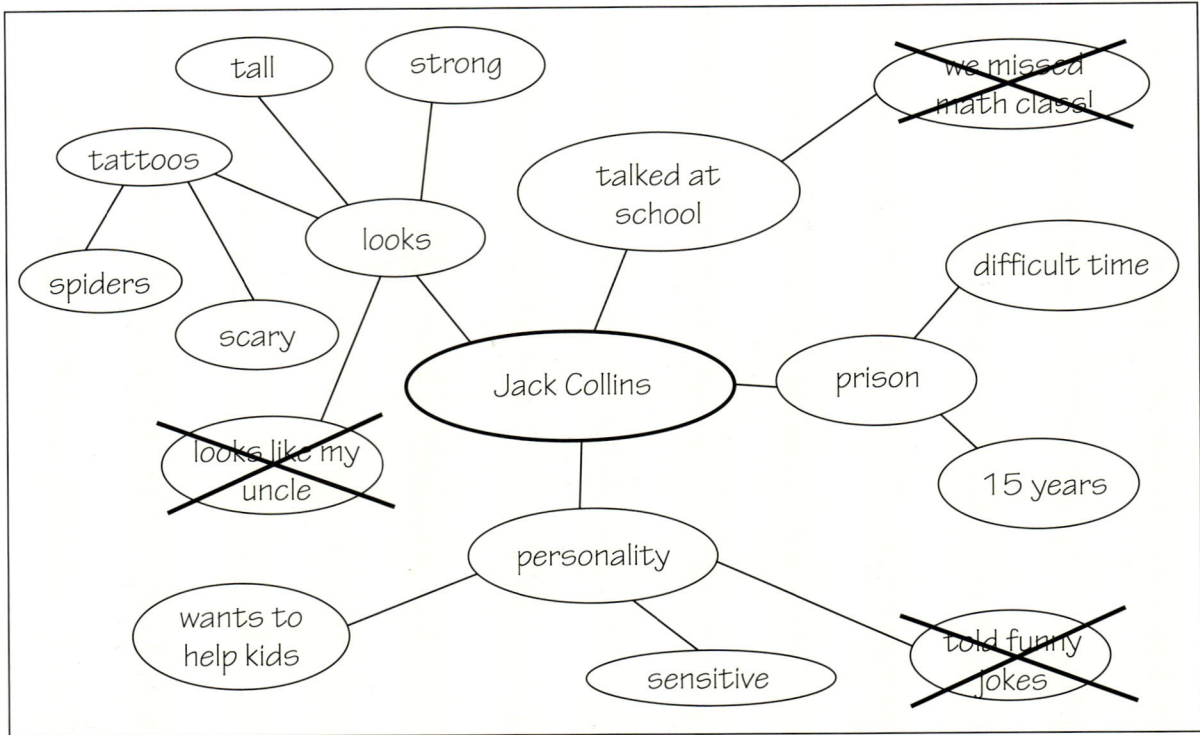

5 On a separate sheet of paper, make a word map for one of the topics below.
- Use plenty of descriptive adjectives.
- Share your word map with a partner.
- How many descriptive adjectives did your partner use?

a. A relative
b. A teacher who helped me
c. A movie / music star

Language focus: Using adjectives in sentences

Adjectives can be used in three different ways:

- before a noun
  *Jack Collins is the most **amazing person** I have ever met.*
- after a form of the *be* verb
  *He made a lot of mistakes when **he was young**.*
- after a verb like *taste, sound, look, feel, smell, seem*
  *He also **looks a little scary**.*

6 Write sentences with each descriptive adjective that you used in your word map. Try to write all three different types of sentence.

7 Look at the pictures and do the following.

a. Write two or three adjectives for each person on a separate sheet of paper. You can write adjectives for their physical appearance or their personality (use your imagination!).

b. Exchange papers with a partner. Write sentences using your partner's adjectives. Then share your sentences.

Writing focus: Concluding sentences

A good paragraph has a clear topic sentence and supporting sentences that explain and support the topic sentence. Many (but not all) paragraphs also have a concluding sentence. The concluding sentence closes the paragraph.

A concluding sentence can …

- restate the topic sentence.
- summarize the main idea of the paragraph.
- make a prediction connected to the paragraph's topic.
- make a suggestion or give advice connected to the topic.

A concluding sentence **does not** state a completely new idea.

Writing Paragraphs

8 Read these concluding sentences for the paragraph on page 136, *Jack Collins*, and decide if they 1 (restate), 2 (summarize), 3 (predict) or 4 (suggest or advise).

a. .... I've never met anyone like Jack before.

b. .... I think Jack will help many teenagers stay out of prison.

c. .... Everyone should talk to someone who has been to prison.

d. .... Jack's experiences, appearance, and personality make him very memorable.

9 The paragraph below is called *My Best Friend's Grandfather*. With a partner, think of three or four things the paragraph could be about.

10 Read the paragraph and find out if any of your guesses were correct.

My Best Friend's Grandfather

1. We can all learn from listening to our grandparents. 2. My best friend's grandfather tells great stories about his life. 3. He's 94 years old, but his voice is still strong and clear. 4. He speaks quietly and slowly when he tells stories. 5. His life was difficult when he was young. 6. His family didn't have much money, and he worked hard. 7. Even though his life was not easy, he is positive and optimistic. 8. I can learn many things from his stories.

....

....

....

---

11 Read the sentences below and do the following.

a. Decide which sentence could not be a concluding sentence for the paragraph *My Best Friend's Grandfather*.

b. Copy the sentence you like best into the paragraph.

c. Tell a partner which concluding sentence you chose and why.

1. My best friend's grandfather is a wonderful storyteller.
2. My best friend's grandfather is a good example for me.
3. My best friend's grandfather never went to college.
4. I think all teenagers should listen to their grandparents' stories.

12 Look at the picture of the soccer player, Iker Casillas, and describe him to a partner.

13 Write a concluding sentence for the paragraph, *A Popular Athlete*, about Iker Casillas. Share your sentence with other students. Decide whether the sentences restate, summarize, predict, or suggest / advise.

A Popular Athlete

Iker Casillas is a famous soccer player from Spain. He is a goalkeeper and also the team captain for the Spanish national team and the club team Real Madrid. He became famous when he was just a teenager, and is now known as one of Europe's best goalkeepers. Casillas is not only a talented player but also a fantastic leader. As team captain, he helped the Spanish national team win their first European Championship in 44 years. In 2010, he led Spain to win their first World Cup ever in an overtime match against the Netherlands. His fans respect him because he is a very hard worker on the field and on the training ground.

....
....
....
....
....

4 Writing Paragraphs

Language focus: Punctuation

○ Capitalization

> **Remember:** In Unit 1, you learned that the first word of a sentence starts with a capital letter.

A word is also capitalized if it is ...

- in the title of a piece of writing (paragraph, essay, book), a movie, a piece of music, etc. Don't capitalize prepositions (*of, to, with*), articles (*a, the*), or conjunctions (*and, but*).
- a name of a group, a place, or a person; that is, a *proper noun*.
- a day of the week or a month.
- a language or a nationality.

> **Note:** A *proper noun* is the name of a specific person, place, or thing. For example, *Picasso* is the name of a specific person, *Paris* is the name of a specific place, *the Olympics* is the name of a specific thing.

14 Find all of the capitalized words in the paragraph on page 141, *A Popular Athlete*. Tell a partner why each word is capitalized.

15 Rewrite the following sentences using correct capitalization.

a. iker, whose full name is iker casillas fernandez, was born on may 20, 1981.

....

b. his father, who worked for the ministry of education, and his mother, a hairdresser, both moved from the town of avila to madrid.

....

c. iker is also known for his work with the children's charity organization known as plan.

....

d. in 2009, iker traveled with plan to mali, where he sponsors a child named bourama.

....

e. after the spanish team won the world cup in 2010, children from peru, indonesia, bangladesh, and senegal sent videos to iker to say "congratulations" and to demonstrate their soccer skills.

....

f. his sponsored child bourama said, "iker casillas can teach me how to play when I grow up, and I'll make wonders just like him."

....

Writing Paragraphs

Put it together

a With a partner, match the topic sentence on the left to the concluding sentence on the right.

a. .... I admire many things about my father.	**1.**	You can easily see that he is friendly, outgoing, and loves to laugh.
b. .... I think my uncle's face shows his personality.	**2.**	She works hard at her job, but she always has time for me.
c. .... Daniel Radcliffe, who plays Harry Potter, is my favorite actor.	**3.**	His poor health is probably why he died young.
d. .... I was always frightened of my history professor.	**4.**	When I grow up, I hope I will be just like my father.
e. .... My mother is a very busy person.	**5.**	She was scary, but I learned a lot from her tough lessons and strict personality!
f. .... Elvis' body and health changed as he got older.	**6.**	I think he will keep improving as he gets older and makes more movies.

b Choose one of the pairs of sentences in exercise a above. Make a word map about the topic. Use your imagination!

c Look at a partner's map and say which ideas are most interesting to you.

d On a separate sheet of paper, write a paragraph.
- Copy the topic sentence and concluding sentence.
- Add supporting sentences by using the details from your word map.

e Check your writing.
Did you ...
- [ ] include a heading on your paper?
- [ ] format the paragraph correctly?
- [ ] start and end each sentence correctly?
- [ ] give the paragraph a title?

f Exchange papers with a partner. Talk with your partner and decide if all the supporting sentences are related to the idea in the topic sentence.

g Hand in your paragraph to your teacher.

AN EXCEPTIONAL PERSON

5 Trends and Fads

In this unit, you will ...
- review descriptive vocabulary.
- use freewriting to brainstorm.
- review what a paragraph contains.
- develop peer feedback skills.
- write a paragraph about a trend.

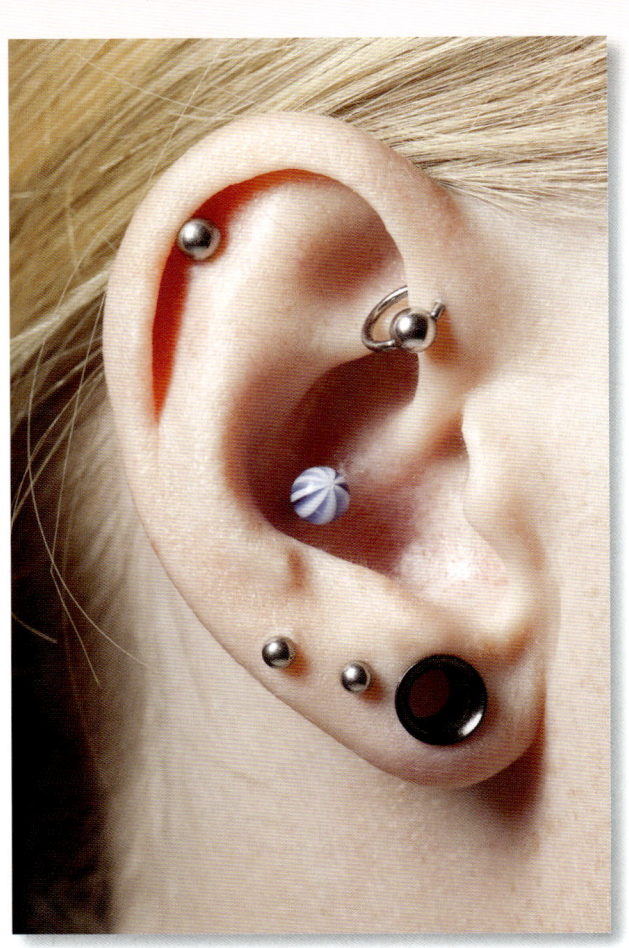

1 Talk with a partner or small group. In many Western countries, it has become popular for young people to get multiple piercings for their ears. Is this true in your country? Do you know anyone with multiple piercings? Would you ever get them?

2 Why do people get multiple piercings for their ears? With your group or partner, make a list of all the reasons you can think of. Then read this paragraph to see if any of your reasons were mentioned.

A Special Look

[1.] My best friend thinks I'm crazy. [2.] My father is sure I'll regret my decision, and my mother says I've been tricked by a fashion fad. [3.] However, I'm glad I got multiple piercings for my ears. [4.] I got the idea from a photo in a magazine of a top model. [5.] She had a row of diamond studs in each ear, and it looked very elegant. [6.] I like being able to wear several earrings at the same time. [7.] It's a way for me to express my personality. [8.] I know that some people don't think that multiple piercings are attractive, but I am very pleased with this special look.

3 Read the paragraph on page 144, *A Special Look,* again and answer the questions.

  a. Which sentence is the topic sentence?

   1 ☐ 2 ☐ 3 ☐ 4 ☐

  b. What do sentences 6 and 7 do?

   1. Say the same information in a different way.

   2. Tell a story about the topic.

   3. Explain the topic sentence by giving more information.

  c. Which of these sentences could be added to the paragraph?

   1. I buy most of my earrings online.

   2. I like looking just a bit different from all of my friends.

   3. I know another girl who also has multiple piercings.

   4. My parents don't like piercings at all.

Language focus: Vocabulary review

4 Work with a partner. Look at these adjectives from Units 1–4. Do they describe people, places, or things? Write the words in the appropriate column. You can use some words in more than one column. Then add two more words of your own to each column.

busy	convenient	comfortable	common
difficult	exciting	fashionable	friendly
humid	noisy	peaceful	perfect
popular	optimistic	salty	shy
spicy	strong	useful	valuable

people	places	things
....	....	....
....	....	....
....	....	....
....	....	....
....	....	....
....	....	....
....	....	....
....	....	....
....	....	....
....	....	....

Writing Paragraphs

Brainstorming: Freewriting

Freewriting is a kind of brainstorming where you write everything you can think of, quickly and without stopping. Freewriting helps to improve your writing fluency, and gives you ideas for your writing.

- Write as much as possible for five or ten minutes.
- Don't worry about spelling, grammar, or punctuation.
- If you make a mistake, just cross it out and continue writing.
- Write continuously, without stopping.

Remember that when you make a list or a word map, you write words or short phrases. When you freewrite, you write sentences.

Look at this example of freewriting on the topic of trends and fashions.

> What is trendy or fashionable now? I can't think of anything. Do I have anything that is fashionable? I don't think so. Everyone has a smart phone now. But smart phones aren't very interesting. What is popular these days? What about ~~televiss~~ TV? Talent shows are popular these days. There are a lot of talent shows on TV these days. With celebrities. "Britain's Next Top Model" is pretty good. I only saw part of last season though because I was out of the country, so I missed the end. I read about it online. But it's better to watch it on TV. Some of those people are really talented, but then some are just dumb. The judges are really funny sometimes. And sometimes they're kind of mean. My roommate likes that show where celebrities compete in a dance contest with real dancers. I forget the name. I saw it a few times, but dancing is boring to me. I can't dance like that. ~~Fashun Fasion~~ Fashion is interesting to me. Modeling is hard, too. It's not an easy job like some people think. A TV show like that is good because it gives some people a chance. Usually only ~~fame~~ famous people or rich people get chances, but this show is for anybody with talent.

5 Choose one of these topics. For five minutes, write as much as you can on a separate sheet of paper. Write everything that comes into your mind, without stopping.

  a. A clothing trend
  b. A fad I don't like
  c. A popular item I own (or would like to own!)

Writing Paragraphs

⟩ Editing your freewriting

After you freewrite, you need to edit what you have written—go back and see which ideas you can use. It is useful to:

- underline the good ideas.
- cross out anything you don't want to use.

6 Look at the edited freewriting below. What topic do you think the writer will use for his / her paragraph? Why did the writer cross out or underline some sentences? Explain to a partner. Use reasons like these:

- The sentence wasn't about the topic.
- The sentence wasn't interesting.
- The sentence was interesting.

> *What is trendy or fashionable now?* ~~I can't think of anything. Do I have anything that is fashionable? I don't think so. Everyone has a smart phone now. But smart phones aren't very interesting. What is popular these days? What about televiss TV?~~ *Talent shows are popular these days. There are a lot of talent shows on TV these days. With celebrities. "Britain's Next Top Model" is pretty good. I only saw part of last season though because I was out of the country, so I missed the end. I read about it online. But it's better to watch it on TV.* <u>Some of those people are really talented, but then some are just dumb. The judges are really funny sometimes. And sometimes they're kind of mean.</u> ~~My roommate likes that show where celebrities compete in a dance contest with real dancers. I forget the name. I saw it a few times, but dancing is boring to me. I can't dance like that.~~ ~~Fashun Fasion~~ *Fashion is interesting to me. Modeling is hard, too. It's not an easy job like some people think.* <u>A TV show like that is good because it gives some people a chance. Usually only ~~fame~~ famous people or rich people get chances, but this show is for anybody with talent.</u>

7 Look at your freewriting from exercise 5 on page 146. Underline sentences that you think are interesting or useful. Cross out anything that is not useful.

8 Spend another five minutes freewriting, starting with a sentence or phrase you have underlined.

9 Look at your two examples of freewriting together. Do you have enough ideas for a paragraph? If not, freewrite some more!

TRENDS AND FADS 147

Writing Paragraphs

Paragraph review

> **Remember:** A paragraph can contain three different types of sentence:
> - A **topic sentence**—tells the reader the topic and main idea of the paragraph.
> - **Supporting sentences**—develop, explain, and give details about the main idea.
> - A **concluding sentence**—restates the topic sentence, summarizes the paragraph, makes a prediction, or gives advice or suggestions.

10 Below are sentences from a paragraph in the wrong order. Decide if the sentences are topic sentences (T), supporting sentences (S), or concluding sentences (C).

- a. .... So, I bought a bike last week for $250 in a second hand bike sale.
- b. .... The colors are bright red, white, and dark blue.
- c. .... It's a great bike, and I'm going to have a lot of fun on it.
- d. .... Mountain bikes are really popular where I live. Everybody has one.
- e. .... The bike is one year old but looks new.
- f. .... It looks like a bike you can ride on very rough mountains and over rocks.

11 Put the sentences above in a logical order. Then write the sentences into a paragraph on a separate sheet of paper. Give the paragraph a title.

Writing focus: Writing the paragraph

After you have chosen a topic and brainstormed ideas, it is time to write your paragraph.

- a topic sentence first.
- Then write the supporting sentences.
- Finish with a concluding sentence.
- Give your paragraph a title.

But this is only the beginning! Good writers follow three steps to improve their writing. They ...

1. check their work.
2. show their work to someone else.
3. make any necessary additions and changes.

These steps can be repeated several times.

Writing Paragraphs

12 With a partner, describe the diagram below. What is happening in each circle?

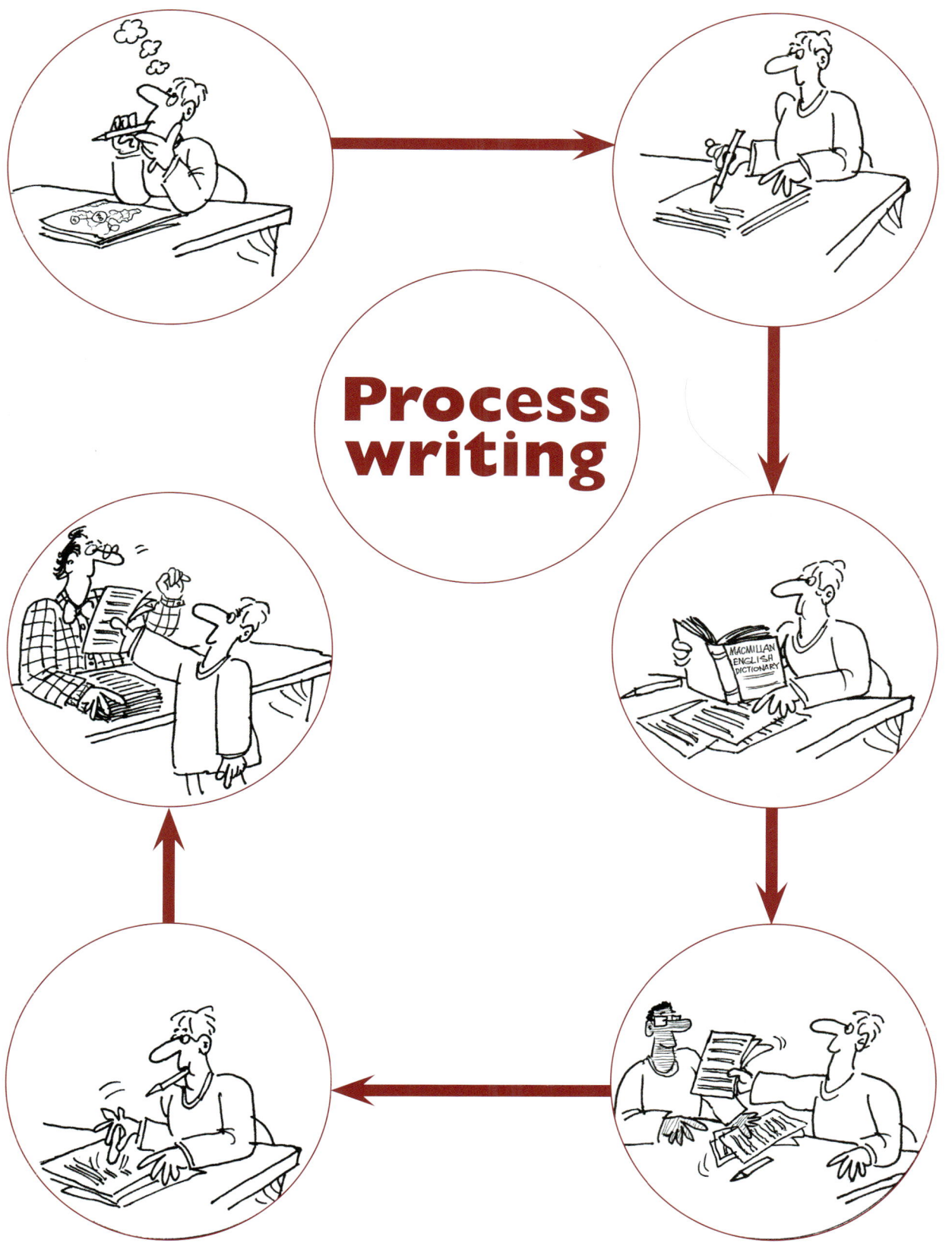

TRENDS AND FADS 149

Writing Paragraphs

Writing focus: Peer reviewing

Exchanging papers with a classmate, reading each other's paper, and making comments is called *peer reviewing*. When you read a classmate's paper, you can …

- practice finding topic sentences, supporting sentences, and concluding sentences.
- notice special vocabulary or grammar.
- see different ways to do the same assignment.
- help the writer by saying what ideas you liked best.
- ask questions to help the writer think of more ideas.
- ask a question if you don't understand something—and maybe the writer will think of a better way to explain.

Many writers—even very good writers—feel nervous or shy about sharing their writing. When you write comments about someone's writing, be kind, useful, and truthful. Remember always to say what you like. Comment on ideas and organization, and not spelling or grammar.

13 With a partner or group, look at the comments below. Put a check (✓) by the ones that are useful for the writer. Put a cross (✗) by the ones that you think aren't useful and give a reason; for example:

- It isn't kind.
- It isn't clear.
- It isn't useful.
- It (probably) isn't true.

a. ☐ The topic sentence was really interesting.
b. ☐ You don't have any examples.
c. ☐ You have one good example. But your paragraph is a little short. Can you write another example?
d. ☐ I liked your paragraph because it was honest. I think you should add a title.
e. ☐ Your topic sentence and concluding sentence are exactly the same. Maybe one should be different.
f. ☐ I think it's OK.
g. ☐ Your paragraph is not very good. I couldn't understand anything.
h. ☐ Your concluding sentence was funny. I liked it a lot!
i. ☐ You used some interesting vocabulary. It was easy for me to imagine that place.
j. ☐ You are a better writer than Shakespeare!
k. ☐ I'm not sure which sentence is the topic sentence. Is it the first one or the second one? Please tell me.

Writing Paragraphs

Put it together

a Use the ideas from your brainstorming from exercises 5 and 8 on pages 146 and 147 to write a paragraph. Write a topic sentence and supporting sentences. Decide if you want to write a concluding sentence.

b Check your writing.

Did you ...

- ☐ include a heading on your paper?
- ☐ format the paragraph properly?
- ☐ start and end each sentence correctly?
- ☐ use capitalization correctly?
- ☐ give the paragraph a title?
- ☐ write a topic sentence?
- ☐ write supporting sentences? How many?
- ☐ use descriptive adjectives?
- ☐ only include one clear idea in each sentence?
- ☐ order the sentences logically?
- ☐ combine sentences logically?
- ☐ write a concluding sentence?

c Exchange papers with a partner. Include your brainstorming.
- Fill out the Peer Review Form on page 202.
- Talk with your partner and go over each form.

d Read your paragraph again.
- Think about the comments from your partner.
- Make any additions or changes to your paragraph that would make it stronger or more interesting.

e Hand in the second draft of your paragraph to your teacher.

6 White Lies

In this unit, you will ...
- identify opinions and examples in supporting sentences.
- use discussion to brainstorm.
- write a paragraph about your opinions.

1 What is a *white lie*?

   a. A mistake about colors, e.g., "Tom's new car is red" when it is actually purple.

   b. A small or unimportant lie you tell not to hurt someone's feelings, e.g., "I think your new car looks cool" when you actually think the new car looks ugly.

   c. A type of lie politicians tell to be popular, e.g., "When I am President, everyone will be able to buy a new car" when the politician knows people will not have more money.

   - Tell a partner about the last time you told a white lie to a friend, a family member or a teacher.
   - Tell your partner if you think it is OK to tell white lies.

2 Now read this paragraph to find out if the writer agrees with you about telling white lies.

White Lies

1. White lies are not always bad. 2. If you tell your girlfriend that her new haircut looks great when it is horrible, she will know you are lying. 3. I think it is better to tell the truth in this case. 4. However, if your girlfriend has a new dress and she really likes it, you should always say it is lovely. 5. If you say you don't like it, you will make her unhappy and angry with you. 6. You can lie if the truth will hurt and it is not important.

Writing Paragraphs

3 Read the paragraph on page 152, *White Lies*, again and answer these questions.
  a. Which sentence is the topic sentence?
  b. What does the concluding sentence do?
    1. It restates the topic sentence.
    2. It makes a prediction.
    3. It makes a suggestion.
  c. What do sentences 2 and 4 do?
    1. They give advice.
    2. They give examples.
    3. They tell a story.

Language focus: Giving an opinion

Your *opinion* is your personal feeling. A *fact* is something that is true. Most writing uses both facts and opinions. When you talk about your opinions, you can start your sentence with phrases such as:

I think *friends should always be honest.*

I don't think *white lies are dangerous.*

I believe *it is better to upset your friends than to lie.*

In my view, *it is often safer to lie than to tell the truth.*

In my opinion, *lying is the same as cheating or stealing.*

When you write, you can use one of the sentence starters above. However, be careful not to use too many, or to use them too often. That can make your writing sound weak. The reader knows that the paragraph is your opinion, because you wrote it!

4 Look at the sentences below. Write F for the facts, and O for the opinions.
  a. ...*O*... Learning English is easier for girls than for boys.
      ...*F*... There are more boys than girls in my English class.
  b. .... Good teachers don't give too much homework.
      .... Our teacher gave us homework last week.
  c. .... Keanu Reeves is a good actor.
      .... Keanu Reeves starred in the *Matrix* movies.
  d. .... Many teens carry cell phones these days.
      .... Cell phones are very convenient.
  e. .... All students have to wear a uniform at my school.
      .... Our school uniforms are not very comfortable.
  f. .... I don't believe that wearing the latest fashions is important.
      .... My favorite clothes are all black.

Writing Paragraphs

5 For each topic below, write one fact and one opinion.
- Read your sentences to a partner.
- partner will tell you which sentence is the fact and which is the opinion.

a. tea

   Green tea is good for your health.   F

   Black tea tastes better than green tea.   O

b. college entrance exams

c. violent video games

d. environmental issues

e. money

f. sports

g. (your choice of topic)

154 WHITE LIES

Brainstorming: Discussion

Talking with other people is a good way to brainstorm:

- You can share ideas with different people.
- You can ask questions to help other students think more deeply.
- When other students ask you questions, you will think of examples to support your opinions.

When you're discussing, it's OK to disagree with your classmates. However, it is important to be respectful of opinions that are different from yours.

6 Work in a group. Choose two of the topics below, and brainstorm opinions.

- Think of as many opinions as you can. You don't have to believe them.
- Someone in your group should write down all the opinions in your group.
- Share your opinions with another group or with the whole class.

a. International marriages
b. Truth and lies
c. Playing video games
d. Cheating in school

Writing focus: Supporting sentences with opinions and examples

In your topic sentence and supporting sentences, you can give an opinion. To support your opinion, you could give *examples*, which can either be facts or experiences you've had.

7 Look again at the paragraph on page 152, *White Lies*. Which sentences are opinions? Which sentences are examples? Are some sentences both?

Writing Paragraphs

8 Decide if these sentences are opinions (O) or examples (E). Write O or E next to each sentence.

- a. .... Smoking should be banned in all restaurants.
- b. .... Smoking is banned in restaurants in California and New York.
- c. .... The air is cleaner and healthier in non-smoking restaurants.
- d. .... I believe that customers prefer non-smoking restaurants.
- e. .... My clothes smelled horrible after I had dinner with a friend who smoked.
- f. .... I went to a smoky restaurant in Paris, and I couldn't eat my food.
- g. .... In my country, smoking is banned on buses and trains, and in all public buildings.

9 Read this paragraph and answer the questions below.

Lying

[1.] In my opinion, exaggeration is the same as lying. [2.] My friend John is always exaggerating. [3.] When we met two years ago, he told me he spoke French fluently. [4.] However, last week we met a French man at a soccer match. [5.] John couldn't say anything to him in French except, "Where are you from?" and "Do you like England?" [6.] I think he lies because he wants to be exciting. [7.] Last night, he told me he has a new millionaire girlfriend. [8.] She probably has a lot of money but isn't a millionaire. [9.] I don't believe John is a good friend.

---

a. Check (✓) the writer's opinions.
   1. ☐ A good friend doesn't exaggerate.
   2. ☐ A good friend has a rich girlfriend.
   3. ☐ A good friend is exciting.
   4. ☐ A good friend tells the truth.

b. Underline two examples used to support the writer's opinions.

c. Work with a partner.
   1. Give an example of a time you have told a white lie or exaggerated.
   2. Tell your partner your opinion about white lies and exaggeration.

Writing Paragraphs

Put it together

a Choose one of the opinions you wrote for exercise 6 on page 155.
- Use this opinion for your topic sentence.
- Brainstorm ideas by discussing the opinion with a small group.
- Write down examples (facts or experiences) to support your opinion.

b Write a paragraph. Use opinions and examples.

c Check your writing.
Did you ...
- [ ] include a heading on your paper?
- [ ] format the paragraph properly?
- [ ] start and end each sentence correctly?
- [ ] use capitalization correctly?
- [ ] give the paragraph a title?
- [ ] write a topic sentence?
- [ ] write supporting sentences? How many?
- [ ] only include one clear idea in each sentence?
- [ ] order the sentences logically?
- [ ] combine the sentences logically?
- [ ] write a concluding sentence?

d Exchange papers with a partner.
- Fill out the Peer Review Form on page 203.
- Talk with your partner and go over each form.

e Read your paragraph again.
- Think about the comments from your partner.
- Make any additions or changes to your paragraph that would make it stronger or more interesting.

f Hand in the second draft of your paragraph to your teacher.

7 Explanations and Excuses

In this unit, you will ...
- develop paragraphs which explain cause and effect / result.
- combine sentences with *so* and *because*.
- practice further with word maps and freewriting.
- write a paragraph about explanations and excuses.

1 Describe this picture to a partner. Guess what the problem is. Tell your partner what you think the people are saying.

2 Read the paragraph and check your guess.

It Wasn't My Fault!

1. Professors should be understanding when students can't complete assignments on time. 2. I couldn't do the writing homework for English class today, and my professor didn't want to hear my reasons. 3. I had good reasons, too. 4. Last night was Evan's birthday. 5. He's my best friend, so I had to go to his party. 6. After the party, I tried to do the homework, but my computer froze and I lost all the information. 7. I was too tired to write it again because it was very late. 8. My professor didn't care. 9. She said, "You had two weeks to do the assignment, so there are no excuses." 10. I think she's angry with me, but it wasn't my fault.

Writing Paragraphs

3 Why didn't the writer do his homework? Write W for the writer's reasons and P for the professor's reasons.

The writer didn't do his homework because ...

a. .... it was his best friend's birthday.
b. .... he is lazy.
c. .... he isn't organized.
d. .... he had a computer problem.
e. .... he isn't a serious student.

Language focus: Giving explanations

Cause and effect / result
- *So* and *because* can be used to join two sentences together:

It was raining. I took an umbrella.
It was raining, **so** *I took an umbrella.*
I took an umbrella **because** *it was raining.*

- *So* and *because* have a similar function.

So tells us the result or effect of a situation:
I took an umbrella.
Because tells us why something happens (the cause):
I took an umbrella. Why? Because it was raining.

- *So* and *because* are often very close in meaning, and you can choose either—but you must use *so* with the result / effect and *because* with the cause:

I had a cold. I didn't go to class.
I had a cold, **so** *I didn't go to class.*
I didn't go to class **because** *I had a cold.*

> **Note:** A comma comes before *so*. There is no comma before *because*.

4 Look again at the paragraph on page 158, *It Wasn't My Fault*, and do the following.

a. Underline the sentences that use *so* or *because*.
b. For each of those sentences, tell a partner what part of the sentence tells the *cause* and what part tells the *effect / result*.

Writing Paragraphs

5 Write a sentence using *so* and another sentence using *because* for these situations.

a. The movie was boring. I left early.
   *The movie was boring, **so** I left early.*
   *I left early **because** the movie was boring.*

b. We played badly. We lost the soccer match.
   ....
   ....

c. I failed the test. I didn't study hard.
   ....
   ....

d. My alarm clock didn't work. I was late for the meeting.
   ....
   ....

e. I am shy. I don't have many friends.
   ....
   ....

f. I won't go to the party. I'm tired.
   ....
   ....

Writing Paragraphs

Language focus: Starting with because

Look at these two sentences:

*I was too tired to write it again **because** it was very late.*

***Because** it was very late, I was too tired to write it again.*

There is no difference in meaning between these two sentences. When you write, use both styles. This will make your writing more varied and more interesting. However, there is a difference in punctuation.

6 With a partner, find the difference in punctuation. Write the explanation here.

....
....
....

7 Rewrite these sentences using *because*.

   a. I couldn't bring my homework. My dog ate my homework.
     *I couldn't bring my homework **because** my dog ate it.*
     ***Because** my dog ate my homework, I couldn't bring it.*

   b. I am too busy. I don't exercise.

   c. I have too much homework. I go to bed late.

   d. I can't give up smoking. I will put on weight.

   e. I lost my friend's book. I was careless.

   f. I'm not going to go to the beach. I have to take an exam.

EXPLANATIONS AND EXCUSES

7 Writing Paragraphs

Brainstorming: Practice with word maps and freewriting

8 Look at this word map and answer the questions below.

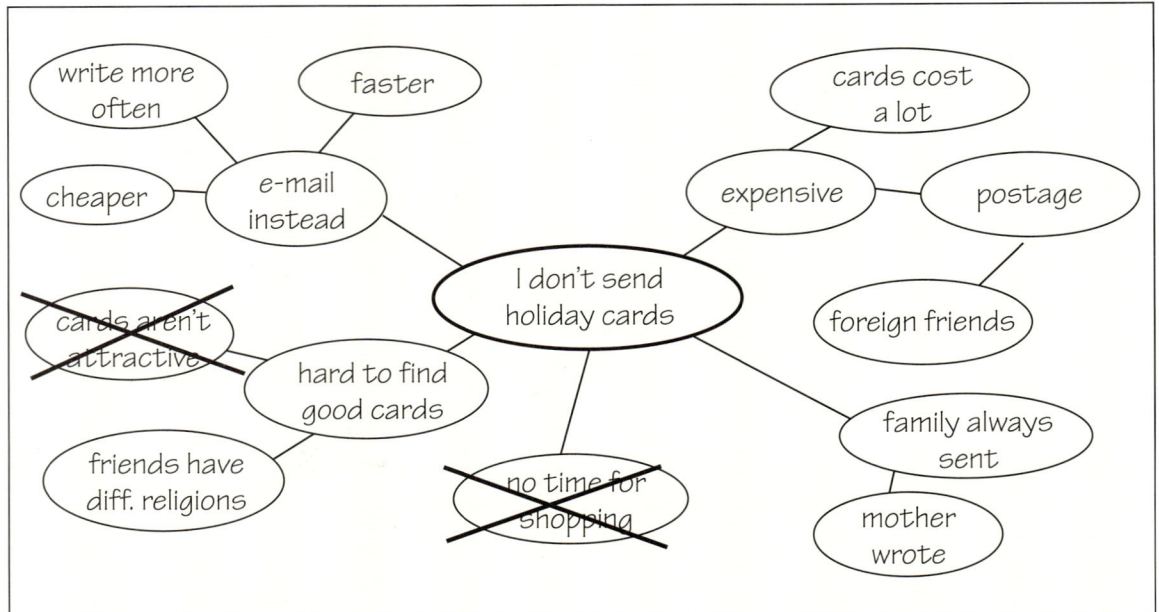

a. What is the writer's topic?

b. How many examples does the writer have?

c. Why did the writer cross out some ideas?

9 Read this paragraph. Were your guesses from exercise 8 above correct? Look at the word map again, and write a topic sentence for the paragraph. Then complete the paragraph with *so* or *because*.

> **Why I Don't Send Holiday Cards**
>
> My family has always sent holiday cards to friends. ....
> ....
> One reason is that I have friends all over the world, a. .... sending cards to them would be expensive. In addition, it's difficult to choose the right cards b. .... my friends have different religious beliefs. Finally, I e-mail my friends almost every week. c. .... I contact them so often, I don't have anything special to say at holiday times. Even though I don't send holiday cards, I am still close to my friends.

10 Look at this picture, and think about what is happening.

11 Freewrite for five minutes about how the driver explains the cause of the accident.

Remember: When you are freewriting, ...
- write for five minutes without stopping.
- write as much as you can. You can cross out ideas you don't like later.
- don't worry about spelling, grammar, or organization.

12 Check and edit your freewriting. Using your ideas, write at least three sentences with *so* or *because*. Then share your sentences with a partner or small group.

Writing Paragraphs

Put it together

a Choose one of these topics and make a word map or freewrite to get some ideas.

　　a. A time I was late

　　b. An accident

　　c. A mistake

　　d. It wasn't my fault!

b Edit your brainstorming. Cross out ideas you don't want to use and add more ideas if necessary.

c Write a paragraph about your topic and then check your writing.

d Exchange papers with a partner. Include your brainstorming.

- Fill out the Peer Review Form on page 204.
- Talk with your partner and go over each form.

e Read your paragraph again.

- Think about the comments from your partner.
- Make any additions or changes to your paragraph that would make it stronger or more interesting.

f Hand in the second draft of your paragraph to your teacher.

8 Problems and Challenges

In this unit, you will ...
- express personal feelings about problems.
- practice using *would like to*, *want to,* and *have to*.
- learn to order supporting sentences logically.
- edit lists by ordering ideas logically.
- write about problems or difficulties.

1. In a small group, describe problems you have with one of the following:

   - family and friends
   - teachers, classes and studying
   - money and budgeting
   - expressing your feelings and ideas

2. This paragraph is about a problem with parents. Read the paragraph to see if you share the problem and if you agree with the writer.

Talking to Parents

1. Talking to friends and classmates is easy for a lot of teenage boys, but talking to parents is more difficult. 2. Many teenage boys would like to talk to their fathers about their feelings, but they don't know how. 3. Sons often want to know how their fathers feel about them. 4. For example, I would like my father to say that he is proud of me. 5. However, my father never talks about his feelings. 6. He only wants to talk about sports or my schoolwork. 7. Parents have to talk to their kids about their feelings, or their children will feel lonely at home.

Writing Paragraphs

3 With a partner, answer these questions.

a. Which sentence is the topic sentence?

b. What does the concluding sentence do? (You can check more than one answer.)

1. ☐ It restates the topic sentence.
2. ☐ It makes a prediction.
3. ☐ It makes a suggestion.
4. ☐ It summarizes the paragraph.

c. Which of these details and examples could be added to the paragraph on page 165? Explain why the others do not belong.

1. ☐ My father is 58 years old.
2. ☐ My father's parents don't talk about their feelings either.
3. ☐ My father is often busy with his job, so I don't have many chances to see him.
4. ☐ Many parents like to play tennis and golf on the weekend.
5. ☐ It's also hard to choose a good birthday gift for my father.
6. ☐ I guess if I want to talk with my father, I will have to start more conversations myself.

Language focus: Want to, would like to, have to

Want to and *would like to* are useful expressions for talking about wishes:

I **want to** get a good job.

Miwa **would like to** travel overseas.

> **Note:** In speech and informal writing, the contraction *I'd like to* is often used. However, in academic writing, contractions are less common. Use *I would like to* when you write.

Have to shows *obligation* (that you must do something, or that it is required):

Mei Mei **has to** get up early to get to school on time.

If you want to drive a car, you **have to** get a driver's license.

4 Read the paragraph on page 165, *Talking to Parents*, again and underline the sentences containing *want to*, *would like to*, and *have to*.

Writing Paragraphs

5 Complete these sentences with the correct form of *want to*, *would like to*, or *have to*.

a. Kelly .... clean her room. It's a mess!

b. Ji Eun .... take dance lessons, but she doesn't have enough money.

c. Ali and Khalid .... go to the party, but they can't find a ride.

d. I .... go out last night, but I .... work at my part-time job.

e. My parents say if I want a new bicycle, I will .... pay for it myself.

f. If you .... work in Spain, you .... learn Spanish.

g. My little sister is always bothering me when I .... be alone.

6 Complete these sentences. Then share with a partner.

a. I would like ....

b. I have to ....

c. I want to .... , but I have to ....

d. When I was a child, I wanted to ....

e. Last year, I had to ....

f. I wish I didn't have to .... !

PROBLEMS AND CHALLENGES 167

Writing Paragraphs

Writing focus: Order of supporting ideas

After brainstorming ideas for a paragraph, you need to decide which ideas to use and the order you will write the ideas.

Ideas and sentences need to be ordered logically.

- Sentences that are part of the same idea go together.
- Sentences can go in *chronological* (time) order.
- Sentences can go in order of importance (see explanation below).

One way to organize your supporting sentences is to decide which ideas are most important. Writers often put the most important ideas last in a paragraph, so the strongest sentences are the last ones the reader sees. When you edit ideas in a list, you can number them in order of importance.

> **Remember:** When brainstorming, ...
> - use a separate, whole sheet of paper.
> - collect as many ideas as possible (don't stop writing).
> - don't worry if you don't like the ideas.
> - write short phrases or single words for lists and word maps, and sentences for freewriting.
> - after you brainstorm, look at the relevant ideas and brainstorm again.
> - edit your brainstorming before you write your paragraph.

7 Look at the list of ideas for a paragraph called *Making Language Classes Interesting*.

- Number the brainstormed ideas in order of importance (write 1 by the most important idea, 2 by the second most important idea, and so on).
- The writer decided not to use two details from the list. Which were they, and why?

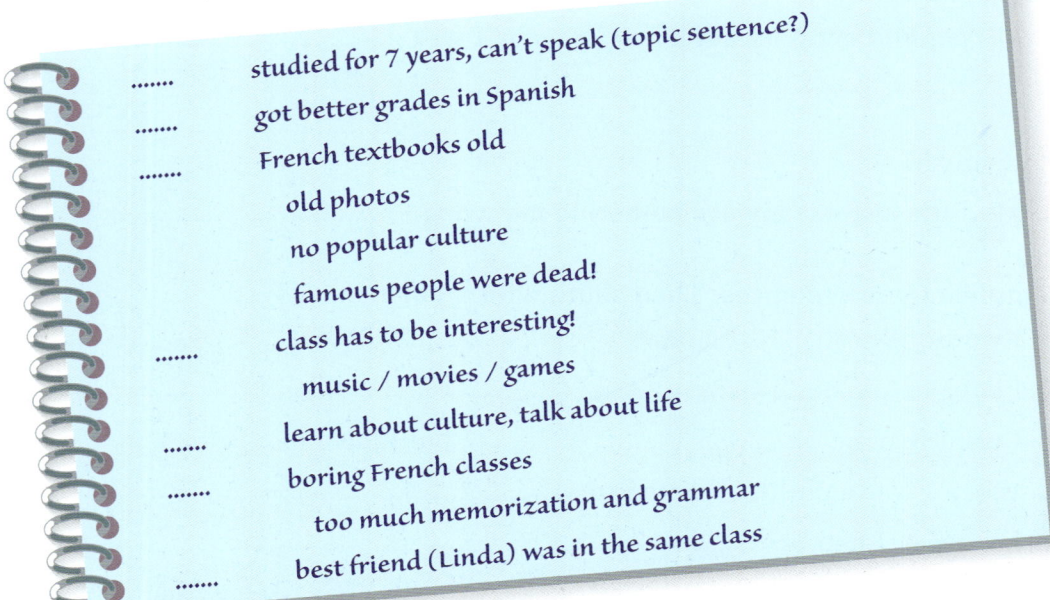

168 PROBLEMS AND CHALLENGES

Writing Paragraphs

8 Read the paragraph *Making Language Classes Interesting* to see if the writer's order of importance was the same as yours.

Making Language Classes Interesting

1. Learning a language is difficult, but it doesn't have to be boring. 2. I studied French at school for seven years, but I cannot speak a word of French now. 3. The problem with learning French was my classes, not the language. 4. One problem was that our textbooks were too old and boring. 5. The pictures were black and white, and the famous singers and movie stars had already died! 6. We also wanted to learn about popular French culture and talk about our lives in French. 7. Students do not want to memorize rules and vocabulary for an hour everyday and nothing else. 8. The most important point is that the classroom has to be interesting. 9. Students need to play games, listen to music, watch movies and talk about them in the foreign language. 10. Teachers need to make language classes useful and interesting if they want students to learn.

9 Look at these sentences for a paragraph called *The Challenge of Running a Marathon*. Number the sentences in chronological order.

- [1] Last year I ran the New York marathon, and it was the hardest thing I've ever done.
- [ ] The twenty-mile point was the worst because I had been running for three hours, I was hungry, and I was in a lot of pain.
- [ ] The beginning of the race was a lot of fun because the crowd was cheering and the sun was shining.
- [ ] I had to spend about six months training for the marathon before it even started.
- [ ] When I crossed the finish line, I could hardly walk and I felt sick.
- [ ] Next year, I would like to watch the marathon but not run it.
- [ ] After thirteen miles, the middle of the marathon, my legs began to hurt and I started to get bored.
- [ ] On the day of the marathon, I had to get up at 5:00 a.m. and get to the starting line. It was cold, and everyone was very tired.

PROBLEMS AND CHALLENGES

8 Writing Paragraphs

10 Look at the paragraph *Not Enough Time below* and do the following.
  a. Choose *three* of the supporting ideas below the paragraph.
  b. Write the sentences into the paragraph.
  c. Put the most important example last.
  d. Share your paragraph with a partner.

> **Note:** It's OK to have a different order—but be sure to explain your choices!

Not Enough Time

Should I quit my part-time job? I like my job as a waiter in a Chinese restaurant because the food is good, the atmosphere is friendly, and I can earn some money. But it is causing some problems for me.

Even though I like my job, I might quit until I finish school, or ask my boss if I can work fewer hours.

- The cooks let me test the food sometimes, and I am gaining weight.
- I would like to see my friends more often, but I have to work almost every night.
- It's hard for me to finish my homework. I want to concentrate on my studies, but I am too tired after work.
- I want to be a journalist and I would like to spend my free time writing stories about the people in my town. I can't do this and work so many hours.
- I have to drive to work, and my car is very old. I'm afraid it will wear out because I am driving it too much.

170 PROBLEMS AND CHALLENGES

11 Look again at the paragraph on page 170, *Not Enough Time*. Why did the writer begin with a question? Share your ideas with a partner or group.

    a. The writer didn't know some information.

    b. The writer wanted to get some advice from another person.

    c. To make the reader interested in the topic.

    d. The writer didn't understand the topic very well.

Put it together

a Choose one of these topics and then brainstorm the topic by making a list.

    a. A problem with a friend

    b. A problem at school

    c. A problem at work

    d. A problem in your city / school

b Edit your list.

- Cross out ideas you don't want to use and add more ideas if necessary.
- Number the other ideas in order of importance.
- Share your list with a partner, and explain your choices.

c Write a paragraph about your topic and then check your writing.

d Exchange papers with a partner. Include your brainstorming.

- Fill out the Peer Review Form on page 95.
- Talk with your partner and go over each form.

e Read your paragraph again.

- Think about the comments from your partner.
- Make any additions or changes to your paragraph that would make it stronger or more interesting.

f Hand in the second draft of your paragraph to your teacher.

9 Strange Stories

In this unit you will ...
- use time expressions: *after*, *before*, and *when*.
- learn to identify the main parts of a narrative.
- practice ordering the events in a narrative in a logical way.
- write a paragraph about interesting or unusual experiences.

1 Look at the picture. What do you think is happening? Share your ideas with a partner or group. Then read the paragraph below and check your guesses.

A UFO Sighting

1. I never believed in aliens before one night last year. 2. It was a cold, dark winter evening, and I was walking home from a friend's house. 3. I stopped to tie my shoe. 4. When I looked up again, I saw a round object coming toward me. 5. It was very large and shiny. 6. I couldn't believe what I was seeing. 7. Before I could shout or run, the object suddenly moved and then disappeared. 8. After the object disappeared, I ran all the way home and called my best friend. 9. When she picked up the phone, I couldn't say anything. 10. I knew she would think I was crazy. 11. I never told anyone about my UFO sighting.

2 Read the paragraph in exercise 1 above again and answer these questions.

a. Which sentence is the topic sentence?

b. How is this paragraph developed?
   1. by telling a story
   2. by giving reasons
   3. by describing objects with details

c. What does sentence 2 do?
   1. It gives details about the topic sentence.
   2. It tells the reader when and where the event happened.
   3. It lets the reader know the paragraph will talk about UFOs.

d. Is sentence 11 a concluding sentence?

Writing Paragraphs

Language focus: Using time expressions

One way to order two events is to use *after, before,* or *when*.

After shows the first event:

*I played soccer **after school**.* (school happened first; not soccer)

After school, *I played soccer.*

Before shows the second event:

*I couldn't play the guitar **before I took lessons**.* (lessons happened first)

Before I took lessons, *I couldn't play the guitar.*

When shows that the first event happened just before the second event:

*I told him the news **when he called**.* (he called first; then I told him the news)

When he called, *I told him the news.*

> **Note:** When *after, before,* or *when* begin a sentence, use a comma after the event.

3 Join these ideas with *after, before,* or *when*. Add a comma if necessary.

a. ...*After*......... the movie, we went home.   d. I left my house .... you called.

b. We left the class .... we turned in our assignments.   e. Please finish your homework .... you watch TV!

c. I woke up .... the alarm clock rang.   f. .... the dog barked, the baby cried.

9 Writing Paragraphs

4 Look at these pictures. What strange thing happened? Share your guesses with a partner.

5 Read the paragraph *Sleeping in a Farmhouse* to see if your guess in exercise 4 above was correct. Then complete the paragraph with *after*, *before*, or *when*.

> Sleeping in a Farmhouse
>
> The strangest experience in my life happened a year a. .... I graduated from high school. I was sixteen years old and my best friend Mark was fifteen. He invited me to visit him during the summer. I was staying with him in his farmhouse in the middle of the countryside. I shared a room with Mark, and our beds were separated by a table. Every morning, Mark's mom brought us a cup of hot tea in bed b. .... we woke up. While we were sleeping one night, I could feel my bed moving. I thought I was dreaming. The next morning, Mark's mother brought us hot tea as usual. c. .... she turned on the lights, we saw that our beds were pushed together and the table had moved. Mark said he didn't do it, and I didn't do it. We still don't know how the beds moved! What do you think?

6 With a partner, think of different explanations for why the beds moved. (You can draw a picture of what happened to help explain.) Then share your ideas with another pair or the whole class.

174 STRANGE STORIES

Writing focus: Narrative paragraphs

Narratives tell stories. Everyone has read narratives, watched them on television or at the movies, or heard them from other people. A narrative paragraph tells a short story or describes an event.

The paragraph *Sleeping in a Farmhouse* is a narrative about two boys on vacation. In the story their beds move in the middle of the night, and they don't know how it happened.

The events (stages of the story) are told in a logical order:

1. **Background information**

   A narrative paragraph usually starts with background information to set the scene for the story and provide context. It can tell **when** and **where** a story happened:

   > The strangest experience in my life happened a year before I graduated from high school. I was sixteen years old and my best friend Mark was fifteen. He invited me to visit him during the summer.

2. **Beginning of the story**

   The beginning of a narrative usually tells what happened first in the story:

   > I was staying with him in his farmhouse in the middle of the countryside. I shared a room with Mark, and our beds were separated by a table. Every morning, Mark's mom brought us a cup of hot tea in bed after we woke up.

3. **Middle of the story**

   The middle of the narrative is usually the main part and tells most of the events in the story:

   > While we were sleeping one night, I could feel my bed moving. I thought I was dreaming. The next morning, Mark's mother brought us hot tea as usual. When she turned on the lights, we saw that our beds were pushed together and the table had moved.

4. **End of the story**

   The end of a narrative concludes the story. It tells the final event, and has a concluding remark:

   > Mark said he didn't do it, and I didn't do it. We still don't know how the beds moved! What do you think?

9 Writing Paragraphs

7 Look at these pictures from a story. In a small group, describe what happened.

8 Read these parts of a paragraph about the pictures in exercise 7 above. Decide if the parts are ...

- background information.
- from the beginning of the story.
- from the middle of the story.
- from the end of the story.

Then number the parts in the correct order. (There are two parts of the middle section.)

a. ☐ ....
A few days later my father was able to go to the window to look for himself. But all he could see was an ugly brick wall.

b. ☐ ....
A strange thing happened to my father when he was in the hospital to have an operation.

c. ☐ ....
The next day he asked the nurse why the man described a beautiful park. The nurse looked confused and told my father, "That man was blind."

d. ☐ ....
My father didn't feel well. He asked the other man to describe the view outside the window because he wanted to feel better. After the man talked about the beautiful view from the window, my father was able to fall asleep. Before my father woke up, the man left the hospital.

e. ☐ ....
After his operation, my father woke up sharing a room with another man. The other man's bed was next to the window.

Writing Paragraphs

9 Read the parts below of two stories, *A Fright in the Forest* and *A Strange Day in Class*. Number the parts in the correct order and decide if they are ...

- background information.
- from the beginning of the story.
- from the middle of the story.
- from the end of the story.

> **Note:** The middle parts are not complete!

A Fright in the Forest

a. ☐ ....
Suddenly, I felt very cold and scared.

b. ☐ ....
I grew up in a small town in the countryside. Near my house was a large forest, and my parents told me not to play there.

c. ☐ ....
After that day, I never went back to the forest.

d. ☐ ....
One day, I was playing in the forest with some of my school friends.

A Strange Day in Class

a. ☐ ....
I have been studying English for a few years and I really enjoy the classes.

b. ☐ ....
I heard everyone laughing. I woke up and realized it was a dream.

c. ☐ ....
One day something unusual happened in class.

d. ☐ ....
The teacher was explaining grammar when I saw something strange out of the window.

10 With a partner, brainstorm what happened in each story. Then write sentences to complete the middle part of each story. Share your paragraph with another pair or the class.

> **Remember:** Brainstorming ...
> - helps you collect ideas.
> - helps you be creative and imaginative.
> - can be done by discussing ideas.

STRANGE STORIES 177

9 *Writing Paragraphs*

Put it together

a **Choose one of these topics.**
   a. A coincidence
   b. A strange experience
   c. A funny story

b **Choose one of the methods of brainstorming you have practiced, and brainstorm the story.**
   - making a list
   - making a word map
   - freewriting
   - discussion

c **Edit your brainstorming.**
   - Cross out ideas you don't want to use and add more ideas if necessary.
   - Share your brainstorming with a partner, and explain your choices.

d **Write a paragraph about your topic and then check your writing.**

e **Exchange papers with a partner. Include your brainstorming.**
   - Fill out the Peer Review Form on page 96.
   - Talk with your partner and go over each form.

f **Work with a new partner. Tell him / her about the story that you read in exercise e above. Listen to your partner tell someone else's story.**

g **Read your paragraph again.**
   - Think about the comments from your partner.
   - Make any additions or changes to your paragraph that would make it stronger or more interesting.

h **Hand in the second draft of your paragraph to your teacher.**

10 Differences

In this unit, you will ...
- use double lists to brainstorm.
- use *whereas* and *however* to make comparisons.
- learn to organize a comparison paragraph.
- compare different situations / events.
- write a paragraph about the changes in your life.

1 Look at the pictures. Tell a partner what you think the differences are between high school and college life for this woman.

2 Read this paragraph and find out the important differences for the writer.

College Life

1. My life changed a lot when I was in college. 2. There were 600 students in my high school and I knew nearly everyone. 3. However, there were thousands of students in my college, and I didn't know anyone. 4. I felt very lonely. 5. In high school, the classes were half boys and half girls. 6. In college, I studied engineering, and there weren't many women in the classes. 7. The biggest change in college was the style of class. 8. We had to do a lot of reading and learning on our own in college, whereas in high school the teacher told us nearly everything to study for the exams. 9. Even though college was more difficult, I enjoyed it more than my school days—after I got used to it!

Writing Paragraphs

3 Read the paragraph on page 179, *College Life*, again and answer these questions with a partner.

   a. How many differences between high school and college does the writer mention? What are they?

   b. The writer says that the biggest difference between high school and college was the style of class. Do you think this was a positive or negative difference? Explain your opinion to a partner.

   c. What are or what will be the differences for you between high school and college?

Brainstorming: Double lists

4 Look at the pictures and tell a partner how you think the summer and winter are different in Maine.

5 Read this paragraph and decide if the writer prefers the summer or winter in Maine.

> ### Winter in Maine
>
> 1. Spend a year in Maine and you'll be amazed by the difference between the summer and winter seasons. 2. The summer season is hot, and everyone likes to swim in the rivers and have barbeques. 3. People also go on hikes in the many mountains and through the national parks. 4. Summer in Maine is very green, and many tourists visit the countryside. 5. However, the winter is even more spectacular. 6. It snows a lot in Maine in the winter, and the scenery looks beautiful. 7. It sometimes snows two feet in one day, which is great for skiing and snowboarding. 8. The best part about the winter is Christmas. 9. There are a lot of parties in December, and people share Christmas presents or cards with friends, family, classmates, and colleagues.

6 Read the paragraph again and look at this brainstormed list. Underline the ideas the writer used from it.

Summer

hot	hiking in mountains / parks	
barbeques	air-conditioning	
shorts / T-Shirts	long, sunny days	
sunglasses	vacation	
swimming in river	my birthday	

Winter

cold	snowboarding / skiing
parties	Christmas parties
scarves / hats / gloves	sharing presents and cards
snow	short, dark days
beautiful scenery	

> **Note:** The writer used a *double list* technique to brainstorm ideas for the paragraph describing differences between summer and winter in Maine. A double list is useful when you are comparing two subjects.

7 Choose one of the topics below. Use a double list to brainstorm ideas.
- Share your list with a partner.
- Discuss which ideas would be good to write about.

a. Elementary school / high school

b. Last year's fashions / this year's fashions

c. My best friend five years ago / my best friend now

d. What was important to me at thirteen years old / what is important now

Language focus: However / whereas

However and *whereas* can be used to connect two different or opposite ideas:

my friends prefer watching movies / I find books more interesting

My friends prefer watching movies. **However,** I find books more interesting.

My friends prefer watching movies, **whereas** I find books more interesting.

Whereas my friends prefer watching movies, I find books more interesting.

> **Note:** You can join two sentences with *whereas*. Use *whereas* at the beginning of a sentence or in the middle, after a comma. Use *however* at the beginning of a sentence.

8 Look again at the paragraph on page 179, *College Life* and the paragraph on page 180, *Winter in Maine*. Underline the sentences that use *however* and *whereas*. Note the punctuation used with these words.

Writing Paragraphs

9 Connect these ideas with *whereas* or *however*. Add punctuation where needed.

   a. (*however*) skiing is a popular winter sport / many young people prefer snowboarding

   b. (*whereas* first) my science class has over 300 people in it / my English seminar has just twelve

   c. (*whereas* in the middle) dogs are more faithful / cats are more independent

   d. (*however*) cars are faster / I'd rather ride my bicycle

   e. (*however*) DVDs are more common these days / I have a huge video tape collection

   f. (*whereas*) (your ideas)

Writing focus: Organizing a comparison paragraph

When you compare two things (high school life and university life; summer and winter weather), you have two choices for organizing your paragraph:

- You can write all about the first subject and then all about the second (*block style*).

First block about the summer in Maine. ⟶

Second block about the winter in Maine. ⟶

> **Winter in Maine**
>
> Spend a year in Maine and you'll be amazed by the difference between the summer and winter seasons. The summer season is hot, and everyone likes to swim in the rivers and have barbeques. People also go on hikes in the many mountains and through the national parks. Summer in Maine is very green, and many tourists visit to see the countryside. However, the winter is even more spectacular. It snows a lot in Maine in the winter, and the scenery looks beautiful. It sometimes snows two feet in one day, which is great for skiing and snowboarding. The best part about the winter is Christmas. There are a lot of parties in December, and people share Christmas presents or cards with friends, family, classmates, and colleagues.

- You choose several points of comparison. Compare first one point about the two topics, then compare a second point about the two topics, and so on (*point-by-point style*).

First point about class size. ⟶

Second point about the number of boys and girls. ⟶

Third point about the class style. ⟶

> **College Life**
>
> My life changed a lot when I was in college. There were 600 students in my high school and I knew nearly everyone. However, there were thousands of students in my college and I didn't know anyone. I felt very lonely. In high school the classes were half boys and half girls. In college I studied engineering and there weren't many women in the classes. The biggest change in college was the style of class. We had to do a lot of reading and learning on our own, whereas in high school the teacher told us nearly everything to study for the exams. Even though college was more difficult, I enjoyed my life more than my school days—after I got used to it!

182 DIFFERENCES

Writing Paragraphs

10

10 **Look at the maps of the UK and Australia.**

a. In a small group, discuss what you think the differences are between London and Sydney in December.

b. Make notes of the differences.

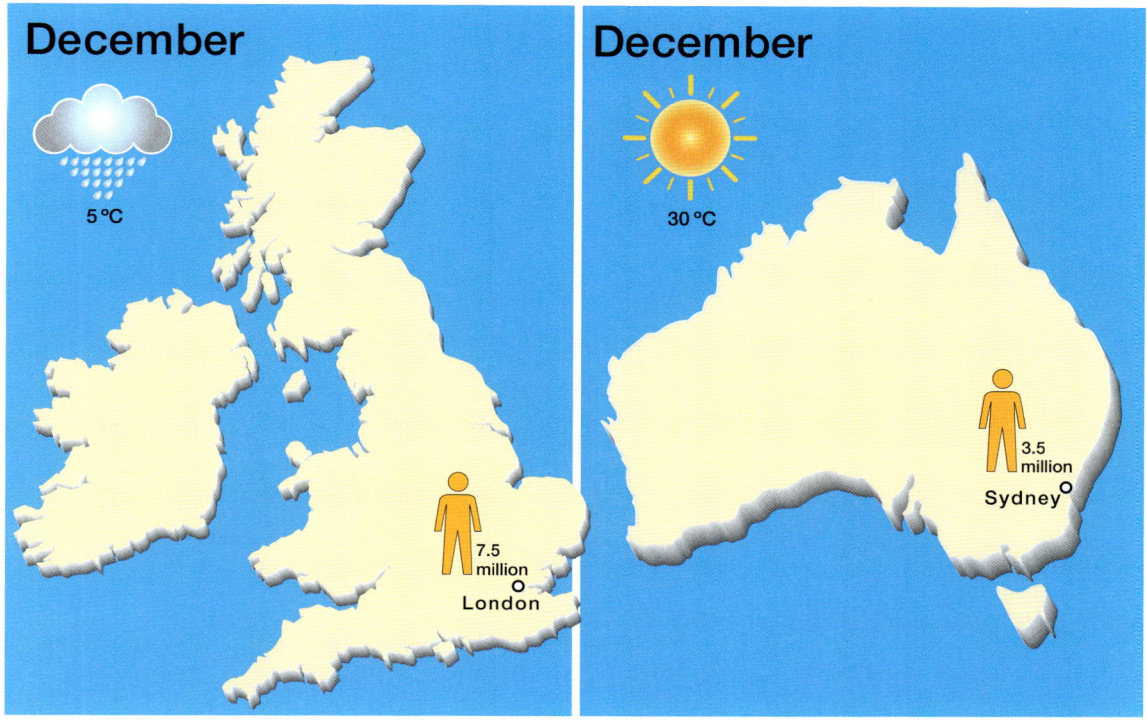

11 **Look at the double list of characteristics of London and Sydney, and add your differences. With a partner, write sentences about the differences using *however* and *whereas*.**

London	Sydney
in the northern hemisphere	in the southern hemisphere
difficult to make friends	easy to make friends
everyone stayed inside and watched TV	everyone was outside surfing and having barbeques

DIFFERENCES 183

Writing Paragraphs

12 On your own, complete the paragraph below, comparing London with Sydney.

- Using exercises 10 and 11 on page 183, write supporting sentences for the paragraph.
- Remember to arrange the ideas in either block style or point-by-point style.
- Connect at least two ideas with *however* or *whereas*.
- Finish the paragraph with a concluding sentence.

> Moving to England
>
> Last December, I moved from Sydney, Australia to London, England with my family, and it was like moving to another planet.

13 Share your paragraph with the same group you were in for exercise 10 on page 183.

- How are your paragraphs similar and different?
- Did the others in your group use block style or point-by-point style?

Put it together

a Look at the brainstorming you did for exercise 7 on page 181.

- Edit your brainstorming for a paragraph (or, if you wish, brainstorm again on one of the other topics).
- Decide if you will organize your paragraph in block style or point-by-point style.
- Number your ideas in order of importance.

b Write your paragraph and then check your writing.

c Exchange papers with a partner. Include your brainstorming.

- Fill out the Peer Review Form on page 207.
- Talk with your partner and go over each form.

d Read your paragraph again and make changes to improve it.

e Hand in the second draft of your paragraph to your teacher.

11 Difficult Decisions

In this unit, you will ...
- practice writing about cause and effect relationships.
- use pair interviews to brainstorm.
- learn how to begin paragraphs with a question.
- write a paragraph about a difficult decision.

1 Talk with a partner or small group. Is it important to keep secrets? Are there any secrets you would tell? Has anyone ever told a secret of yours? Why? How did you feel about it?

> Telling a Secret
>
> Do you think it's OK to tell your best friend's secret? Last year, my best friend told me a secret, and she made me promise not to tell anyone. My friend is slim, but she thought she was fat. Consequently, she wouldn't eat any food, and she became anorexic. I didn't know what to do. Because I thought she might get angry, I hesitated to tell her parents or teachers. However, I finally decided to tell her parents. As a result, they made sure my friend ate all her meals. They also took her to a psychologist every week for six months. Because of her parents' and the psychologist's help, my friend is much healthier now. I thought my friend would hate me for telling her parents about her problem, but last week she thanked me. I'm glad I told her secret.

2 Read the paragraph above and discuss with a partner. Which of these events happened first? Write 1 by the first one and 2 by the second.

a. .... My friend thought she was fat. .... My friend wouldn't eat any food.

b. .... I hesitated to tell her parents. .... I thought she might get angry.

c. .... Her parents made sure she ate all her meals. .... I told her parents her secret.

d. .... My friend is healthier now. .... Her parents and the psychologist helped her.

3 Why did the writer start her paragraph with a question?
   a. She wanted her readers' opinions about her decision.
   b. She needed some information she didn't have.
   c. She wanted her readers to think deeply about her topic.
   d. She is worried she made the wrong decision.

4 How did the writer develop her paragraph?
   a. She gave a lot of examples.
   b. She used a narrative.
   c. She described her friend carefully.

11 Writing Paragraphs

Language focus: Cause and effect

> **Remember:** In Unit 7, you used *so* and *because* to write about cause and effect.
> *Because* tells us the cause of an action or a situation.
> *So* tells us the effect.

Below are some words and expressions, which, like *so*, show effect.
Use a variety of expressions in your writing to keep it interesting.

As a result, consequently, and *therefore* are all used to connect two ideas. They all have a similar meaning. They show that the second sentence was the effect, or result, of the first one. They can be used at the beginning of the second sentence or they can join the two sentences with the word *and* before them.

as a result
I finally decided to tell her parents. **As a result,** they made sure my friend ate all her meals.
I finally decided to tell her parents, and **as a result** they made sure my friend ate all her meals.

consequently
My friend thought she was fat. **Consequently,** she wouldn't eat any food.
My friend thought she was fat, and **consequently** she wouldn't eat any food.

therefore
My friend thought she was fat. **Therefore,** she wouldn't eat any food.
My friend thought she was fat, and **therefore** she wouldn't eat any food.

5 Look at the example sentences above.
   a. If *as a result, consequently,* or *therefore* begin a sentence, where is a comma used?
   b. If they join two sentences with *and*, where is a comma used?

6 Connect these sentences with *as a result, consequently*, or *therefore*. Think about the correct order of the sentences and use correct punctuation.
   a. I didn't go to college right away. I wanted to travel for a year after high school.
   b. My parents needed help in their restaurant. I moved back home and worked for them.
   c. Cars are very convenient. People use them more than they should.
   d. My visa wasn't issued in time. I had to change my airplane ticket.
   e. Our school didn't have a lot of money. The administration decided to cancel some after-school clubs.
   f. I joined a social networking site that I don't actually like. My friends complained that it was hard to communicate with me.

Brainstorming: Pair interviews

You have already used discussion for brainstorming in Unit 6. Talking with just one person can also help you think of ideas for writing because that person can ask you focused questions about your topic. Your partner might ask you questions that begin with words like *what, why, how long, when,* and so on.

For example, when the writer of *Telling a Secret* told her partner about her difficult decision, her partner asked her questions such as *When did this happen? How did you find out about her problem? Why didn't you tell her parents immediately? What happened next? How did you feel? Do you think you made the right decision?*

To use pair interviews effectively, follow these steps:

- Tell your partner as much as you can about your topic.
- When you run out of things to say, your partner will ask you questions to help you continue.
- Write down the ideas that you talk about.

You won't use all of the ideas for your paragraph. However, it's always better to have too many ideas and then edit them.

7 **With a partner, look at the pictures of a woman who had to make a difficult decision, and do the following.**

   a. Tell your partner what's happening in each picture.

   b. Write a list of questions that you could ask the woman about her difficult decision.

   c. Share your list of questions with another pair.

Writing Paragraphs

8 Read this paragraph. Did the writer answer any of the questions you wrote with your partner?

> *Studying Abroad*
>
> *Going to Australia was a difficult decision for me. I wanted to go to Australia to get a degree in Business Administration, but my parents didn't want me to leave home. I knew I would miss my friends and family too, because I would be in Australia for four years. In the end, I decided to study in Australia to improve my career. As a result, I now speak English very well, and I work for a large international company. Because of all the languages I speak, I also travel around the world a lot with my company. Therefore, I don't regret going to Australia.*

9 Choose one of these topics. Then work with a partner. Your partner will ask you questions about your topic. Write down your partner's questions. At the end of the exercise, tell your partner which questions were the most helpful (helped you think of the most or the best ideas).

   a. Telling a secret / keeping a secret

   b. A time I changed my mind

   c. Choosing a job

   d. Choosing a school / university

   e. Starting / stopping an activity

Writing focus: Using questions to catch attention

A question at the beginning of your paragraph can encourage your reader to think deeply about your topic. Questions can be used to start paragraphs about a difficult decision, opinions, or personal feelings. In the opening paragraph in this unit, the writer asked, *Do you think it's OK to tell your best friend's secret?* This question helps the reader to think about the topic of secrets and telling them.

However, questions can be difficult to use effectively. The best questions are ones that help the reader to focus on and think about your topic. You need to imagine your audience (the people who will read your writing) and imagine how they might answer the question.

- Will the answer be too easy or too obvious?
- Could the reader give an answer very different from yours?

If the writer of *Telling a Secret* had asked *Have you ever told your best friend's secret?* or *Have you ever had a friend with anorexia?*, the reader might have answered "No" in his / her mind, and then lost interest in the topic.

If the writer had asked, *Do you know what anorexia is?*, the reader might have answered *Of course!* and thought that the paragraph topic would be too simple.

Writing Paragraphs

10 Below are several topics and some questions for the first sentence. Check (✔) the questions that are good. Discuss your choices with a partner.

Studying in Australia

☐ Have you ever been to Australia?
☐ Is it more important to be safe or to follow your dream?
☐ Where do you want to go to college?
☐ Can where you study change your life?

Quitting smoking

☐ Is smoking a choice or a disease?
☐ Do you smoke?
☐ Do you know how to quit smoking?
☐ Is it possible to be completely free of an addiction?

Breaking up with a girlfriend

☐ Do you have a girlfriend?
☐ Do you want to break up with your girlfriend?
☐ Can a former girlfriend really become your friend?
☐ Is there a kind way to tell someone you no longer love her?

Put it together

a Look at the paragraph topics from exercise 9 on page 188, and choose a new one (or choose your own topic about a difficult decision).

b Talk with a partner about your paragraph topic. Write down any good ideas that come from your discussion. If you need more ideas, talk with another partner, or try your favorite method of brainstorming.

c Write your paragraph and then check your writing.

d Exchange papers with a partner.
- Fill out the Peer Review Form on page 208.
- Talk with your partner and go over each form.

e Read your paragraph again and make changes to improve it.

f Hand in the second draft of your paragraph to your teacher.

12 Fate or Choice?

In this unit you will ...
- write about hopes and plans for the future.
- review brainstorming techniques.
- review connecting words and phrases.
- write a paragraph about the future.

1 Look at the pictures. Tell a partner what is happening. What will happen next?

2 Have you ever bought a lottery ticket or entered a drawing? Why, or why not? Have you ever won? Share your experiences with a group.

3 Read this paragraph to find out if the writer believes in luck.

> ### Do You Believe in Luck?
>
> 1. My parents and friends think that buying lottery tickets is foolish. 2. They say that ordinary people like me never win, and that it's just a waste of money. 3. However, I don't agree with this because I know that ordinary people win things. 4. For example, I've entered drawings before, and I've won several times. 5. I won a T-shirt at my school festival once, and also a gift certificate in a department store. 6. In addition, my uncle won a free dinner for two people by putting his business card in a drawing at a restaurant. 7. I hope to win a lot of money in the lottery in the future, so I'm going to buy a few lottery tickets. 8. After all, someone has to win the lottery, and it could be me one day!

4 Look again at the paragraph on page 190, *Do You Believe in Luck?* Then answer these questions with a partner.
   a. Does the author have the same opinion as you?
   b. Which sentence is the topic sentence?
      1 ☐   2 ☐   3 ☐
   c. Which sentence shows the writer's opinion?
   d. Which sentences support the writer's opinion?
   e. Which sentences conclude the paragraph?
      5 and 6 ☐   6 and 7 ☐   7 and 8 ☐
   f. Underline the sentences where the writer talks about the future.

Language focus: Writing about hopes and plans

To talk about your hopes and plans for the future you can use expressions such as *I would like to, I hope to,* and *I want to.*

I would like to be a journalist.
I hope to get a job in engineering when I finish college.
I want to live a long life, so I never take risks on the road.

Two verb phrases to write about definite plans for the future are *be going to* and *plan to.*

I'm going to buy a few lottery tickets.
I plan to buy a few lottery tickets.

5 Write sentences expressing each of the following personal wishes or plans. Use a variety of forms.
   a. Tomas / professional race car driver
      Tomas wants to be a professional race car driver.
   b. Sandra / politician
      ....
   c. Cooper / married with children in ten years
      ....
   d. Diana / Olympic medal in 2016
      ....
   e. Andrea / a sports car soon
      ....
   f. Write a sentence about a dream / hope that you have.
      ....
   g. Write a sentence about a plan that you have.
      ....

Writing Paragraphs

Brainstorming: Review

6 Work with a partner and do the following.

a. Take turns describing how to do these different types of brainstorming:
1. list
2. word map
3. freewriting
4. discussion
5. list showing order of importance
6. list showing chronological order
7. double list
8. pair interview

b. Explain to your partner which type of brainstorming ...
- is the easiest for you to begin.
- helps you get the most ideas.
- helps you get the most useful ideas.
- is the most difficult for you.
- is your favorite.

7 Choose two or three of these topics. Do a different type of brainstorming for each topic.
a. A career goal
b. Marriage or career?
c. Why I would / wouldn't like to have children
d. An unusual plan for the future
e. A crazy dream?
f. The best place to live
g. A travel plan

8 Exchange two examples of brainstorming from exercise 7 on page 192 with a partner. Answer these questions.

  a. Did the writer get a lot of ideas?

  b. Which brainstorming method gave the most ideas?

  c. Which ideas do you think are most interesting for a paragraph?

Writing focus: Review of connectors

9 Work with a partner and do the following.

- Take turns explaining what the words and expressions below mean, and how they are used.
- Write sentences for at least four of the words / expressions.

Example:
I've nearly finished my English writing textbook, Writing Paragraphs. **As a result,** *I can write very good paragraphs.*

after
and
as a result
in addition
because
before
but
consequently
for example
however
I think
in my opinion
so
therefore
when

10 With the same partner, answer these questions about connecting words and expressions.

  a. Why do writers use connectors?

  b. Should there be a connector in each sentence? Why, or why not?

  c. Which of the expressions in exercise 9 mean almost the same thing?

  d. Choose three expressions and tell about the rules for using commas with them.

  e. Which two expressions cannot start a new sentence (in academic writing)?

  f. What other connectors do you know? Make a list, and share it with another pair or the whole class.

12 Writing Paragraphs

11 Read this paragraph. With a partner, add connectors where needed. Compare your answers in groups. (There could be more than one right answer for each space.)

Changing my Future

I hope to be a successful artist someday soon. I have been painting since I was a young child ᵃ·...................... all my family said I had great talent. ᵇ·...................... , I couldn't get a job as an artist or make enough money selling my art. I really want to be an artist, ᶜ·...................... I need to make some changes to achieve my dream. First, I plan to study for a graduate degree in Fine Art to learn more about color and to make my paintings more original. ᵈ·...................... , I will have more confidence about trying to sell my work. ᵉ·...................... , I am going to design a website to show and sell my paintings. If you have dreams, don't wait for fate. You have to do something yourself to achieve your dreams. Going back to school or exploring different business opportunities are just two ways to change your future.

12 Read the paragraph again to underline any future wishes and plans.

Put it together

a Use one of the topics from exercise 7 on page 192 for which you brainstormed ideas.

b Write a paragraph, using connectors and some of the future forms you practiced. Then check your writing.

c Exchange papers with a partner.
- Fill out the Peer Review Form on page 209.
- Talk with your partner and go over each form.

d Read your paragraph again and make changes to improve it.

e Hand in the second draft of your paragraph to your teacher.

Grammar for Writers

This is not a grammar book; this is a writing book. However, good writers should be able to talk about grammar. Then they can talk about their writing. If you know some basic grammar terms, you can learn how to write correct and interesting sentences more easily. You can understand, talk about, and ask questions about the grammatical mistakes you make in your writing, and you can correct them more easily. At the same time, it is important to develop a "feeling" or intuition about English grammar: you can do this by exposing yourself to English. Read English stories, magazines, and web pages. Listen to English songs; watch English movies; have conversations in English. You will be surprised at how these activities also help your writing!

Parts of Speech

- **Noun**

    A *noun* names something: a person or animal (*teacher, Anne, bird*), a place (*mountain, New York, bedroom*), a thing (*computer, dress, cell phone*), or idea (*love, honesty, happiness*).

    Writers need to think about *noun phrases* in addition to simple nouns. A noun phrase includes the main noun and some words that describe it.

    bag (noun)

    The bag that my mother gave me. (noun phrase)

    Note: *Pronouns* (*I, you, he, she, it, we,* and *they*) are words that replace nouns, and are used in the same way.

    The topic of your sentences and paragraphs will be a noun or noun phrase.

- **Verb**

    The *verb* tells about the action or condition in the sentence.

    He **runs**.   (action)
    They **are eating** *dinner.*

    She **seems** *lonely.*   (condition)
    I **feel** *tired.*

    Verbs change slightly according to who is doing the action (*he runs; they run*) and the tense or time (*he runs every day; he ran yesterday*). We say that a verb must *agree* with the person or thing that the sentence is about.

    A *verb phrase* is the main verb (*run*) plus any auxiliary verbs (*does run, is running, has run, could be running*).

    Verb phrases show your feelings about your topic. You also use verbs when you write to tell stories and to explain what happened.

Writing Paragraphs

Preposition

Prepositions are short words (*at, on, for*) that connect ideas. They tell about time, place, or purpose (reason).

We eat dinner **at** *seven o'clock.* (time)
My book is **on** *the desk.* (place)
She bought a gift **for** *her friend.* (purpose)

A *prepositional phrase* includes a preposition and a noun. The prepositional phrases in the examples above are at *seven o'clock, on the desk,* and *for her friend.*

Adding prepositional phrases to your sentences is an easy way to write longer, more detailed sentences.

Adjective

An *adjective* describes, or tells about, a noun. It answers the question *What kind of* or *Which?*

She has a **red** *bag.* (What kind of bag does she have?)
The **small brown** *dog is mine.* (Which dog is yours?)

Adjective phrases—several words—do the same thing. Notice that there can be several adjective phrases for one noun.

She has a bag **from Peru.**
The dog **over there by that tree** *is mine.*

Many adjective phrases are prepositional phrases. Since adjectives and adjective phrases describe nouns, you will often see adjective phrases in noun phrases:

The red bag **with the black handles** *is mine.*

Using adjectives when you write helps you paint a picture of the nouns you are describing. They help your reader to see what you are describing.

Adverb

An *adverb* describes, or tells about, a verb. It answers the questions *Where, When, How, For how long / How often,* and *Why?*

It rained **yesterday.** (When did it rain?)
She eats **slowly.** (How does she eat?)
I **sometimes** *play tennis.* (How often do you play tennis?)

Adverb phrases contain several words. These may also be prepositional phrases. There can be more than one adverb phrase in a sentence.

She went **to the bank to get some money.** (Where did she go? Why did she go there?)

Adverbs add power to your verb phrases. They add more information and support to your ideas.

Use both adjectives and adverbs to make your writing more sophisticated, interesting, and accurate.

⊃ **Article**

There are three articles in English: *a*, *an*, and *the*. All of the articles signal nouns: *She is* **a friend**; *Would you like* **an apple**?; *Meet me in* **the classroom**. However, not all nouns have articles before them: *I will see you on* **Friday**; *I didn't see that* **movie**; *I don't believe in* **magic**. Using English articles correctly takes a lot of practice. Do not be discouraged if you make mistakes with articles while learning to write in English.

Parts of a Sentence

A complete sentence must have a subject and a predicate.

⊃ **Subject**

The subject of a sentence is the person, thing, or idea that the sentence is about. It is always a noun or a noun phrase. In a statement, it usually comes before the verb. To check if your subject agrees with the verb, find the *head noun*—the most basic noun that the sentence is about.

Amy *is my sister.*
She *is my sister.*
The girl *with the long hair is my sister.* (*girl* is the head noun)
The *young* **girl** *with the long hair sitting over there is my sister.* (*girl* is the head noun)

⊃ **Predicate**

The predicate tells what the subject does, what happens to the subject, or how the subject is. The predicate contains at least the verb, and often other words that follow the verb.

Amy **studies.**
Amy **studies English.**
Amy **studies English in her room for several hours every night.**

Finding the subject and predicate of your sentences helps you see whether you have a complete sentence, and whether the subject and verb of your sentence agree.

Writing Paragraphs

Punctuation

Here are some common rules for using punctuation in your writing. Of course, this is not a complete list. If you have further questions, check a grammar book or ask your teacher.

Capitalization

Always capitalize:
- the first word of every sentence.
- days of the week (*Tuesday*) and months of the year (*April*).
- the first letter (only) of the names of people and places (*Bangkok, Ayaka Seo*).
- the main words of a title, but not articles (*a, an, the*) or prepositions (words like *to, of, for*) or conjunctions (*and, but*), unless they are the first word in the title: *The Three Things I Do in the Morning.*

Period (.)

A period comes at the end of a statement:
An electronic dictionary is more convenient than a paper one.

If the sentence ends with an abbreviation, don't use more than one period:
RIGHT: *My mother just finished her Ph.D.*
WRONG: *My mother just finished her Ph.D..*

Comma (,)

Use a comma to separate a series of three or more items:
I take a dictionary, a notebook, and some paper to class every day.

Use a comma before words like *and, but, or,* and *so* to separate two parts of a sentence that each have a subject and a verb.
She needed some work experience, so she got a part-time job.
He did not study at all, but he still got an 87 on the test.

Use a comma after an introductory word or expression, such as *However, Therefore,* and *In conclusion*:
However, the high price of electric cars means that most people cannot afford one.

Quotation marks (" ")

Use quotation marks when you type or write the title of a book or movie:
"Hamlet" was written by Shakespeare.

When you use a word processor, you can use italics instead:
Hamlet was written by Shakespeare.

Use quotation marks to show the exact words someone spoke or wrote:
The professor announced, "We're going to have an exam next week."
Shakespeare wrote, "All the world's a stage."

Do not use quotation marks if you're reporting what another person said:
The professor said that we should study hard this week.

Writing Paragraphs

⊃ **Punctuation when using quotation marks**

If you are using expressions like *he said* or *the girl remarked* after the quotation, then use a comma and not a period at the end of the quoted sentence:
"We're going to have an exam next week," announced the professor.

Use a period if the quoted sentence comes at the end:
The professor announced, "We're going to have an exam next week."

Notice how a comma is used after *announced*, above, to introduce the quotation.

⊃ **Quotation marks and capitalization**

Capitalize the first letter of the word that begins a quotation. However, if an expression like *she said* interrupts the quotation and divides the sentence, then do not capitalize the first word of the part that finishes the quotation:
"Next week," said the professor, "we are going to have an exam."

The comma after *week* separates the quotation from the rest of the sentence.

Use a capital letter only if the second part is a new, complete sentence:
"We'll have an exam next week," explained the teacher. "It will take thirty minutes."

⊃ **Advice for academic writing**

The following are not usually used in academic writing, although they are fine in informal situations, such as letters to your friends.

- Parentheses that give information which is not part of your main sentence:
  Smart phones are useful (and besides, I think they look great).

  If your idea is important, it should be in a sentence of its own. If it is not important, it should not be in your paper.

- The abbreviation *etc.* to continue a list. Instead, use a phrase like *such as* in your sentence:
  Students in my university come from countries such as China, India, and Australia.

- Exclamation points (!). Instead, write strong sentences with plenty of details to show your reader your feelings:
  Angel Falls is one of the most spectacular natural wonders you will ever see.

- An ellipsis (...) at the end of a sentence, to show that the sentence is not finished:
  The professor said that I should study hard, so ...

  Instead, finish your sentence:

  The professor said that I should study hard, so I should not go to the party tonight.

Writing Paragraphs

Sample paragraph: Brainstorming

Assignment: Write a paragraph about a person who is important to you. Explain why that person is special. Use a word map to brainstorm ideas, edit your map, and then write your first draft. Then exchange papers with a classmate and fill out a Peer Review Form. After you receive your classmate's form, write a second draft using ideas from your classmate and your own ideas.

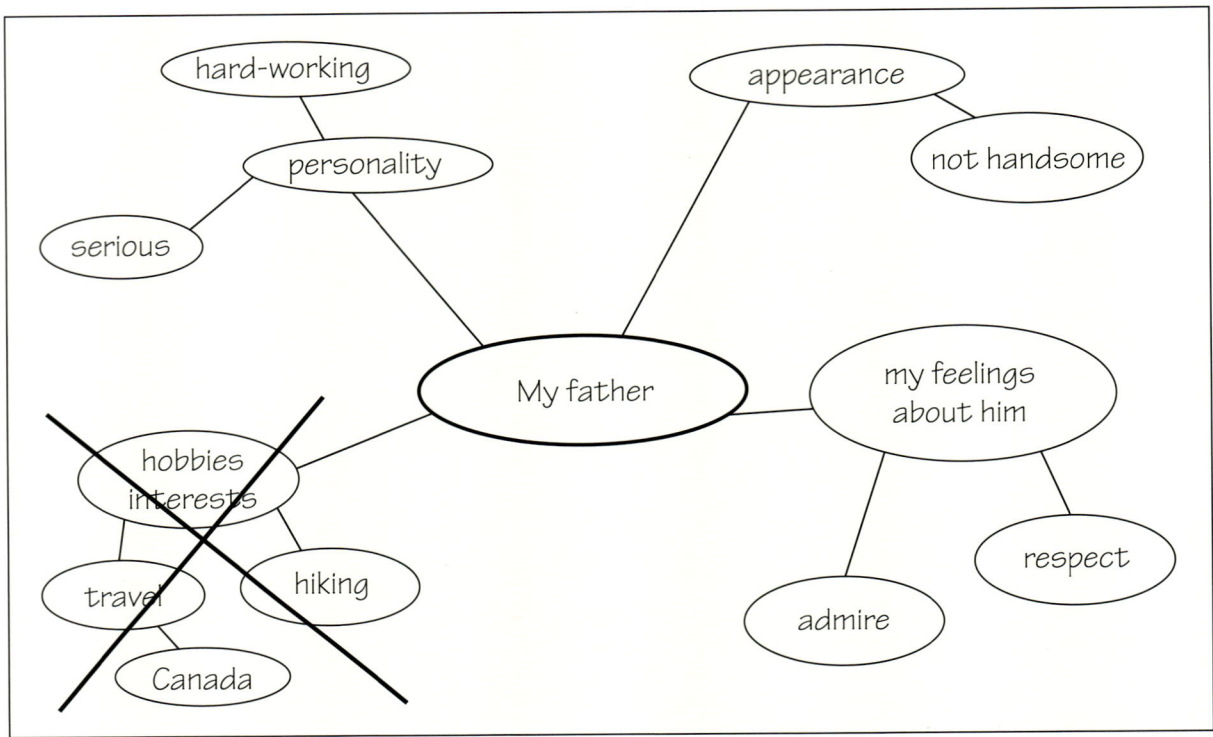

Sample paragraph: First draft

Kensaku Isagawa
May 11, 2011
Writing Class
Instructor: Carlos Islam

1st Draft

I admire many things about my father. He does not have any special qualities. He would be easy to overlook because he is not special. He is a good person. I get bored when I work with him. He has strong opinions, and he is tough and generous to other peoples. He always looks at the future. He never regrets something. I learned a lot from him.

Peer Review Form

Writer's name: Kensaku Isagawa
Reviewer's name: Yumika Hara
Title: ?
Date: May 12, 2011

1. What is the topic of the paragraph? What is the writer's opinion about that topic?

   Topic = Ken's father   Opinion = Ken admires his father

2. Look at the word map. Were any ideas crossed out? Why, do you think?

   Yes, he crossed out "hobbies." I don't know why, but maybe there were too many ideas for one paragraph. "Hobbies" is not why he admires his father, I guess.

3. Read the paragraph again. What is the topic sentence? Write it here.

   I admire many things about (my father).

   Circle the topic and underline the main idea.

4. How many supporting sentences are there?

   seven

5. Is there a concluding sentence? If so, what does it do (for example, restate the topic sentence, give advice, make a prediction, offer a final comment)?

   Yes, it offers a final comment.

6. Which sentence is your favourite? Write it here.

   He has strong opinions, and he is tough and generous to other peoples.

7. Do you have any questions or comments for the writer?

   This is interesting. I want to know more about your father. Also, I think it is better to be specific. Why is he a "good" person and why isn't he "special"?
   I think the sentence, "I get bored when I work with him" is not connected to your idea. The concluding sentence would be stronger if you said what you learned from your father, or if said something like, "I hope I can be like my father when I have children." Also, I want to know what doesn't he regret? Can you tell me examples? What have you learned from him?

Sample paragraph: Final draft

Kensaku Isagawa
May 15, 2011
Writing Class
Instructor: Carlos Islam

I Respect My Father

I admire many things about my father, but he does not have any special qualities. He would be easy to overlook because he is not outstandingly handsome or striking in appearance. However, he is a careful, serious, and hard working person. He has strong opinions, and he is tough and generous to other people. He always looks to the future. He never regrets anything. I think I learned a lot from him.

Peer Review Form—Unit 5

Writer's name: ....

Reviewer's name: ....

Title: ....

Date: ....

1. What is the topic of the paragraph? What is the writer's opinion about that topic?

2. Look at the freewriting. Is it long or short? Have any ideas been crossed out? Why, do you think?

3. Read the paragraph again. What is the topic sentence? Write it here.

   ....

   ....

   Circle the topic and underline the main idea.

4. How many supporting sentences are there?

5. Is there a concluding sentence? If so, what does it do (for example, restate the topic sentence, give advice, make a prediction, offer a final comment)?

6. Does the paragraph have these things?

	yes	no
• writer's name and date		
• paragraph title		
• descriptive adjectives		
• some sentences or adjectives combined with *and*		
• some sentences or adjectives combined with *but*		

7. Do you have any questions or comments for the writer?

Peer Review Form—Unit 6

Writer's name: ....

Reviewer's name: ....

Title: ....

Date: ....

1. What is the topic of the paragraph? What is the writer's opinion about that topic?

2. Read the paragraph again. What is the topic sentence? Write it here.

   ....

   ....

   Circle the topic and underline the main idea.

3. How many supporting sentences are there?

4. Underline supporting sentences that state an opinion.

5. Double underline sentences that support an opinion.

6. How many sentences state facts?

7. Is there a concluding sentence? If so, what does it do (for example, restate the topic sentence, make a prediction, give a suggestion)?

8. Which sentence is your favorite? Write it here.

   ....

   ....

9. Do you have any questions or comments for the writer?

© Macmillan Publishers Limited, 2016. This page may be photocopied and used within the class.

Peer Review Form—Unit 7

Writer's name: ....

Reviewer's name: ....

Title: ....

Date: ....

1. What is the topic of the paragraph?

2. Look at the brainstorming.
   a. What kind of brainstorming did the writer use?
   b. Was the brainstorming edited?
   c. Do you think that method helped the writer think of a lot of ideas?

3. Read the paragraph again.
   a. What do you think about the writer's explanation or excuse?
   b. Would you make the same choice, do you think? Why, or why not?

4. <u>Underline</u> the topic sentence.

5. Did the writer combine any sentences with *so* or *because*? If so, write them here.
   ....
   ....
   ....

6. Which sentence is your favorite? Write it here.
   ....
   ....

7. Do you have any questions or comments for the writer?

Peer Review Form—Unit 8

Writer's name: ....

Reviewer's name: ....

Title: ....

Date: ....

1. What is the topic? What problem does the writer explain?

2. Look at the writer's list.
   a. Which idea do you think is the most important?
   b. Were any ideas crossed out? Why, do you think?
   c. Did the writer number his / her ideas in order of importance?

3. Read the paragraph again. What is the topic sentence? Write it here.

   ....

   ....

   Circle the topic and underline the main idea.

4. How many supporting sentences are there?

5. Is there a concluding sentence? If so, what does it do?

6. Write the last supporting sentence. Is it the most important supporting idea?

   ....

   ....

7. Does the paragraph have these things?

	yes	no
• at least three supporting ideas		
• supporting sentences expressing desire or obligation		

8. Do you have any questions or comments for the writer?

ADDITIONAL MATERIALS **205**

© Macmillan Publishers Limited, 2016. This page may be photocopied and used within the class.

PHOTOCOPIABLE

Peer Review Form—Unit 9

Writer's name: ....

Reviewer's name: ....

Title: ....

Date: ....

1. What is the topic of the paragraph?

2. Write one or two words to describe the feeling or mood of the narrative (for example, *scary, strange, happy, sad*).

3. Look at the brainstorming.
    a. What kind of brainstorming did the writer use?
    b. Was the brainstorming edited?
    c. Do you think that method helped the writer think of a lot of ideas?

4. Read the paragraph again. Make a list of the main events, in the order they happened.

5. Is there a concluding sentence? If so, what does it do?

6. Which sentence is your favorite? Write it here.

   ....

   ....

7. Does the paragraph have these things?

	yes	no
• some sentences or adjectives combined with *after*		
• some sentences or adjectives combined with *before*		
• some sentences or adjectives combined with *when*		

8. Do you have any questions or comments for the writer?

Peer Review Form—Unit 10

Writer's name: ....

Reviewer's name: ....

Title: ....

Date: ....

1. What two things is the writer comparing? What is the writer's opinion about each of the things?

2. Look at the double list the writer used to brainstorm.
   a. Was it long or short?
   b. Which ideas were used?
   c. Were they the most interesting to you?

3. Read the paragraph again. What is the topic sentence? Write it here.
   ....
   ....
   Circle the topic and underline the main idea.

4. How many supporting sentences are there?

5. Is there a concluding sentence? If so, what does it do?

6. Does the paragraph have these things?

	yes	no
• point-by-point style		
• block style		
• two ideas joined using *whereas*		
• two ideas joined using *however*		

7. Do you have any questions or comments for the writer?

ADDITIONAL MATERIALS 207

© Macmillan Publishers Limited, 2016. This page may be photocopied and used within the class.

PHOTOCOPIABLE

Peer Review Form—Unit 11

Writer's name: ....

Reviewer's name: ....

Title: ....

Date: ....

1. What is the difficult decision the writer made? Why was it difficult?

2. What is the topic sentence? Write it here.

   ....

   ....

3. Did the writer begin with a question? If so, how did you answer it?

4. Read the paragraph again. <u>Underline</u> the words and expressions the writer used to link sentences and ideas (such as *and, but, because, so, therefore, as a result, consequently*).

   Do you think the writer used commas correctly in those sentences? If you are not sure, make a star (*) next to the sentence.

5. Was it easy to understand the paragraph? Were all the events told in a logical order?

6. Is there a concluding sentence? If so, what does it do?

7. Which sentence is your favorite? Write it here.

   ....

   ....

8. Do you have any questions or comments for the writer?

Peer Review Form—Unit 12

Writer's name: ....

Reviewer's name: ....

Title: ....

Date: ....

1. What is the topic of the paragraph? What is the writer's opinion about that topic?

2. Look at the brainstorming.
    a. Would you have used a different technique? Why, or why not?
    b. Did the writer get a lot of ideas from the brainstorming?

3. Read the paragraph again. What does the writer hope or desire for the future?

4. How many supporting sentences are there?

5. Do the supporting sentences include any of these things?

	yes	no
• connecting words and expressions • facts • opinions • examples		

6. Is there a concluding sentence? If so, what does it do?

7. Which sentence is your favorite? Write it here.

   ....

   ....

8. Do you have any questions or comments for the writer?

© Macmillan Publishers Limited, 2016. This page may be photocopied and used within the class.

DOROTHY E ZEMACH
& LISA A GHULLDU

writing
ESSAYS
FROM PARAGRAPH TO ESSAY

Contents

To the Teacher ccxiv
To the Student ccxv

Introduction: Process Writing — 216
- Understanding process writing

1 Pre-Writing: Getting Ready to Write — 219
- Choosing and narrowing a topic
- Gathering ideas
- Editing ideas

2 The Structure of a Paragraph — 225
- The definition of a paragraph
- The parts of a paragraph
- Identifying and writing topic sentences

3 The Development of a Paragraph — 231
- Paragraph support and development
- Writing concluding sentences
- Peer editing

4 Descriptive Paragraphs — 239
- Descriptive paragraphs and reasons for writing them
- Organizing and writing descriptive paragraphs using adjectives and prepositions
- Using connecting words and phrases to write a paragraph that describes a process

5 Opinion Paragraphs — 247
- Distinguishing between fact and opinion
- Organizing and writing paragraphs expressing opinions and arguments
- Using transition words to express causality
- Modal expressions to make recommendations

6 Comparison / Contrast Paragraphs — 254
- Comparison / contrast paragraphs and reasons for writing them
- Organizing comparison / contrast paragraphs
- Connecting words used for comparing and contrasting topics
- Writing about the advantages and disadvantages of a topic

| **7 Problem / Solution Paragraphs** | **264** |

- Writing about problems and solutions
- Using real conditionals
- Writing a two-paragraph paper with linking phrases

| **8 The Structure of an Essay** | **270** |

- The definition of an essay
- Formatting an essay
- Writing a thesis statement

| **9 Outlining an Essay** | **277** |

- The purpose of an outline
- Writing an outline

| **10 Introductions and Conclusions** | **285** |

- The purpose of an introduction
- Types of information in introductions
- The purpose of a conclusion
- Writing conclusions

| **11 Unity and Coherence** | **292** |

- The importance of unity in essay writing
- Editing an essay for unity
- The importance of coherence in essay writing
- Creating coherence

| **12 Essays for Examinations** | **302** |

- Common instructions for essay tests
- Writing timed essays and managing time

| **Additional Materials** | **309** |

- Sample essay: brainstorming
- Sample essay: first draft
- Sample essay: second draft
- Punctuation
- Sample information letter
- Sample statement of purpose
- Sample résumé

| **Photocopiable Materials** | **320** |

To the Teacher

Non-native English speakers who enroll in a college or university want to develop writing skills that will lead to academic success. This book is a combination text and workbook. Its focused lessons, specific exercises, and ample opportunities for practice are designed to help your students gain confidence in writing academic prose.

Writing Essays is designed to take university-level students with an intermediate ability in English as a second language from paragraph writing through essay writing. The course combines a process approach to writing (where students work on invention, peer response, editing, and writing multiple drafts) with a pragmatic approach to teaching the basics of writing (with direct instruction on such elements as topic sentences, thesis statements, and outlines).

The Introduction presents process writing to students. The tasks in the main units are graded. Students first work on recognizing and identifying key writing structures from model paragraphs and essays. Then they manipulate the structures in short, manageable tasks. Finally, they apply the structures to their own writing. There are opportunities for students to work independently, with a partner, and with a group. The exercises can be done either in class or as homework. Critical thinking is emphasized, so that students become aware of the impact of their choice of words, sentences, and organizational techniques on the effectiveness of their writing. The focus throughout is on academic writing—the type of writing used in university courses and exams in English-speaking institutions of higher learning.

In Units 1–6, students analyze and write the types of paragraphs that commonly occur in academic contexts. They practice writing topic sentences and concluding sentences, organizing the paragraph coherently, and using appropriate vocabulary, grammar, and transitional devices in the paragraph body. In Unit 7, students write two-paragraph papers, in preparation for longer assignments. In Units 8–11, students apply what they have learned about paragraphs to essay writing. They work on developing and supporting a central thesis, organizing an outline from which to write, and writing effective introductions and conclusions. Unit 12 discusses strategies for timed essay writing, including understanding standard instructions, time-management techniques, and methods for organizing information.

Included in *Writing Essays* are samples of the development of an essay from brainstorming to the final draft. There is also a guide to punctuation and examples of a letter requesting information, a personal essay of the type commonly required in college applications, and a résumé.

The Teacher's Guide supports the instructor by offering teaching suggestions, a discussion of marking and grading writing, ideas for supplemental activities for each unit, and photocopiable exercises and activities.

To the Student

Writing is a very important part of your university study. You will write assignments that may range from one paragraph to several pages long, and will write answers on tests and exams that may be a few sentences long or a complete essay.

Academic writing in English may be different not only from academic writing in your own language, but even from other writing in English. The purpose of *Writing Essays* is to help you recognize and produce the sort of writing that you will do for your university courses.

During this course, you will have many opportunities to study and discuss examples of English academic writing. Naturally, you will also have many opportunities to discuss your own academic writing and the writing of your classmates. You will learn how important the reader is to the writer, and how to express clearly and directly what you mean to communicate. We hope that what you learn in this course will help you throughout your academic studies and beyond.

You should come to your writing class every day with energy and a willingness to work and learn. Your instructor and your classmates have much to share with you, and you have much to share with them. By coming to class with your questions, taking chances and trying new ways, and expressing your ideas in another language, you will add not only to your own world but to the world of those around you.

Good luck!

Dorothy E Zemach
Lisa A Ghulldu

Introduction: Process Writing

In this unit, you will ...
- learn about process writing, the writing method used in most English-speaking university classes.

The writing process

I These words are important for understanding the writing process. Match each word with the correct definition.

a. step
b. topic
c. gather
d. organize
e. paragraph
f. essay
g. proofread
h. edit

1. to check a piece of writing for errors
2. a group of related sentences
3. one thing in a series of things you do
4. subject; what the piece of writing is about
5. to change or correct a piece of writing
6. a short piece of writing, at least three paragraphs long
7. to arrange in a clear, logical way
8. to find and collect together

Writing Essays

The six steps of the writing process

2 Read about the writing process. These are the steps you will practice in this book.

⊃ **Process writing**

When we write, we do more than just put words together to make sentences. Good writers go through several steps to produce a piece of writing.

Pre-writing

> **STEP ONE: Choose a topic.** Before you write, your teacher gives you a specific assignment or some ideas of what to write about. If not, choose your topic yourself.
>
> **STEP TWO: Gather ideas.** When you have a topic, think about what you will write about that topic.
>
> **STEP THREE: Organize.** Decide which of the ideas you want to use and where you want to use them. Choose which idea to talk about first, which to talk about next, and which to talk about last.

Drafting

> **STEP FOUR: Write.** Write your paragraph or essay from start to finish. Use your notes about your ideas and organization.

Reviewing and revising

> **STEP FIVE: Review structure and content.** Check what you have written. Read your writing silently to yourself or aloud, perhaps to a friend. Look for places where you can add more information, and check to see if you have any unnecessary information. Ask a classmate to exchange papers with you. Your classmate reads your paper, and you read his or hers. Getting a reader's opinion is a good way to know if your writing is clear and effective. Learning to give opinions about other people's writing helps you to improve your own. You may want to go on to step six now and revise the structure and content of your paper before you proofread it.

Rewriting

> **STEP SIX:**
>
> **Revise structure and content.** Use your ideas from step five to re-write your text, making improvements to the structure and content. You might need to explain something more clearly, or add more details. You may even need to change your organization so that your paper is more logical. Together, steps five and six can be called *editing*.
>
> **Proofread.** Read your paper again. This time, check your spelling and grammar and think about the words you have chosen to use.
>
> **Make final corrections.** Check that you have corrected the errors you discovered in steps five and six and make any other changes you want to make. Now your text is finished!

Steps five and six can be repeated many times.

Writing Essays

Review

3 Complete this chart, summarizing the steps of the writing process.

Pre-writing

- **STEP ONE:** Choose a ....
- **STEP TWO:** Gather ....
- **STEP THREE:** Decide ....

Drafting

- **STEP FOUR:** Write ....

Reviewing and revising

- **STEP FIVE:** Check ....

Rewriting

- **STEP SIX:**
May need to …
  - explain ....
  - add ....
  - change ....

Steps .... and .... may be .... many times.

218 INTRODUCTION: PROCESS WRITING

Pre-Writing: Getting Ready to Write

In this unit, you will learn how to ...
- choose and narrow a topic.
- gather ideas.
- edit ideas.

⊃ **What is pre-writing?**

Before you begin writing, you decide what you are going to write about. Then you plan what you are going to write. This process is called *pre-writing*.

Choosing and narrowing a topic

⊃ How to choose a topic for a paragraph

A paragraph is a group of five to ten sentences that give information about a topic. Before you write, you must choose a topic for your paragraph.

- Choose a topic that isn't too *narrow* (limited, brief). A narrow topic will not have enough ideas to write about. *The ages of my brothers and sisters* is too narrow. You can't write very much about it.
- Choose a topic that isn't too *broad* (general). A broad topic will have too many ideas for just one paragraph. Most paragraphs are five to ten sentences long. *Schools* is too general. There are thousands of things you could say about it.

A student could narrow this topic by choosing one aspect of schools to discuss.

schools ⟶ *high schools in my country*
popular school clubs
university entrance exams

1 Choose three topics from this list. Narrow each of the three down to a paragraph topic. Then compare with a partner.

a. holidays
b. friends
c. my country
d. dancing
e. cars

1

Writing Essays

Brainstorming

⟳ **What is brainstorming?**

Brainstorming is a way of gathering ideas about a topic. Think of a storm: thousands of drops of rain, all coming down together. Now, imagine thousands of ideas "raining" down onto your paper! When you brainstorm, write down every idea that comes to you. Don't worry now about whether the ideas are good or silly, useful or not. You can decide that later. Right now, you are gathering as many ideas as you can.

You will learn three types of brainstorming in this unit: *making a list*, *freewriting*, and *mapping*.

⟳ **Making a list**

Write single words, phrases, or sentences that are connected to your topic. Look at this list a student made when brainstorming ideas to write about her topic, "What should I study in college?"

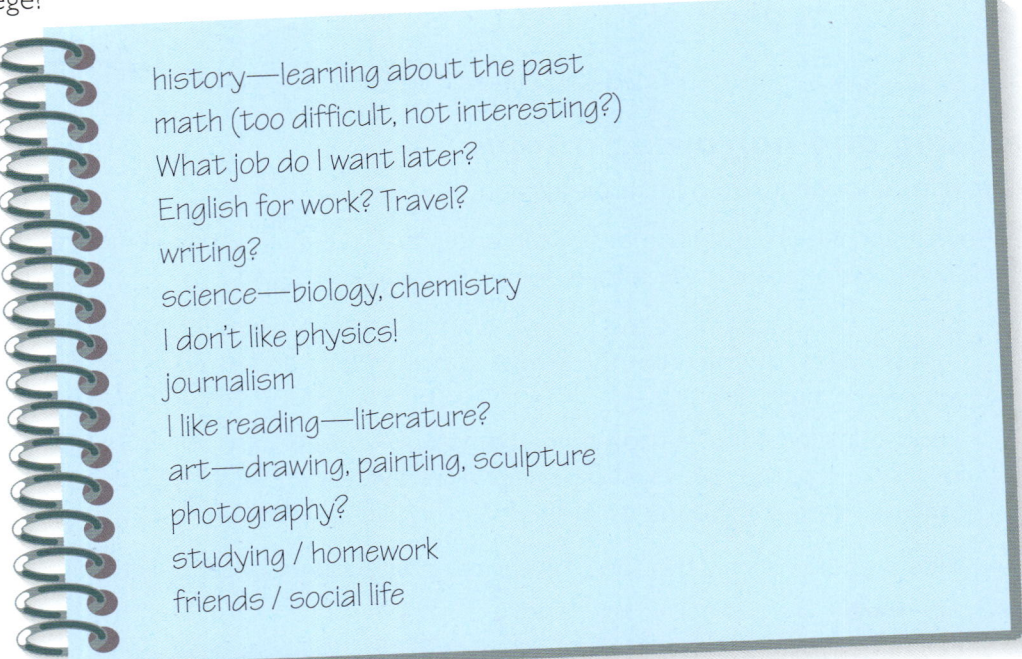

2 Work with a partner or small group. Choose one of these topics. List as many ideas as you can in five minutes.
   a. teenage fashions
   b. social networking
   c. driving a motorcycle

3 Work alone. Choose a topic from exercise 1 on page 219, and list as many ideas as you can in five minutes.

220 PRE-WRITING: GETTING READY TO WRITE

↻ **Freewriting**

When you freewrite, you write whatever comes into your head about your topic, without stopping. Most freewriting exercises are short—just five or ten minutes.

Freewriting helps you practice *fluency* (writing quickly and easily). When you freewrite, you do not need to worry about *accuracy* (having correct grammar and spelling). Don't check your dictionary when you freewrite. Don't stop if you make a mistake. Just keep writing!

Here is an example of a student's freewriting:

> There are ~~too~~ so many subjects to study at university, it is difficult to choose one for my major. I've always made good grades in math, but I don't like it very much. I don't like ~~physical~~ physics or any science very much. Writing—I've always liked writing. Would journalism be a good course to take? Newspapers have pictures, too, so maybe photography would be good. I'm ~~maybe~~ definitely looking forward to meeting new friends at university. And what about reading? Reading is a part of any course, but literature includes a lot of reading and it probably includes a lot of writing, too.

Notice how the writer's ideas jump around. When she makes a mistake, she just crosses it out and continues writing. One thought (*writing*) leads to another (*journalism*), and then to another (*photography*). There are some details that are not exactly about her topic (*looking forward to meeting new friends*), but that's OK in freewriting. You want to get as many ideas on paper as you can. You can take out unnecessary words and sentences later.

4 **Choose one of the narrowed topics you thought of for exercise 1 on page 219. Practice freewriting for five minutes. Remember, do not stop, erase, or go back. Just write as much as you can.**

1 Writing Essays

◯ **Mapping**

To make a map, use a whole sheet of paper, and write your topic in the middle, with a circle around it. Then put the next idea in a circle above or below your topic, and connect the circles with lines. The lines show that the two ideas are related.

The example below shows a map of "What should I study in college?" The writer connected *favorite subjects* to the main idea. *Art* and *English* are connected to *favorite subjects* to show that they are related.

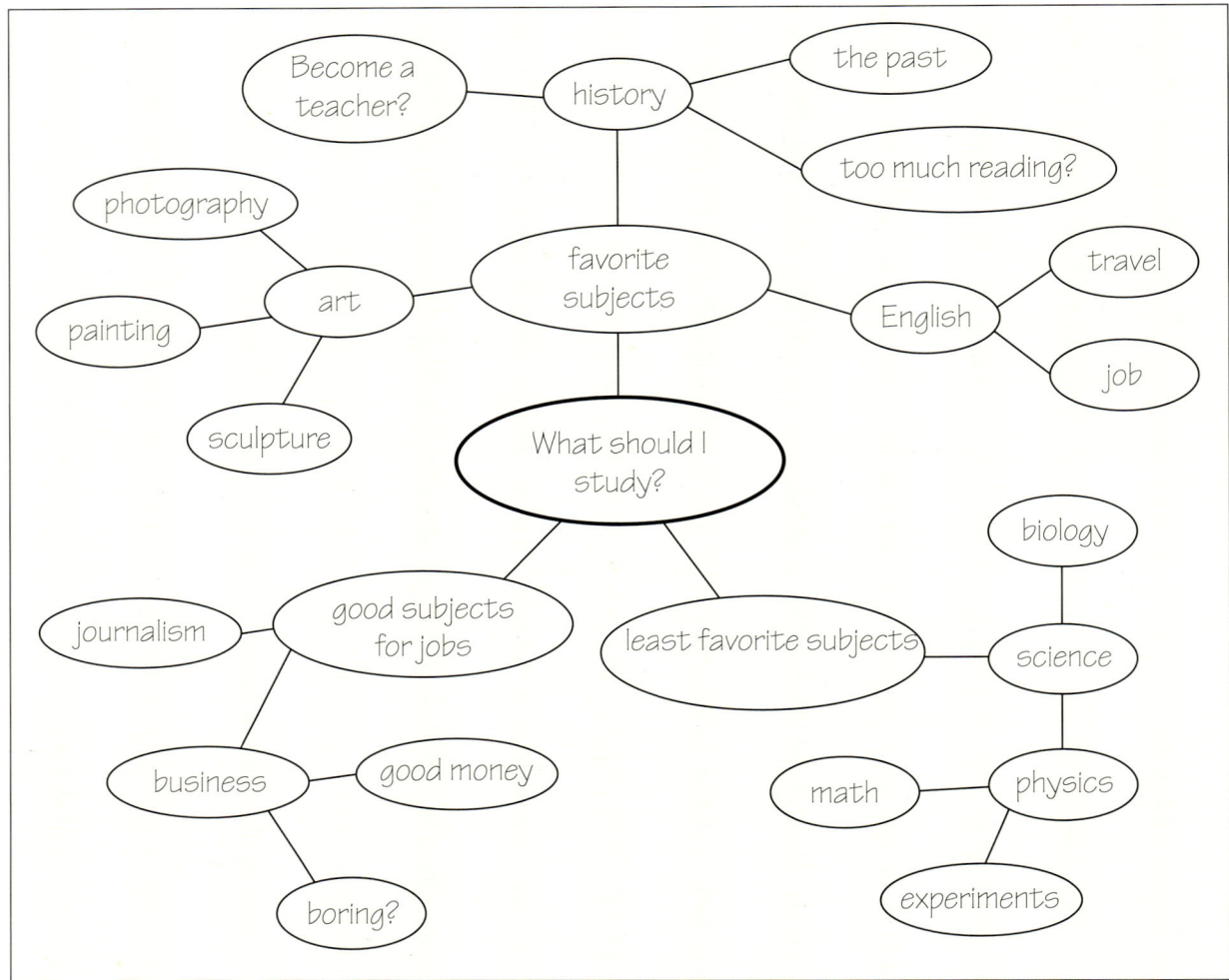

5 Choose another narrowed topic you thought of for exercise 1 on page 219. Make a map in five minutes. Share your map with a partner. Explain how the circles are related to each other.

◯ **What's the best way to brainstorm?**

There is no best method of brainstorming. Some writers like to use lists because they don't have to write complete sentences. Some writers like freewriting because they can write quickly and ideas come easily. Some writers prefer mapping because they can easily see the relationship between ideas. Experiment with all three methods, and then choose the one that works best for you.

Editing

⊃ **How to edit**

After you have gathered plenty of ideas, you will need to go back and edit them. This is the time to choose which ideas are the most interesting, and which are the most *relevant to* (important or necessary for) your topic. Of course, you can still add new ideas if you think of something else while you are re-reading your list. For example, the student writing "What should I study in college?" edited her list like this:

> history—learning about the past
> ~~math (too difficult, not interesting?)~~ **Not interesting to me.**
> What job do I want later? **Describe more.**
> English for work? Travel?
> writing? **Important in many subjects.**
> ~~science—biology, chemistry~~
> ~~I don't like physics!~~ **I don't want to study science!**
> journalism
> I like reading—literature?
> art—drawing, painting, sculpture
> photography?
> studying / homework **What about it?**
> ~~friends / social life~~ **Not related.**

To edit freewriting, cross out sentences or parts of sentences that aren't related. You can add more ideas in the margin or add more sentences at the bottom. To edit a map, cross out circles that don't belong, and add new ones if you get more ideas. You might also change the lines you have drawn.

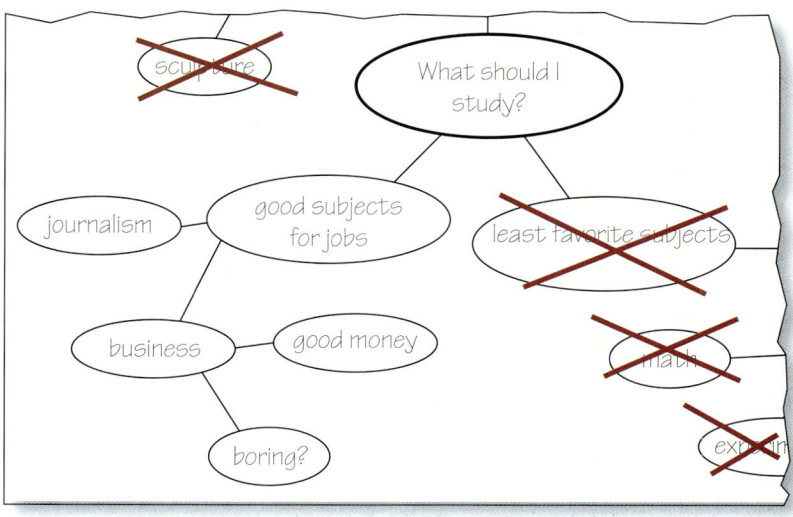

6 Look at the list you made in exercise 3 on page 220, the freewriting you did in exercise 4 on page 221, or the map you made in exercise 5 on page 222. Edit your brainstorming. Show your work to a partner. Explain how you edited your brainstorming.

1

Writing Essays

Review

7 Complete the crossword puzzle.

Each paragraph has only one topic. If the topic is too [1.] n___, you will not be able to write enough about it. On the other hand, if the topic is too [2.] b___, you will have too many ideas for just one paragraph.

After you choose a topic, you will need to [3.] b___ some ideas to write about in your paragraph. One way to do this is to make a [4.] l___. Another way of brainstorming is [5.] m___. After you have written down many ideas, you can go back and decide which ones are the most interesting and the most [6.] r___ to your topic.

[7.] F___ is a useful way to help you write more easily and naturally. In this kind of writing, you are working on [8.] f___, and not [9.] a___.

8 Look again at the note about brainstorming at the bottom of page 222. Brainstorm a list of pros (good things) and cons (bad things) about each of the three methods of brainstorming.

2 The Structure of a Paragraph

In this unit, you will learn ...
- the definition of a paragraph.
- the parts of a paragraph.
- how to identify and write topic sentences.

⊃ What is a paragraph?

As you learned in Unit 1, a paragraph is a group of sentences about a single *topic*. Together, the sentences of the paragraph explain the writer's *main idea* (most important idea) about the topic. In academic writing, a paragraph is often between five and ten sentences long, but it can be longer or shorter, depending on the topic. The first sentence of a paragraph is usually indented (moved in) a few spaces.

Understanding a paragraph

1 Read this paragraph. It is the beginning of an article about Switzerland in a student newspaper. Then answer the questions.

Switzerland—Something Interesting at Every Turn
By Ken Jones

If you dream of traveling to a country with beautiful mountains, delicious food, wonderful places to go sight-seeing, and polite people, you should visit Switzerland. If you look at the map, the first thing you notice is that Switzerland has many mountains, including some of the highest in Europe. Climbing or skiing down the mountains is great fun. Another thing you will notice is that Switzerland shares its borders with five different countries: France, Germany, Italy, Austria, and Lichtenstein. In fact, there are four official languages in Switzerland: German, French, Italian, and Romansch. All these groups of people make Swiss culture very interesting. Finally, Switzerland has many cities and interesting places to visit. Cities such as Bern have modern buildings like the Paul Klee Zentrum, yet the traditional alpine refuges in the mountains show that the country's old traditions are still alive. All the people, places, and things to see make Switzerland a great place for a holiday.

2 Writing Essays

a. What is the topic of the paragraph?
....

b. What is the main idea about the topic?
....

c. What ideas help explain the main idea?
....
....
....

Paragraph organization

⊃ What makes a paragraph?

A paragraph has three basic parts:

1. The topic sentence. This is the main idea of the paragraph. It is usually the first sentence of the paragraph, and it is the most general sentence of the paragraph.

2. The supporting sentences. These are sentences that talk about or explain the topic sentence. They are more detailed ideas that follow the topic sentence.

3. The concluding sentence. This may be found as the last sentence of a paragraph. It can finish a paragraph by repeating the main idea or just giving a final comment about the topic.2

226 THE STRUCTURE OF A PARAGRAPH

Writing Essays

2

2 Read the paragraph about Switzerland in exercise 1 on page 225 again. Circle the topic sentence, put one line under the supporting sentences, and put two lines under the concluding sentence.

3 Put a check (✓) next to the group of sentences that makes a good paragraph. Why are the other groups of sentences not good paragraphs?

a. ☐

> Many people suffer from insomnia, which is the inability to fall asleep or stay asleep. There are several causes of insomnia. One of the main causes is stress. When people feel stressed or nervous about their work, for example, they may not be able to fall asleep for many hours or they may wake up during the night and not be able to fall asleep again. When people do not have enough sleep, it can affect their mood, making them irritable or depressed. Insomnia can also have a negative effect on concentration and job performance. Therefore, finding help for insomnia is very important for people who suffer from it.

b. ☐

> Classes in literature are useful no matter what job you intend to have when you finish university. Books are about life. People who study literature learn the skill of reading carefully and understanding characters, situations, and relationships. This kind of understanding can be useful to teachers and business people alike. Literature classes also require a lot of writing, so they help students develop the skill of clear communication. Of course, a professional writer needs to have this skill, but it is an equally important skill for an engineer. Finally, reading literature helps develop an understanding of many different points of view. Reading a novel by a Russian author, for example, will help a reader learn more about Russian culture. For anyone whose job may bring them into contact with Russian colleagues, this insight can help encourage better cross-cultural understanding. Studying literature is studying life, so it is relevant to almost any job you can think of.

c. ☐

> One good way to learn another language is to live in a country where that language is used. When you live in another country, the language is around you all the time, so you can learn to listen to and speak it more easily.

THE STRUCTURE OF A PARAGRAPH 227

2 Writing Essays

The topic and the main idea

⊃ The topic sentence …
- usually comes first in a paragraph.
- gives the writer's main idea or opinion about the topic and helps the reader understand what the paragraph is going to talk about.

4 Circle the topic of the sentence. Underline the main idea about the topic.

a. (Switzerland) is a <u>very interesting country to visit</u>.

b. One cause of insomnia is stress.

c. A library is a good place to study.

d. Learning a second language creates job opportunities.

e. Watching and playing sports can both be good forms of relaxation.

f. One of the most valuable tools for students is the computer.

g. People with different personalities may find it difficult to live together.

h. The summer season is a good time for travel.

i. There are several advantages to living in a larger city.

5 For each of these paragraphs, choose the sentence from the list below that would make the best topic sentence.

a.

…………………………………………………………………………
………………………………………………… When Ken wanted to enter a good university, he studied hard to pass the examination. The first time he took the exam, he did not do well, and he felt very discouraged. But he knew he wanted to study at that university, so he studied more. The next year, he tried taking the exam again. The second time, he did very well, and now he is studying engineering. I believe Ken is a good role model for me, and he has taught me that never giving up is the best way to succeed.

1. One of my closest friends, named Ken, is a person I can trust.
2. My friend Ken is a very successful student.
3. I admire my friend Ken because he doesn't give up.

228 THE STRUCTURE OF A PARAGRAPH

Writing Essays 2

b.

.... Many children begin learning to play soccer when they are very young. You often can see them playing at school or in the streets around their houses. In high school, students may play soccer on a team and compete in tournaments. If a player is very good, he might go on to play for a professional team. People in my country love to watch soccer on television and also go to the games whenever they can. Many people have a favorite team or player, and everyone loves to talk about matches and competitions. Soccer is really like a national sport in my country.

1. I love to play soccer, and I hope I can become a professional player one day.
2. There are many popular sports in my country, but the most popular sport is soccer.
3. Soccer is a difficult sport to learn to play well.

6 Write a topic sentence for three of these topics.
a. A benefit of doing physical exercise
b. A popular holiday or celebration
c. A healthy food to eat
d. A benefit of learning a second language
e. Playing a musical instrument

topic: ....
....
....

topic: ....
....
....

topic: ....
....
....

THE STRUCTURE OF A PARAGRAPH 229

2 Writing Essays

Review

7 These sentences are mixed up parts of one paragraph. Number the parts in order: 1. topic sentence, 2. supporting sentences, and 3. concluding sentence.

> What should I study at university?
>
> a. .... It wasn't an easy decision, but for the reasons listed above, I have decided to study journalism.
>
> b. .... It can be difficult to choose a subject to study in college because there are so many choices, but by considering my skills and interests, I have decided to study journalism.
>
> c. .... I have always enjoyed writing, so it is sensible to choose a major that involves writing. When I begin working, I would like to have the opportunity to travel, and travel is often an important part of a journalist's job. Finally, I am also interested in photography, and pictures are very important in journalism.

8 Use words or phrases in the box to complete the sentences.

| concluding sentence | indented | main idea | paragraph |
| supporting sentences | topic | topic sentence | |

a. The .... is usually the first sentence in a .... It gives the .... and the ....

b. The first sentence of a paragraph should be ....

c. The .... come after the topic sentence, and they explain the topic sentence.

d. The .... comes at the end of a paragraph.

3 The Development of a Paragraph

In this unit, you will learn ...
- methods of paragraph support and development.
- how to write concluding sentences.
- how to do peer editing.

↪ Paragraph development

After you have chosen a topic and written a topic sentence, you *develop* your main idea by adding more information to explain what you mean. This unit will explain three common ways to develop a paragraph: giving *details*, giving an *explanation*, and giving an *example*.

Details

1 Details are specific points that tell more about a general statement. Read this brochure from a health club. Notice the details that help develop the paragraph.

ATLAS HEALTH CENTER

You'll love working out at the Atlas Health Center, and you'll love what it does for you! We have state-of-the-art exercise equipment in large, air-conditioned rooms. You can work out alone or with the help of one of our professional personal trainers. If you like to exercise with friends, join an aerobics or swimming class—or even try kickboxing! Our staff nutrition experts are always on hand to talk with you about health issues. When you've finished, you can relax with a whirlpool bath or a sauna. Come exercise with us at Atlas, and you'll soon be feeling strong and looking good.

2 In the paragraph above, underline the topic sentence. Below, list the details used to support the topic sentence. Compare your answers with a partner.

a. ....
b. ....
c. ....
d. ....
e. ....
f. ....

Writing Essays

Explanation

3 An explanation tells what something means or how something works. In this paragraph, underline the topic sentence. Then answer the questions.

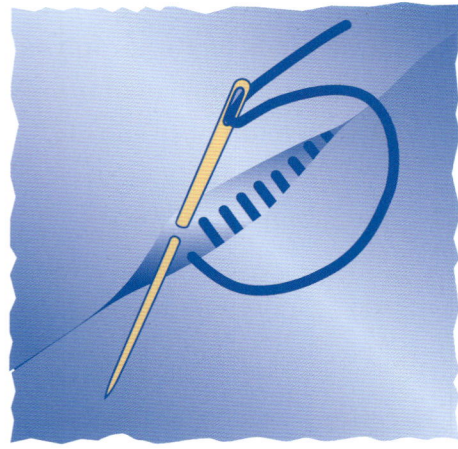

"A stitch in time saves nine." My mother, who likes to sew, used this simple saying to teach me the value of working on problems when they are still small. Originally, the saying referred to sewing—if you have a small hole in a shirt, you can repair it with one stitch. But if you wait, the hole will get larger, and it will take you nine stitches. This simple sentence reminds me to take care of small problems before they become big problems.

a. What is the writer trying to explain? ....
b. Is she successful? Do you understand the explanation?   yes / no

Example

4 An example is a specific person, place, thing, or event that supports an idea or statement. This paragraph includes an example from the writer's own experience. Underline the topic sentence.

Even when two people get off on the wrong foot, they can become good friends. When I was a university student, I lived in the dormitory for the first year, with a roommate. I arrived a few days before he did. When he first came, he woke me up at 3:00 in the morning making a lot of noise. He was cooking dinner! When I got up in the morning to make myself breakfast, I found his dirty dishes left on the counters and in the sink. I was very annoyed. However, when I met him later that afternoon, he was very nice. He apologized for leaving a mess, and explained that he had had some trouble with his airplane flights and had been traveling for a long time. He was hungry when he arrived and very sleepy. After that, he was always good about washing his dishes. He was in two of my classes, and we often studied together. We're not roommates anymore, but we are still friends.

5 Why do you think the writer chose to use an example to develop the paragraph in exercise 4 above? Write your reason here, and then compare with a partner.

....

Writing Essays

Choosing a means of support

6 Would you develop each of these topics with details, an explanation, or an example? Explain your choices to a partner. (More than one answer is possible.)
   a. what freedom means to me
   b. an unusual vacation
   c. weddings in my country
   d. why I don't like to swim
   e. the ideal job

7 Develop your own paragraph. Look back at the topic sentences you wrote in Unit 2, exercise 6 on page 229. Follow these steps.
   Step one: Choose one that you would like to develop into a paragraph.
   Step two: Brainstorm some ideas using any method you like.
   Step three: Develop your paragraph with supporting sentences.
   Step four: Exchange paragraphs with a partner. Say what kind of support your partner used. Could your partner tell what kind of support you used?

Concluding sentences

⊃ How to end a paragraph

The final sentence of a paragraph is called the *concluding sentence*. It sums up the main points or restates the main idea in a different way. A sentence that sums up the paragraph reminds the reader of what the writer's main idea and supporting points were. A sentence that restates the main idea should give the same information in a slightly different way, perhaps by using different words or by using different word order. A concluding sentence should not introduce a new point.

8 Read the example paragraphs in exercises 3 and 4 on page 232 again. Underline the concluding sentences. Do the concluding sentences sum up the information in the paragraph or restate the main idea?

9 Work with a partner. Take turns reading these paragraphs aloud. Is the main idea developed by details, an explanation, or an example? Is there a concluding sentence? Circle *yes* or *no*. If there is no concluding sentence, write one with your partner.

> Even simple study habits can improve your grades. In college, I learned how important it is to get enough sleep. When you are well-rested, it is easier to learn. Research shows that when people don't get enough sleep, their memories aren't as effective. If students are really tired, they might even fall asleep in class! It's easy to see how getting enough sleep can improve your performance in school.

   a. means of support: ....
      concluding sentence? yes / no

3 Writing Essays

> My favorite class is psychology. I enjoy learning about the ways people think and behave. I also am interested in learning about the way children's minds develop.

b. means of support: ....
concluding sentence? yes / no

....

> I am too nervous to sing karaoke songs with my friends. The last time I tried was on my birthday, when my friends took me to a karaoke club. I told my friends I didn't want to sing, but they encouraged me until I said yes. When I stood up in front of the microphone, I was so scared, I felt dizzy. It was hard to hear the music, and my mouth was too dry to make a sound. I just stood there until a friend jumped up next to me and finished the song.

c. means of support: ....
concluding sentence? yes / no

....

> I will never eat dinner at The Little French Bistro again. The restaurant is not very clean. You can see dust in the corners and on the shelves. The food is expensive, but the portions are small. I never feel full after I've finished eating. In addition, the waiters are not very friendly. For these reasons, I will not visit that restaurant again.

d. means of support: ....
concluding sentence? yes / no

....

> For me, a friend is someone who accepts you the way you are. A friend doesn't want you to change your personality or your style. I like people who don't care if the people they are with are wearing popular clothes or listening to trendy music.

e. means of support: ....
concluding sentence? yes / no

....

Peer editing

⊃ What is peer editing?

Showing your work to another student is a very useful way to improve your writing. This is called *peer editing*. You read your partner's writing and your partner reads yours. You comment on your partner's writing and your partner comments on yours. You might talk together, write comments on a sheet that your instructor gives you, or write directly on your partner's paper.

Here is the first draft of the paragraph about the writer and his friend. The writer has shown the paragraph to another student, who wrote some comments.

Topic sentence

I don't know the meaning of this idiom.
Even when two people <u>get off on the wrong foot</u>, they can still

Developed by example become good friends. When I was a university student, I lived in the

What was his name?
dormitory for the first year, with a <u>roommate</u>. I arrived a few days before

Did you meet him then?
he did. When he first came, <u>he woke me up at 3:00</u> in the morning making

How did you know he was cooking?
a lot of noise. <u>He was cooking dinner!</u> When I got up in the morning to

How did you feel about that?
make myself breakfast, <u>I found his dirty dishes</u> left on the counters and in

Explain how you noticed this
the sink. However, <u>later</u>, he was very nice. He apologized for leaving a

but why did he arrive so late?
mess, and explained that he <u>was hungry when he arrived and very sleepy</u>.

After that, he was always good about washing his dishes. He was in two

good example
of my classes, and we often studied together. We're not roommates

anymore, but we are still friends.

---

10 Look at the handwritten comments on the paragraph above, and answer these questions with a partner.

a. Why do you think the peer editor sometimes wrote questions instead of statements? For example, why did she write "What was his name?" instead of "Tell me his name"?

b. Why do you think the peer editor marked the topic sentence and the concluding sentence?

c. The peer editor didn't understand a phrase in the topic sentence. Do you think the writer should change that sentence? Why or why not?

d. Go back to exercise 4 on page 18 and read the paragraph again. Did the writer use the reader's suggestions?

Writing Essays

◌ Why do writers use peer editing?

There are two reasons for peer editing. The first is to get a reader's opinion about your writing. A reader can tell you that …

- you should add more details or explanation.
- something is not organized clearly.
- you have some information that is not relevant.
- there is something that is hard to understand.

These comments will help you write your next draft. Remember that suggestions from a peer editor are just suggestions. You don't have to make every change that is suggested. However, you should think about all of the comments that you receive.

The second reason to share writing with others is for you to read more examples of writing. Other people will have had experiences that you haven't. They may show you fresh ways of writing about experiences. Reading their paragraphs and essays can give you good ideas to use yourself in the future.

◌ How do I peer edit?

- Read your partner's paper several times. The first time, just read from the beginning through to the end. Ask yourself, "What is it about? What is the writer's purpose?"
- On your second reading, go more slowly and look at specific parts of the writing and make notes.
  - Look for topic sentences and concluding sentences.
  - Note places where you have trouble understanding something, where there seems to be unnecessary information, or where there is not enough information.
  - Let the writer know which parts of the paper are especially strong or interesting.
  - Ask questions. This is a good way to let the writer know where he or she could add more information.
  - Circle or underline words, phrases, and sentences that you wish to comment on.
- Don't look for grammar or spelling mistakes. Pay attention just to the content and organization of the paper.

Writing Essays

Giving constructive suggestions

11 For each pair of sentences, check (✓) the one that you feel would be most helpful to the writer. Share your answers with a partner, and explain your choices.

a. ☐ This is a weak topic sentence.
☐ Can you make this topic sentence stronger?

b. ☐ Did you remember a concluding sentence?
☐ Why didn't you write a concluding sentence?

c. ☐ You didn't write enough.
☐ Please explain more about your vacation. Where did you stay? What did you do during the day?

d. ☐ I'm not sure what this part means.
☐ This must be wrong. I can't understand it.

e. ☐ I think this sentence should come before the next one.
☐ Your organization is pretty bad. You'd better change it.

f. ☐ Why do you keep saying the same thing over and over again?
☐ I think these two sentences are really saying the same thing.

g. ☐ I can't understand why you're talking about your sister.
☐ Your paragraph is about your brother, but this sentence is about your sister. Are you sure it's relevant?

h. ☐ This is a good paragraph. Nice job! I wish I could write as well as you.
☐ I like your topic sentence because it has a strong main idea. Your example is funny. I wish I could meet your brother!

12 Read this paragraph aloud with a partner. Then peer edit it together. Then join another pair and share your comments.

> My father is a teacher. I admire him a lot. I am considering becoming a teacher, too. My older brother works for a big company. My father really loves learning, so he is a natural teacher. My father always helped me with my homework. I guess I will become a teacher.

THE DEVELOPMENT OF A PARAGRAPH 237

Writing Essays

13 Write a second draft of the paragraph in exercise 12 on page 237. Use the comments you and your partner made. Then exchange paragraphs with your partner. Discuss how your versions are different from the original. Do you think the second drafts are better? Why or why not?

Review

14 Read these statements. Write T (true) or F (false). If the statement is false, change it to make it true. Then compare your answers with a partner.

    a. .... Details give more specific information than the topic sentence.

    b. .... An explanation tells what something is or how it works.

    c. .... A detail is usually a short, personal story.

    d. .... The concluding sentence uses the same words as the topic sentence.

    e. .... The concluding sentence should finish the paragraph with a new idea.

    f. .... A peer editor should mark any spelling and grammatical mistakes carefully.

    g. .... A peer editor should give some positive comments.

    h. .... Peer editing helps the writer, not the reader.

    i. .... If a peer editor can't understand something that you wrote, then you know he or she isn't a very good reader.

    j. .... A peer editor should be able to identify your topic sentence, main idea, and concluding sentence easily.

4 Descriptive Paragraphs

In this unit, you will learn about …
- descriptive paragraphs and reasons for writing them.
- organizing and writing descriptive paragraphs using adjectives and prepositions.
- using connecting words and phrases to write a paragraph that describes a process.

⊃ Describing people, places, and processes

A descriptive paragraph explains how someone or something looks or feels. A process paragraph explains how something is done.

Describing a place

⊃ Using adjectives

Adjectives are words that tell us how things look, feel, taste, sound, or smell. Adjectives also describe how you feel about something. Here are a few common adjectives.

shape and size	atmosphere	how you feel	appearance
large / small	cozy	amazed	colorful
wide / narrow	comfortable	surprised	unforgettable
round	warm / cool	happy	beautiful
rectangular	cold / hot	nostalgic	unattractive

A description of a place may answer some of these questions:
- Where is the place?
- How big is it?
- How warm or cold is the place?
- How does the place make you feel? Why?
- What things can you see in this place?
- What colors do you see?

1 List some words to describe these places.

4 Writing Essays

2 Read this description from a travel brochure. Circle the adjectives.

Niagara Falls, a popular destination for thousands of visitors each year, is a beautiful place. When you stand at the edge and look down at the 188 feet of white waterfalls, you feel amazed at the power of nature. The tree-lined river that leads into the falls is fast-moving, pouring over the edge of the falls and crashing to the bottom in a loud roar. If you want to experience the falls close up, go for a boat ride. You'll come near enough to look up at the roaring streams of water flowing over the edge and feel the cool mist that rises as the water hits the rocks below. Seeing Niagara Falls is an unforgettable experience!

Using prepositions

Prepositions tell us how a space is organized. These are some common and useful prepositions and phrasal prepositions:

in front of / in back of, behind	to the right of / to the left of
on top of / on the bottom of	in the middle of
next to	around
above / below, underneath	between

3 Read this paragraph that describes someone's favorite place. Underline the prepositions.

My favorite place to relax is a small café down the street from where I live. This café is on a small side street and as soon as you see it, you feel like going in. There are three windows on either side of the door, and each window has a small window box with brightly colored flowers. There is a small wooden door that opens into the café, and as you go in, you can see a dozen small tables all around the room. Even though it isn't a big place, its size makes it very cozy and comfortable. I always like to sit at a small table in the corner near the front windows. From here, I can look at the artwork on the walls and at the pretty green plants hanging from the ceiling. With a strong cup of coffee and a good book, I feel very happy and relaxed in my favorite café.

240 DESCRIPTIVE PARAGRAPHS

NIAGARA FALLS

4 Write six sentences to describe the place where you are right now. Try to answer some of the questions under "Using adjectives" on page 239. Use adjectives and prepositions.

Describing a character

⊃ Describing people

Here are some common adjectives for describing people:

Personality	Physical characteristics
happy, satisfied	big, large, tall
relaxed	small, tiny, short
exciting	thin
nervous	heavy
angry	strong
serious	weak
sad, depressed	brown-, black-, blond-, red-haired
outgoing	light-, dark-skinned
....	....
....	....

A description of a person may answer some of the following questions:

- Who is the person?
- What does the person do?
- What does he or she look like?
- How does the person act—how is his or her personality?
- How does he or she make others feel?

5 With a partner, add at least two other adjectives to the two lists above.

DESCRIPTIVE PARAGRAPHS **241**

Writing Essays

6 Read this description written by a young woman about her grandmother. Circle the adjectives that describe the grandmother.

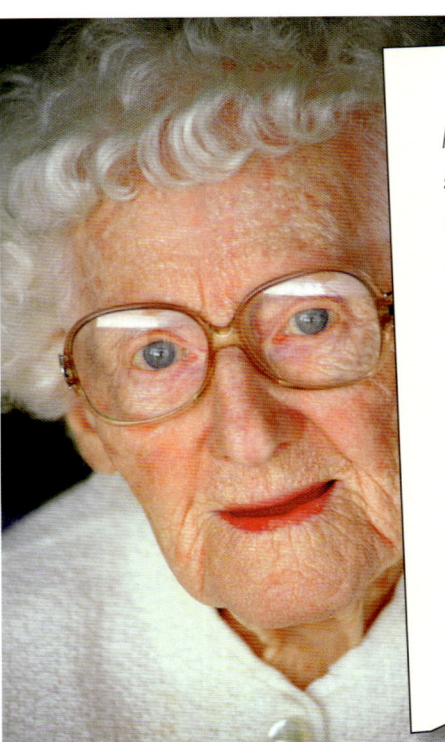

When I was young, I admired my grandmother for her strength and kindness. She was not very big. In fact, she was tiny and very thin. She was strong, though. She lived by herself and still did a lot of the chores around her house. When I was a child, I saw her almost every day, and she and I would talk about everything. She was a very happy person and was always smiling and joking, and she often made me laugh. My grandmother was also very patient, and she would listen to all of my problems. She gave me very good advice whenever I needed it. I didn't need to be afraid to tell her anything, because she never got mad at me. She just listened and tried to help. I also liked to spend time with her because she had interesting stories to tell about her own childhood and life experiences. When I was young, my grandmother was my favorite friend.

7 Describe one of these people. Write eight sentences. Try to answer three or more of the questions at the bottom of page 241. Use your imagination!

8 Think of a person or place you know well. Then brainstorm your ideas, narrow your topic, and write a descriptive paragraph.

Writing Essays 4

Describing a process

9 A process paragraph is a description of how something works or how something is done. It explains the steps you need to follow to complete an activity. Read the following science experiment and do the exercises below.

> Evaporation is the process of changing from a liquid to a vapor. A simple experiment can be done to learn more about how evaporation works. First, collect the necessary supplies to complete the experiment: one sheet of black construction paper, a small paint brush, a small cup of water, and a watch with a second hand. Next, place the paper on a dry, flat surface in the shade. Now wet the paint brush in the water and dab a drop of water onto the black paper. Immediately after wetting the paper, begin timing how long it takes for the water stain to dry up, or evaporate. When the water has dried, write the time down. At this point, begin the same experiment again by completing all of the steps, except that the paper should be placed under direct sunlight, or some type of heat source. Time how long the water takes to evaporate again. Finally, compare the two times, and answer the following questions: Where did the water go? Did a heat source, such as sunlight, make the water evaporate more slowly or more quickly? Why? By completing this simple experiment, it is possible to easily learn about the process of evaporation.

a. Underline the topic sentence and the concluding sentence of the paragraph.

b. List the steps for completing the experiment in the order you find them.

1. *Collect the necessary supplies to complete the experiment.*
2. ....
3. ....
4. ....
5. ....
6. ....
7. ....

c. How are the steps in the paragraph connected together? What words do you see that help show the sequence to follow? Underline them.

DESCRIPTIVE PARAGRAPHS 243

4 Writing Essays

Connectors

What are connectors?

Connectors are words and phrases that help tie sentences together in a paragraph. They show the relationships between the ideas in a paragraph. They are not used between every sentence, but are used often enough to make the order clear. Here are some common connectors that show time order or the order of steps:

first, second, third, etc.	finally, at last	until
next	the last step	as
then	before, prior to	
after, after that	while	
now, at this point	when	

10 Choose appropriate connectors to connect the steps in this paragraph about preparing for a trip.

Planning a vacation abroad? Here are some suggestions to make your trip successful. a. ...., find out if you need a visa for the country that you want to visit. Make sure you have enough time to apply for it b. .... you buy your ticket. c. .... you've found out about visas, you should research airfares and schedules. d. ...., look for the best flight for you. Remember, the cheapest flight may stop over in several cities and reduce the amount of time you have to spend at your destination. You might want to fly direct. e. .... you're researching flights, you can also ask your travel agent about getting a good deal on a hotel. It's a good idea to book your flight and hotel early if you're sure of your destination. If you haven't already done it, the f. .... step is to learn about places to visit, the weather, the food, and other details about the country. The Internet can be a very useful source of information. g. ...., on the day of your flight, make sure you go to the airport at least two hours before your flight. Now you are ready to start enjoying your vacation!

244 DESCRIPTIVE PARAGRAPHS

Ordering sentences

11 Order the steps to form a process paragraph. Write 1 next to the first step, 2 for the second step, and so on.

> **Introduction to linguistics: language-learning research project**
>
> Conduct an experiment to find out whether learners of English use English more correctly on a written test or in informal conversation.
>
> a. .... Next, make a written test that checks the grammar point you are researching. This could be a fill-in-the-blanks test, a correct-the-errors test, or another style. It should have at least ten questions, but it should not be too long.
>
> b. .... After giving the written test, interview each learner individually for about ten minutes. Try to make the interviews informal and friendly. Be sure to ask questions that will encourage learners to use the grammar point you are researching. Record the interviews. (Ask for learners' permission first!)
>
> c. .... After you have counted the errors, calculate the score as a percentage. Do this for the written test and the spoken inteview.
>
> d. .... Next, read the tests and listen to the recordings. Make a note of how many times your chosen grammar point was used, and how many times it was used incorrectly. Do this for both the written test and the recorded conversation.
>
> e. .... Third, find about ten intermediate-level English learners who will agree to take your test. Arrange a time to give the test to each learner.
>
> f. .... Finally, prepare two graphs to compare your results. Did learners make more mistakes on the written test or while they were speaking?
>
> g. ..... First, choose a common English grammar point you would like to use in your research. Ask your teacher for a suggestion if you need help choosing one.

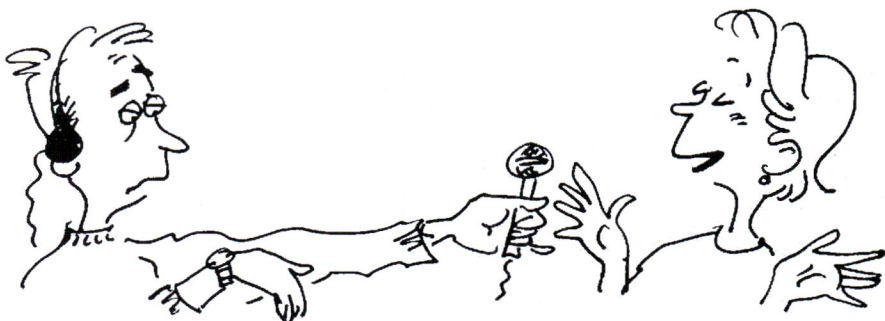

12 Write a process paragraph about a topic that you know well. First, brainstorm all the steps that need to be followed. Then write the paragraph. Remember to use transitions.

4 Writing Essays

Review

13 This paragraph describes a city park, but it doesn't have enough descriptive details. Imagine that you live next to a park. Rewrite the paragraph, adding description, to make it more interesting.

> I live next to a park. The park is large and has trees and grass. There is a lake in the park where you can see people enjoying many activities. There are many places to sit and relax. There are many paths that you can walk on, and everywhere you walk you can see flowers. I really enjoy spending time in this park.

5 Opinion Paragraphs

In this unit, you will learn how to ...
- distinguish between fact and opinion.
- organize and write paragraphs expressing opinions and arguments.
- use transition words to express causality.
- use modal expressions to make recommendations.

⟳ Facts and opinions

A *fact* is a piece of information that is true: *That movie was three hours long.*
An *opinion* is an idea or belief about a particular subject: *That movie was boring.*
Writers use facts to support their opinions and to show why they hold their beliefs.

An opinion paragraph

1 Read this letter to the editor of a newspaper. Answer the questions.

Dear Editor,
   More people should ride bicycles into town. Last year, seventy-three percent of all workers drove their own car to work. Car traffic in town is terrible, parking places are hard to find, and pollution from cars is a real problem. Citizens who want a cleaner, nicer place to live ought to try this non-polluting form of transportation. Cycling is good exercise, too! The city must not allow this problem to get worse. Instead, people should ride bicycles to work and school—and enjoy the health benefits of daily exercise.

Bill Adams
Bellingham

a. What is the main idea of this paragraph? Circle the sentence.
b. What is the writer's purpose? Why did he write this letter?
c. Underline the sentences or parts of sentences that show an opinion.
d. Why do you think the writer included a fact in this paragraph?

OPINION PARAGRAPHS **247**

Writing Essays

2 Do these types of writing use mostly facts, mostly opinions, or an even mixture of both? Write F for fact, O for opinion, or B for both. Explain your choices to a partner.

  a. .... movie review
  b. .... advice column
  c. .... police report of a crime
  d. .... travel brochure
  e. .... news report
  f. .... book report for a college literature class
  g. .... magazine advertisement
  h. .... personal e-mail to a friend

3 Can you think of other types of writing that use opinions? Make a list. Then make a list of types of writing that use facts.

Use opinions ....

Use facts ....

4 Read these sentences. Write F if the sentence is a fact, and O if the sentence is an opinion.

  a. .... Airfares have become too expensive.
  b. .... English is an easier language to learn than Arabic.
  c. .... Owls are birds that hunt at night.
  d. .... I was born in New York City.
  e. .... Exercise is the best way to stay healthy.
  f. .... Internet use has increased every year since its beginning.
  g. .... Engineering is the best career choice.
  h. .... Big cities are dangerous at night.

5 Write three fact sentences and three opinion sentences.

  a. ....
  b. ....
  c. ....
  d. ....
  e. ....
  f. ....

6 Share your sentences with a partner. Decide which of your partner's sentences are fact and which are opinion.

Writing Essays 5

Modal auxiliaries

⊃ Using modal auxiliaries

When you speak, you introduce opinions with phrases like *I think, In my opinion,* and *I believe*. In general, these introductory phrases are not needed in writing. They can even make you sound less sure of your ideas. Instead, writers use grammatical methods such as modal auxiliary verbs to express their opinions. Modal auxiliary verbs show the strength of a writer's opinion or argument.

AFFIRMATIVE:			
The city	could	add more bike paths.	weakest
	should		▼
	ought to		
	has to / must		strongest
NEGATIVE:			
The city	doesn't have to	allow more cars.	weakest
	shouldn't		▼
	can't / must not		strongest

7 Look again at the paragraph in exercise 1 on page 247. Circle the modal auxilaries. How strong do you think the writer's opinions were? Discuss with a partner.

8 Read the paragraph below. Circle the most appropriate modal auxiliary in each sentence.

Dear Editor,

I agree with Bill Adams's opinion in his recent letter saying that people ^{a.} *should / don't have to* ride their bicycles into town. However, there is one problem with this idea. The roads in town are so narrow and full of cars that you ^{b.} *can't / ought to* ride safely on them. If people are going to ride bicycles into town, the city ^{c.} *could / must* make some bike paths for people to use. Maybe the city ^{d.} *could / mustn't* charge a small additional tax on fuel to pay for the bike paths. Motorists have created the problem, so motorists ^{e.} *could / should* pay for the solution. The city ^{f.} *ought to / doesn't have to* support cyclists like Bill Adams by building more bike paths.

Melissa Green
Parkville

OPINION PARAGRAPHS **249**

Writing Essays

Expressing opinions: class survey

9 Read these statements that express opinions. Add three of your own.

Name:	....	....	....
1. Grocery stores and shops shouldn't give plastic bags to customers.	☐ agree ☐ disagree	☐ agree ☐ disagree	☐ agree ☐ disagree
2. University students should not have part-time jobs.	☐ agree ☐ disagree	☐ agree ☐ disagree	☐ agree ☐ disagree
3.	☐ agree ☐ disagree	☐ agree ☐ disagree	☐ agree ☐ disagree
4.	☐ agree ☐ disagree	☐ agree ☐ disagree	☐ agree ☐ disagree
5.	☐ agree ☐ disagree	☐ agree ☐ disagree	☐ agree ☐ disagree

10 Share your statements with three classmates. Say how you feel about your partners' statements by saying, "I agree" or "I disagree," and then adding one sentence. Check (✓) your partners' opinions about your statements.

Grocery stores and shops shouldn't give plastic bags to customers.

I agree. Shoppers should bring their own reusable bags.

or

I disagree. Plastic bags are very useful and convenient.

11 Read the opinion paragraphs in exercise 1 on page 247 and exercise 8 on page 249 again. Then write a paragraph about one of the opinions you expressed in exercise 10 above. Brainstorm ideas, narrow your topic, and then write. Remember to use modal auxiliaries.

Writing Essays

Causal adverbs

▷ **How to use causal adverbs for expressing opinions**

Because, since, and *so* are causal adverbs. They join two ideas when one idea causes or explains the other. *Because* and *since* introduce the cause or reason, and *so* and *therefore* introduce the effect or result:

cause / reason	effect / result
gasoline is becoming scarce and expensive	we should develop electric cars

For example:

Because *gasoline is becoming scarce and expensive, we should develop electric cars.*

We should develop electric cars **since** *gasoline is becoming scarce and expensive.*

Gasoline is becoming scarce and expensive, **so** *we should develop electric cars.*

Therefore is slightly different. It joins the ideas in two sentences:

Gasoline is becoming scarce and expensive. **Therefore***, we should develop electric cars.*

12 In the examples above, underline the causes. Circle the results. Do the causal adverbs come before the cause or before the result? Share your answers with a partner.

▷ **Punctuation note**
- When *because* or *since* begin a sentence, use a comma after the first part of the sentence (the cause).
- When the effect or result comes first, don't use a comma before *because* and *since*.
- A result or effect beginning with *so* is usually the second part of a sentence. Use a comma before *so*.
- Use *Therefore* after a period.
- Use a comma after *Therefore*.

13 Complete this opinion paragraph using *because* or *since*, *so*, or *Therefore*. Add punctuation where necessary.

Bruce Lee (1940–1973), the greatest action movie star of all time, should be given a lifetime achievement award for his work in the movies. Bruce died tragically in 1973 ᵃ· .... he wouldn't be able to receive the award himself, but his fans all over the world would love to see him honored. Why was Bruce Lee so great? The fight scenes in his films were amazing ᵇ· .... Bruce was always in top physical condition. His body was almost perfect. He was also a great actor. ᶜ· .... he started acting when he was just six years old, he was very comfortable and natural in front of the camera. His face was very expressive ᵈ· .... he was able to communicate a lot of feeling with a simple look. Bruce always looked good on film ᵉ· .... he was so charming. Bruce Lee was a talented actor, a brilliant fighter, and an almost perfect example of physical fitness. ᶠ· .... he should receive an award that recognizes his great contribution to the art of film making.

OPINION PARAGRAPHS

Writing Essays

14 Use the causal adverbs in parentheses to join these ideas. You may change the order of ideas. You may make one sentence or two. Use appropriate punctuation.

  a. the city doesn't have enough money / we ought to increase city taxes (so)

  ....

  b. I'm going to quit my part-time job / I don't have enough time for my homework (because)

  ....

  c. some plants and trees are dying / this summer has been very dry (since)

  ....

  d. many students are graduating with nursing degrees / it might be hard for nurses to find jobs in the future (Therefore)

  ....

  e. my friends all recommend that restaurant / I will try it this weekend (so)

  ....

15 Look again at the opinions that were expressed in exercise 9 on page 250. Complete these sentences in your notebook with your own ideas about these opinions. Use appropriate punctuation.

  a. Because ....
  b. .... since ....
  c. .... so ....
  d. Since ....
  e. .... because ....
  f. .... Therefore ....

Writing an opinion paragraph

16 Write an opinion paragraph. First, answer this question: *What do I want my reader to think or do?* Then brainstorm ideas and narrow your topic. Use modal auxiliaries and causal adverbs.

252 OPINION PARAGRAPHS

Writing Essays

Review

17 Put these sentences in order to make a paragraph. Write 1 in front of the first sentence, 2 in front of the second sentence, and so on.

a. .... He was receiving a call.
b. .... My friend and I leaned forward, listening carefully to the movie.
c. .... It was very distracting.
d. .... Last night, I went to see a movie with my friend. It was a suspense movie.
e. .... He decided to answer the call.
f. .... We think that people should turn off their cell phones when they watch a movie, or not bring them at all!
g. .... It was very exciting.
h. .... The man next to us had a cell phone, and it was vibrating.
i. .... Suddenly, we heard a buzzing sound.
j. .... He was whispering but we could still hear him.
k. .... Cell phones should not be allowed in theaters.
l. .... My friend and I felt annoyed.
m. .... At the most exciting moment, the actors didn't speak. Only quiet music was playing.

18 With a partner, write a paragraph using the sentences in exercise 17 above. Remember to join some of the sentences with causal adverbs and with connectors from the top of page 244. Read your paragraph to another pair. How were your paragraphs the same? How were they different?

OPINION PARAGRAPHS 253

6 Comparison / Contrast Paragraphs

In this unit, you will learn about ...
- comparison / contrast paragraphs and reasons for writing them.
- how to organize comparison / contrast paragraphs.
- connecting words used for comparing and contrasting topics.
- how to write about the advantages and disadvantages of a topic.

⊃ Paragraphs that compare and contrast

To *compare* means to discuss how two people, places, or things are *similar:* Both teachers and students need to spend a lot of time preparing for classes. To *contrast* means to discuss how two people, places, or things are *different:* One main advantage of a bicycle over a car is that a bicycle doesn't create air pollution.

Comparing and contrasting

1 Look at the following pairs and decide whether you would *compare* them, *contrast* them, or both.
   a. a large city / a small town
   b. studying in one's country / studying abroad
   c. using cash / using a credit card
   d. the role of a mother / the role of a father
   e. buses / trains

254 COMPARISON / CONTRAST PARAGRAPHS

2 Read the following paragraph and answer the questions.
   a. What two things does the paragraph talk about?
   b. Is the paragraph mostly comparing or contrasting? How do you know?

In recent years, new technology such as cellular telephones and the Internet have made life more convenient. Cellular telephones allow people to talk to one another almost anywhere. Likewise, the Internet gives people the ability to talk to one another very easily, even across countries. Second, cellular phones and the Internet are available 24 hours per day, so people can speak or connect at any time, day or night. Another convenient quality of these two types of technology is that they both allow people to find out information without even leaving one's home. A person can access the Internet through most types of cellular phones, and the Internet can be used to look up virtually any topic of interest. Clearly, cellular phones, the Internet, and other new types of technology that exist today provide a great deal of convenience for people.

6 Writing Essays

Comparative and contrastive structures

> Using comparative structures

These words and phrases are used for writing comparisons:

and	The man **and** the woman are tall.
both	**Both** of the tables have broken legs.
both … and	**Both** my neighbor **and** I are selling our cars.
also	The stores are closing for the holiday. The bank is **also** closing.
too	Kathy is planning to go to the party, and I am, **too**.
neither … nor	**Neither** Joe **nor** Steve went to the meeting last night.
similar to	Their new computer is **similar to** the one my brother bought.
the same as	Is the restaurant where you had dinner **the same as** the place where I ate last month?
(just) as + adjective + as.	His coat is **just as warm as** the more expensive one.
likewise	My parents were born in a small village. **Likewise**, my brothers and I also grew up in a small town.
similarly	There are many parks to visit in that city. **Similarly**, there are several parks in my hometown, too.

3 Complete these sentences with phrases from above.

a. .... cell phones .... computers will work without a power source.

b. To access the Internet on my laptop, I need to connect to a wireless signal. .... , my cell phone needs to connect to a network.

c. I pay a monthly fee for .... my cell phone and my Internet services.

256 COMPARISON / CONTRAST PARAGRAPHS

Using contrastive structures

These words and phrases are used for writing contrasts:

more / less + adjective / adverb + than	Eating out is usually **more expensive than** cooking at home.
adjective + er + than	My bedroom is **bigger than** my sister's room.
but, while, though	I enjoy eating fruit for dessert, **but / while / though** my friend likes chocolate.
not the same as	This book **isn't the same as** the one you bought.
not as … as	Some people feel that doing exercise **isn't as fun as** watching TV.
different from	That style of shirt is **different from** the styles most people wear.
in contrast	The lakes we swam in were very clean and beautiful. **In contrast**, the lakes in my country are polluted.
however	The new store sells its clothing at low prices. **However**, other stores have better quality clothing.
on the other hand	My brother likes to play sports. **On the other hand**, I prefer to do yoga.

4 **Complete these sentences with phrases from above.**

a. The climate in the northern region of my country is very .... the weather in the southern region.

b. In the north, there are four distinct seasons .... in the south of the country, the seasons are not that different.

c. The northern area has mountains and the temperatures in the winter are extremely cold; .... , the south is much more flat and has warm to hot temperatures throughout the year.

d. Heavy rains and high humidity in the summer are common in the south, ... the north has only moderate rainfall throughout the year and much lower humidity.

COMPARISON / CONTRAST PARAGRAPHS 257

6 Writing Essays

Similarities and differences

5 Write eight sentences about these two cars. Write about four similarities and four differences.

Comparison / contrast organization

↪ Two methods for organizing a comparison / contrast paragraph

Method 1: Block organization

First, write about supporting points for the first topic. Then compare or contrast those same points to the second topic. This type of organization could be outlined like this:

Topic sentence comparing / contrasting two topics (A & B)

Points of comparison / contrast about Topic A

Points of comparison / contrast about Topic B

Concluding sentence

> Reading a story in a book is often very different from seeing it as a movie. When you read a story, you need to use your imagination. A book usually gives a lot of description about the people, places, and things in the story, so you can create pictures in your mind. In addition, the conversations between people are always written with details that describe how the people look or feel while they are talking. When you read, you use a lot of imagination to help "see" the characters in the story. However, when you see a movie, it is a different experience. When you watch a movie, you don't need to use your imagination. The pictures on the screen give all the details about the people, places, and things in the story. The conversations are spoken out loud, so you just listen and watch. The feelings of the people come through their faces, body movements, and voices. Although a book and a movie might tell the same story, reading a book and watching a movie are very different experiences.

258 COMPARISON / CONTRAST PARAGRAPHS

Writing Essays

Method 2: Point-by-point organization

Compare or contrast one point about the two topics, then a second point, then a third point, and so on. This type of organization could be outlined like this:

Topic sentence comparing or contrasting two topics (A & B)

First point of comparison / contrast (A1, B1)

Second point of comparison / contrast (A2, B2)

Third point of comparison / contrast (A3, B3)

Fourth point of comparison / contrast (A4, B4)

Fifth point of comparison / contrast (A5, B5)

Concluding sentence

> Marilyn Monroe and Princess Diana lived at different times in different countries, but their lives had some surprising similarities. First of all, both women had a difficult childhood. Monroe spent many years without parents in an orphanage, and Diana's mother left the family when she was only six. Later in their lives, both women married famous men. Princess Diana married Prince Charles, and Marilyn Monroe married a famous baseball player and later a famous writer. They also had difficult marriages and eventually separated from their husbands. Another similarity between Marilyn Monroe and Princess Diana was that they were both very popular. Diana was called "The people's princess" because she was so friendly. Although Monroe was famously beautiful, she was well-liked because she seemed very innocent. However, although they both seemed to have very happy lives, both women actually had emotional problems and often felt sad and depressed. Monroe went through serious depression and had to go to a hospital for treatment. Likewise, Diana suffered from an eating problem and was depressed during parts of her marriage. A last similarity between Marilyn Monroe and Princess Diana was their deaths at an early age. In fact, they were both thirty-six years old when they died, Monroe in 1962 and Diana in 1997. Maybe their similar life circumstances and lifestyles explain why Princess Diana and Marilyn Monroe also had similar personalities.

6 Read the two paragraphs above then answer the questions.

    a. Which paragraph mostly compares and which mostly contrasts?

    b. Finish filling in the outlines on page 260 for each paragraph.

COMPARISON / CONTRAST PARAGRAPHS

6 Writing Essays

Block organization: Paragraph 1

Topic sentence: Reading a story in a book is often very different from seeing it as a movie.

Topic A—reading a book
Supporting points:

1. ....

2. ....

Topic B— ....
Supporting points:

1. ....

2. ....

Point-by-point organization: Paragraph 2

Topic sentence: Marilyn Monroe and Princess Diana lived at different times in different countries, but their lives had some surprising similarities.

First point of comparison—difficult childhood
A1: ....
B1: Princess Diana—mother left family

Second point of comparison— ....
A2: Princess Diana—married Prince Charles, later separated from him
B2: ....

Third point of comparison— ....
A3: ....
B3: ....

Fourth point of comparison—had emotional problems
A4: Marilyn Monroe— ....
B4: ....

Fifth point of comparison— ....
A5: ....
B5: ....

7 Look again at the paragraph in exercise 2 on page 255. Does it use point-by-point or block organization? How do you know?

8 Read this list of details about two types of sports. Then make a list of similarities and a list of differences below. Discuss your answers with a partner.

Team sports
- teach the skills needed for working with others
- individual strengths benefit the group's success
- players rely on each other and close relationships can develop
- coaches are important for managing the group's diverse talent and personalities
- individual talent may not be developed
- take time and practice to improve skills
- popular with fans

Individual sports
- teach the skills for working independently
- players rely on their own skills for success
- individual talent can be developed
- take time and practice to improve skills
- popular with fans
- a coach and player can develop a very close relationship

Similarities between the sports
....
....
....
....
....
....
....
....

Differences between the sports
....
....
....
....
....
....
....
....

9 Write a comparison or contrast paragraph. Use either point-by-point organization or block organization.

6 Writing Essays

Advantages and disadvantages

⊃ Writing about advantages and disadvantages

Another way to compare or contrast is to talk about *advantages* (positive points) or *disadvantages* (negative points) of a topic. If you are writing about one topic, it is usually best to discuss advantages and disadvantages in two separate paragraphs. If you are comparing or contrasting two topics, you could organize the paragraph in either point-by-point or block style.

10 Read this paragraph from a school newspaper. List the supporting points. Does the paragraph discuss advantages or disadvantages?

> Studying abroad and studying in your own country both have definite benefits for a student. Living in another country can be an exciting experience because everything seems new and different. The challenge of living in a new environment can give you courage and self-confidence, too. If you want to learn another language, living abroad is a great way to do that because you can read magazines or newspapers, watch television programs, or make friends with people who are native speakers. Another good reason to live abroad is to learn more about another culture. On the other hand, there are also advantages to staying in your own country to study. It is cheaper than living abroad, so you can save more money. Also, in your home country, everything is familiar. You don't need to worry about taking classes in a foreign language, and you can understand the culture and the expectations of teachers. Finally, if you stay in your own country, you can be close to your family and friends. So, if you are thinking about where to study, consider all of these benefits and make a decision that is right for you.

11 Write one or two paragraphs comparing or contrasting topics of your choice or one of these.

- the advantages and disadvantages of taking online / distance education courses
- living in a small town / living in a large city
- the advantages and disadvantages of having a job while in college
- using gas-powered vehicles / electric vehicles

Writing Essays 6

Review

12 List five words or phrases of comparison and five of contrast. Use them to compare and contrast two things in your college. Share your sentences with the rest of the class.

Comparison	Contrast
....	....
....	....
....	....
....	....
....	....
....	....
....	....

13 Work with a partner. Separate these ideas into advantages (A) and disadvantages (D).

Studying English
- **a.** .... takes a lot of time
- **b.** .... classes are fun
- **c.** .... grammar is difficult
- **d.** .... useful for talking to people from other countries
- **e.** .... good for using the Internet
- **f.** .... lots of vocabulary to learn
- **g.** .... too many tests to take
- **h.** .... helps to understand English-language movies
- **i.** .... my friends like English
- **j.** .... pronunciation is difficult

14 Now, in pairs, one person should write a paragraph about the advantages and the other person should write about the disadvantages of studying English. Add one new idea of your own to your paragraph.

15 Share your paragraphs with another pair of students.

7 Problem / Solution Paragraphs

In this unit, you will ...
- write about problems and solutions.
- use real conditionals.
- write a two-paragraph paper with linking phrases.

↪ Problems and solutions

Problem / solution writing first explains a problem and then proposes one or more solutions to that problem. Often this type of writing requires more than one paragraph. In this unit, you will write a two-paragraph discussion of a problem and solution.

Problems and solutions

1 Read the article from a website on page 265. What is the main idea of the first paragraph? What is the topic sentence?

2 Answer these questions.
  a. How is the first paragraph developed? What are the supporting ideas?
  b. What do the supporting ideas show?
  c. What is the main idea of the second paragraph? What is the topic sentence?
  d. What solution does the writer offer? What details support or explain the solution?
  e. Is there a concluding sentence in the first paragraph? In the second paragraph?

Writing about problems

↪ How to write a *problem paragraph*

A *problem paragraph* describes and discusses a problem issue. The topic sentence names the issue you will discuss. The supporting sentences show why this issue is a problem.

3 Work with a partner or small group. Discuss why these issues are problems. Then add two more issues and discuss them.
  a. air pollution
  b. traffic
  c. overcrowded classrooms
  d. ....
  e. ....

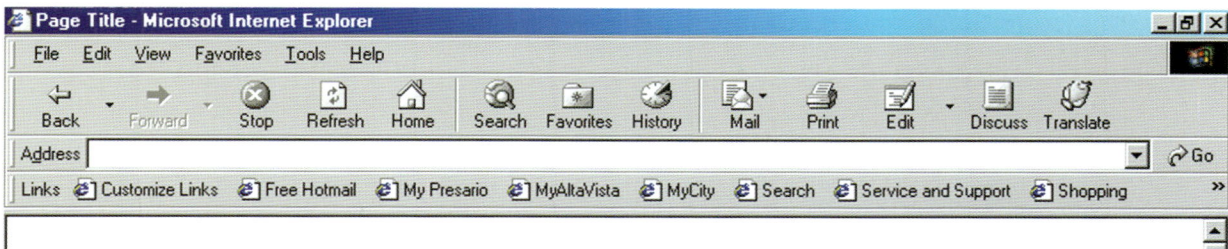

Deforestation is a serious problem because forests and trees aren't just pretty to look at, they do an important job making the earth's environment suitable for life. They clean the air, store water, preserve soil, and provide homes for animals. They also supply food, fuel, wood products, and paper products for humans. In the past fifty years, more than half of the world's rain forests have been destroyed. Today, the forests of the world are being cut down at a rate of fifty acres every minute! Scientists say that if deforestation continues, the world's climate may change, floods may become more common, and animals will die.

One solution to the problem of deforestation is to use less paper. If you use less paper, fewer trees will be cut for paper making. How can you use less paper? One answer is to reduce your paper use by using both sides of the paper when you photocopy, write a letter, or write a paper for school. A second answer is to reuse old paper when you can, rather than using a new sheet of paper. The backs of old envelopes are perfect for shopping lists or phone messages, and when you write a rough draft of an essay, write it on the back of something else. A final answer is to recycle used paper products instead of throwing them away. Most schools, offices, and neighborhoods have some kind of recycling center. If you follow the three Rs—reduce, reuse, and recycle—you can help save the world's forests.

7 Writing Essays

⊃ **Using conditional structures**

The *real* (or *first*) conditional is a useful way to talk about both problems and solutions:

Fish **will get** *sick if factories* **dump** *their waste into streams.*
   modal + main verb   present
   (will, can, could,
   should, etc.)

If you **eat** *fish from polluted waters, you* **could get** *sick too.*
   present   modal + main verb
                                   (will, can, could, should, etc.)

Punctuation note: No comma is needed when the *if*-clause comes second:
People can become sick if they eat the sick fish.

The event in the *if*-clause is possible, or is likely to happen. The event in the result clause would logically follow. There are other types of conditional sentences, but real conditionals are the most common in writing about problems and solutions.

4 Read the paragraphs on page 265 again. Underline the conditional sentences.

5 Complete these sentences by circling the correct form of the verb.
  a. It's difficult these days to be a university student. If you *want to / will want to* study full-time, it *costs / will cost* a lot of money.
  b. If you *are / could be* in class all day, you *might not have / might have* enough time to get a part-time job.
  c. If students *work / will work* part-time, it *could take / couldn't take* them more years to finish their studies because they are so busy.
  d. If universities *don't stop / stop* increasing their tuition rates, only rich students *are / will be* able to study full-time.
  e. We *must keep / mustn't keep* higher education affordable if we *want / will want* to have an educated population.

6 Complete these sentences with your own ideas. Then compare with a partner.
  a. If it rains this weekend, ...
  b. If the library isn't open tomorrow, ...
  c. If gas prices increase even more, ...
  d. .... , I will call you tonight.
  e. .... , you can make a lot of money.
  f. .... , I won't take a vacation.

7 For each topic in exercise 3 on page 264, write one or two conditional sentences that explain the problem. Compare your sentences with a partner. Did you have similar or different ideas?

8 Choose one topic from exercise 3 on page 264. Brainstorm more ideas if necessary, then write a paragraph about it. Use conditional sentences.

Linking problems with solutions

⊃ How to link a solution paragraph to a problem paragraph

The first paragraph—the problem paragraph—explains the problem. The topic sentence of the second paragraph—the *solution paragraph*—introduces your solution or solutions. The supporting sentences show how your solution(s) will solve the problem. Use these phrases:

In order to solve these problems, …	*In order to overcome these problems, …*
To meet this need, …	*One solution is …*
One answer is …	*One thing we can do is …*
A second / third / final answer is …	

9 Read the solution paragraph on page 265 again. Circle the linking phrases.

10 Work with a group. For each of these topic sentences, brainstorm solutions. Introduce each solution with one of the phrases above. Then think of one more problem together, and give it to another group to discuss.

   a. We must reduce exam stress for high school students.
   b. Teenagers spend so much time using their cell phones that they are no longer skilled at face-to-face interaction.

   c. In the next five to ten years, experts predict that there won't be enough doctors and nurses to meet hospitals' needs.
   d. We have to find ways to protect young children from violence on television.
   e. ....

7 Writing Essays

Writing solutions

⊃ Finding the best solution

After you have brainstormed solutions to your problem, you need to select the best one or ones to write about in your solution paragraph. A strong solution clearly and reasonably solves the problem. A weak solution doesn't really solve the problem or is not practical or not logical.

11 With a partner, talk about the solutions that this student brainstormed for her topic. Mark each one *strong, OK,* or *weak*.

Topic sentence: I need more spending money while I am in college.

.... borrow money from my friends

.... sell some of my things

.... ask my parents for money

.... play my guitar on the streets

.... get a part-time job

.... drop out of college and get a full-time job

.... buy lottery tickets

.... ride my bike to school instead of using public transportation

.... ask my professors for money

.... buy fewer CDs and new clothes

12 Use at least three solutions from the list in exercise 11 above to write a solution paragraph. Use linking phrases and conditional sentences to explain how the solutions will solve the problem. Share your paragraph with your partner.

13 For the problem paragraph you wrote in exercise 8 on page 267, brainstorm solutions. Edit your brainstorming, then write a solution paragraph. Use linking phrases and conditional sentences.

Writing Essays

Review

14 Look at this list of ideas that a student brainstormed about his topic. Work with a partner to divide the ideas into problems and solutions. Try to add one more problem and solution to the list.

> *Topic:* getting along with a roommate
>
> noisy roommate
>
> make cleaning schedule
>
> roommate is messy
>
> argue about how to decorate room
>
> fighting causes stress
>
> set aside quiet time for studying
>
> each person decorates half of the room
>
> talk each week about concerns

problems
a. ....
b. ....
c. ....
d. ....
e. ....

solutions
f. ....
g. ....
h. ....
i. ....
j. ....

15 Work alone. Use the ideas above to write a problem paragraph and a solution paragraph. Remember to write a topic sentence for each paragraph, and a concluding sentence for the solution paragraph. Use conditional sentences and linking phrases where you can. Then compare your paragraphs with your partner. What parts were similar? What parts were different?

PROBLEM / SOLUTION PARAGRAPHS

8 The Structure of an Essay

In this unit, you will learn …
- the definition of an essay.
- how to format an essay.
- how to write a thesis statement.

What is an essay?

An essay is a group of paragraphs written about a single topic and a central main idea. It must have at least three paragraphs, but a five-paragraph essay is a common assignment for academic writing.

The structure of an essay

The three main parts of an essay

The introduction

This is the first paragraph of an essay. It explains the topic with general ideas. It also has a *thesis statement*. This is a sentence that gives the main idea. It usually comes at or near the end of the paragraph.

The body

These are the paragraphs that explain and support the thesis statement and come between the introduction and the conclusion. There must be one or more body paragraphs in an essay.

The conclusion

This is the last paragraph of an essay. It summarizes or restates the thesis and the supporting ideas of the essay.

How to format an essay

1. Use double spacing (leave a blank line between each line of writing).
2. Leave 2.5 centimeters (1 inch) of space on the sides, and the top and bottom of the page. This space is called the **margin**.
3. If you type your essay, start the first line of each paragraph with five spaces (one tab). This is called **indenting**. If you write by hand, indent about 2 centimeters ($^3/_4$ inch).
4. Put the title of your essay at the top of the first page in the center.

1 Label the three parts of this essay: introduction, body paragraphs, and conclusion.

American and British English: One Language with Many Differences

The English language came to be the world language that it is today by events that happened hundreds of years ago. British colonization and trade led to the spread of the English language to many areas around the world, and by the early 1600's English was introduced to North America. Although the English used in the United States and the United Kingdom is generally mutually intelligible, it has developed several differences, including pronunciation, grammar, punctuation, and spelling. Certain differences in vocabulary and the use of idioms between American and British English can cause misunderstandings between speakers.

Vocabulary is one area where many differences can be found between American and British English. There are many examples of a particular vocabulary word having different meanings. Words such as *bill* (AmE = paper money or invoice, BrE = invoice), *biscuit* (AmE = slightly salty, thick pastry, BrE = sweet dessert, like an American cookie) and *football* (AmE = soccer) are three well-known examples. Other examples of vocabulary that are entirely different words for the same meaning include *elevator* (AmE) and *lift* (BrE); *gas* (AmE) and *petrol* (BrE); *period* (AmE) and *full stop* (BrE); *apartment* (AmE) and *flat* (BrE); *potato chips* (AmE) and *crisps* (BrE); *subway* (AmE) and *underground* (BrE); *line* (AmE) and *queue* (BrE); and *intersection* (AmE) and *crossroads* (BrE).

In addition to words, there are certain idioms, or phrases, that differ between the two forms of English. Most of the phrases differ by only one or two words and can sometimes cause misunderstandings between speakers of American and British English. Some examples include (BrE) *a drop in the ocean* and (AmE) *a drop in the bucket*, which mean "a small part of something that is much larger"; (BrE) *blow one's trumpet* and (AmE) *blow (or toot) one's horn*, which mean "to brag about one's own accomplishments"; and (BrE) *tuppence worth* and (AmE) *two cents' worth*, which mean "to offer one's opinion or advice". One phrase that can cause some confusion in conversation is *I don't mind*. If a person is asked whether he would like tea or coffee, for example, the BrE response "I don't mind" means that either choice is acceptable, while the AmE response would most likely be "I don't care."

The examples above are only a small sample of the various ways American English and British English differ. However, although vocabulary differences can cause some misunderstandings, generally speakers of both forms of English can understand one another with little difficulty. Differences between American and British English have developed over the centuries, and these differences will likely continue to develop and change into the future.

8 Writing Essays

Thesis statements

1 What is a thesis statement?

The *thesis statement* is the sentence that tells the main idea of the essay. It can be compared to a topic sentence, which gives the main idea of a paragraph. The thesis statement can express an opinion: *Travel is an effective way to bring people of different cultures together and learn about one another.* It can also state an argument or fact to be defended or explained: *There are several ways that technology has made classroom instruction more effective.* It usually comes at or near the end of the introductory paragraph.

2 Look at the essay in exercise 1 on page 271 again. Underline the thesis statement.

3 In these introductory paragraphs, underline the thesis statement. Then circle the topic and draw another line under the main idea in each thesis statement. Share your answers with a partner.

a.

> The British eat many different kinds of food, but the typical diet of many people includes eating a lot of fast food and ready-made dishes. The popularity of hamburger and pizza restaurants has increased greatly over the years. As a result of this diet, many British people have food-related health problems. To create a healthier society, people should learn about eating a good diet and should teach their children to do the same.

b.

> Everybody knows the koala, that cute Australian animal that resembles a teddy bear. Although koalas look like toys, they are actually strong climbers and spend their days in the treetops. Mother koalas carry their babies around from tree to tree in a pouch, or pocket, on their stomach. Although there were millions of koalas in Australia in the past, they are now a protected species of animal. As a result of human population growth, deforestation, and hunting, the number of koalas has declined.

c.

> Taoism is an ancient philosophy from Asia that places great importance on the natural world. Taoists believe that spirit can be found in every person or thing, living or non-living. For the Taoist, even a mountain or a stone contains spirit. Lao Tsu, a Taoist writer and philosopher, said "People follow earth. Earth follows heaven. Heaven follows the Tao. The Tao follows what is natural." For thousands of years in China and other Asian countries, gardens have been an important way to create a place where people can feel the spirit of the natural world. Creating a Taoist garden is an art. No two Taoist gardens are exactly alike, but all Taoist gardens include four essential elements: water, mountains, buildings, and bridges.

Writing Essays

⊃ Writing a strong thesis statement

- A thesis statement gives the author's opinion or states an important idea about the topic. It should give an idea that can be discussed and explained with supporting ideas:

  The qualifications for entering a university in my country are unreasonable.

  When studying a second language, there are several ways to improve your use of the language.

  These are strong thesis statements. They can be discussed or explained.

- A thesis statement should not be a sentence that only gives a fact about the topic:

  In the Northern Hemisphere, the summer months are warmer than the winter months.

  This is not a strong thesis statement. It cannot be discussed or argued about.

- A thesis statement should not state two sides of an argument equally:

  There are advantages and disadvantages to using nuclear power.

  This could be a topic sentence, but it is not a thesis statement. It gives two sides of an argument without giving a clear opinion of support or disagreement. It could be revised like this:

  Although there are some advantages, using nuclear power has many disadvantages and should not be a part of our country's energy plan.

  This is a strong thesis statement. It clearly gives the writer's opinion about nuclear power.

4 Read these thesis statements below. Write ✓ (strong thesis statement), F (fact only—a weak thesis statement), or N (no clear opinion—a weak thesis statement).

a. .... The top government official in my country is the prime minister.
b. .... Many diseases are caused by both genetic and environmental factors.
c. .... India became an independent country in 1947.
d. .... To be a successful student, good study habits are more important than intelligence.
e. .... There are several advantages of owning a car, but there are also many disadvantages.
f. .... Half of the families in my country own a house.
g. .... Using public transportation would be one of the best ways to solve the traffic and pollution problems in cities around the world.
h. .... While traveling, staying in a hotel offers more comfort, but sleeping in a tent is less expensive.
i. .... Classical music concerts are very popular in my country.
j. .... In order to create a successful advertisement, it is necessary to consider three issues: who should be targeted, where the ad should be placed, and what type of ad should be made.

Writing Essays

Writing thesis statements

How to connect the thesis statement and the essay

The body paragraphs of an essay should always explain the thesis statement. In addition, each body paragraph should discuss *one* part of the thesis. Look at the following thesis statement. The topics to be discussed are underlined:

To create a successful advertisement, it is necessary for advertisers to answer three questions: <u>What are we selling?</u>, <u>Who are we selling it to?</u>, and <u>How can we make people want to buy it?</u>

Possible topic sentences for each body paragraph:

1. The first step in creating a successful advertisement is to completely understand the product that is being sold and how it can be used.

2. A second important part of creating an advertisement is deciding who is expected to buy the product.

3. Finally, a way must be found to create an ad that will make people want to buy the product.

5 Look at the introductory paragraphs in exercise 3 on page 272. What should the body paragraphs discuss for each thesis statement? Write your ideas and then compare your answers with a partner.

⊃ How to develop a thesis statement

One way to develop a thesis statement for an essay is to write opinions you have about the topic. Begin, *I think that …* and complete the sentence with your opinion. Then remove *I think that …* and the remaining words make a possible thesis statement.

Topic: diet / food

~~I think that~~ a vegetarian diet is one of the best ways to live a healthy life.

~~I think that~~ governments should restrict the use of chemicals in agriculture and food production.

After you have written several opinion statements, choose the one that would make the best thesis. Remember to decide if the sentence gives a clear opinion, states a fact, or presents two sides without a clear argument.

6 For each of these topics, write two or three opinions you have, starting with *I think that*.

a. exercise

....
....
....

b. university study

....
....
....

c. the Internet

....
....
....

d. music

....
....
....

Writing Essays

7 Now cross out the *I think that* in the statements you wrote in exercise 6 on page 275. Choose the best thesis statement for each topic. Share these with a partner. Decide which ones are good thesis statements.

8 Choose one of your thesis statements from exercise 7 above. Circle the topics that must be explained in the essay. Write a topic sentence for each of the circled ideas.

Review

9 Complete the crossword.

The topic sentence gives the ¹·m___ idea of a ²·p___ . Likewise, the thesis statement gives the main ³·i___ of an ⁴·e___.

The ⁵·s___ sentences of a paragraph explain the topic sentence, just as the ⁶·b___ paragraphs of an essay explain the thesis statement.

The last sentence of a paragraph is called the ⁷·c___ sentence, and the last paragraph of an essay is called the ⁸·c___.

9 Outlining an Essay

In this unit, you will learn …
- **the purpose of an outline.**
- **how to write an outline.**

↪ **What is an outline?**

An outline is a list of the information you will put in your essay. You can see an example of an outline on page 279.

An outline …

- begins with the essay's thesis statement.
- shows the organization of the essay.
- tells what ideas you will discuss and shows which ideas will come first, second, and so on.
- ends with the essay's conclusion.

Writing an outline before you write an essay will …

- show you what to write before you actually begin writing.
- help make your essay well organized and clearly focused.
- keep you from forgetting any important points.

Imagine your skeleton: although you don't see it, it supports your body. In the same way, although a reader won't see your outline, making an outline in advance will support your essay by providing its structure. In fact, adding more information to an outline is called "fleshing it out."

Writing Essays

Looking at an outline

1 Read the outline on page 279. Answer the questions.
   a. What will be the thesis statement of the essay?
   b. How many body paragraphs will the essay have?
   c. How many supporting points will the third paragraph have? What will they be?
   d. How many details will the fourth paragraph have? What will they be?

Writing an outline

⊃ How to write an outline

Before writing an outline, you must go through the usual process of gathering ideas, editing them, and deciding on a topic for your writing. Writing an outline can be a very useful way of organizing your ideas and seeing how they will work together.

To show how the ideas work together, number them. To avoid confusion, use several different types of numbers and letters to show the organization of the ideas. Use roman numerals (I, II, III, IV, V, VI, etc.) for your essay's main ideas: your introduction and thesis statement, your body paragraphs, and your conclusion. Write all of these first, before going into more detail anywhere.

   I. Introduction
   II. First main idea
   III. Second main idea
   IV. Third main idea
   V. Conclusion

Next, fill in more information for your body paragraphs by using capital roman letters (A, B, C, etc.). Use one letter for each supporting idea in your body paragraph. Complete this information for each body paragraph before going into more detail.

   I. Introduction
   II. First main idea
      A. First supporting point
      B. Second supporting point
      … and so on.

Finally, use Arabic numerals (1, 2, 3, etc.) to give details for your supporting points. Not every supporting point will have details, and some points will have several. It is not important to have the same number of details for every supporting point.

   I. Introduction
   II. First main idea
      A. First supporting point
         1. First detail
         2. Second detail
      B. Second supporting point
         1. First detail
         2. Second detail
         … and so on.

Don't Support Nuclear Energy!

I. Nuclear power is not a good energy source for the world.

II. Very expensive
   A. Nuclear fuel is expensive
   B. Nuclear power plants are expensive to build and operate
      1. Cost of construction
      2. Cost of training workers
      3. Cost of safety features

III. Nuclear materials are not safe
   A. Nuclear fuels are dangerous
      1. Mining fuels produces radioactive gas
      2. Working with radioactive fuels can harm workers
   B. Nuclear waste products are dangerous
      1. Very radioactive
      2. Difficult to dispose of or store safely

IV. There is a possibility of disastrous accidents
   A. Nuclear power plants can fail
      1. Three Mile Island, U.S.A. (1979)
      2. Darlington, Canada (1992)
      3. Sellafield, England (2005)
   B. Workers can make mistakes
      1. Chernobyl, U.S.S.R. (1986)
      2. Tokaimura, Japan (1999)
      3. Asco, Spain (2007–2008)
   C. Natural disasters can occur
      1. Tornado: Mururoa, the Pacific (1981)
      2. Earthquake: Fukushima, Japan (2011)

V. Because of the cost and the danger, the world should develop different types of energy to replace nuclear power.

9 Writing Essays

2 Fill in this outline for the essay in Unit 8, exercise 1 on page 271. Then compare with a partner.

The differences between American and British English.

I. Thesis statement: ……………………………………………………………………………………

II. Vocabulary differences

    A. …………………………………………

        1. bill

        2. …………………………………………

        3. …………………………………………

    B. Different words with same meaning

        1. elevator/lift

        2. gas/…………………………………………

        3. period/…………………………………………

        4. …………………………………………

III. …………………………………………

    A. a drop in the ocean/bucket

    B. …………………………………………

    C. …………………………………………

    D. …………………………………………

IV. Conclusion: …………………………………………

……………………………………………………………

……………………………………………………………

……………………………………………………………

3 Label each statement T for thesis statement, M for main idea, S for supporting point, or C for conclusion.

Title: The Benefits of Yoga
- **a.** ...... Develops clear thinking
- **b.** ...... Physical benefits
- **c.** ...... Improves concentration
- **d.** ...... Reduces fear, anger, and worry
- **e.** ...... Mental benefits
- **f.** ...... Improves blood circulation
- **g.** ...... Improves digestion
- **h.** ...... Helps you feel calm and peaceful
- **i.** ...... Develops self-confidence
- **j.** ...... Practicing yoga regularly can be good for your mind, your body, and your emotions.
- **k.** ...... Makes you strong and flexible
- **l.** ...... Therefore, to build mental, physical, and emotional health, consider practicing yoga.
- **m.** ...... Emotional benefits

4 Arrange the ideas in exercise 3 above into an outline. Compare your finished outline with a partner.

I. ....

II. ....

    A. ....

    B. ....

III. ....

    A. ....

    B. ....

    C. ....

IV. ....

    A. ....

    B. ....

    C. ....

V. ....

9 Writing Essays

Evaluating an outline

⊃ The outline checklist

Before you start writing your essay, check your outline for organization, support, and topic development. If possible, have a friend or your instructor check your outline too.

Organization

❏ paragraphs in the right order
❏ supporting points and details in the right order

Support

❏ each main idea related to the thesis statement
❏ each supporting point related to the paragraph's main idea
❏ each detail related to the paragraph's supporting points

Topic development

❏ enough (and not too many) main ideas to develop the thesis statement
❏ enough (and not too many) supporting points for each main point
❏ enough (and not too many) details for each supporting point

5 With a partner, check the outline on page 283 for organization, support, and topic development. What should the author add, subtract, or change in this outline? Share your ideas with another pair. Did you make the same recommendations?

In 1848, gold was discovered in California. People from all over the world rushed to California to look for gold—they wanted to become rich. This was called "the gold rush."

The Effects of the California Gold Rush on the City of San Francisco

I. The California gold rush changed San Francisco in ways that we can still see today.

II. History of the gold rush
   A. 1848
      1. Gold was discovered near San Francisco
      2. The U.S. president tells the country there's gold in California
   B. 1864: the gold rush ends
   C. 1849: the gold rush begins as people from all over the world go to California to look for gold. Gold is very easy to find.
   D. 1850s: gold becomes more difficult to find; big, expensive machines are now needed to find gold
   E. Gold rushes in other countries
      1. Australia (1851–53)
      2. South Africa (1884)
      3. Canada (1897–98)

III. Effects on San Francisco today
   A. People still come to San Francisco hoping to get rich
      1. Computer industry
   B. Sightseeing is very popular in San Francisco
   C. San Francisco is still an expensive city
      1. Houses and land
      2. Food & clothing
      3. Many new fast-food restaurants sell cheap hamburgers
   D. Still problems in the city
   E. Technological development is still important
   F. There is no gold mining today
   G. Character of San Francisco today

IV. Changes in California in the 1800s
   A. Population increased—more than 40,000 people moved to California in 1848–50
   B. Everything became more expensive
      1. Houses and land
   C. Problems with crime and violence
   D. Technology to find gold improved

V. The special personality of San Francisco can be traced in part to the famous gold rush of the 1800s.

Writing Essays

6. Look at the thesis statement and topic sentences you wrote in Unit 8, exercise 8 on page 276. Write an outline for your essay. Then write the essay.

7. Exchange the essay you wrote for exercise 6 above with a partner. As you read your partner's essay, write an outline of the main ideas, supporting points, and details. Your partner will outline your essay. Discuss the outlines.

Review

8. Write a simple outline of yourself or your life. First, outline only the body paragraphs. Your main ideas could include physical characteristics, your personality, your habits, your family, places you have lived, jobs you have had, things you like and dislike, and so on.

9. Explain your outline to a partner. Your partner will then add a thesis statement and concluding statement.

10. Join another pair and present your complete outlines.

284 OUTLINING AN ESSAY

10 Introductions and Conclusions

In this unit, you will learn about …
- the purpose of an introduction.
- types of information in introductions.
- the purpose of a conclusion.
- techniques for writing conclusions.

The importance of introductions and conclusions

Unit 8 explained that the introduction and the conclusion are two of the three main parts of an essay. Without an introduction and a conclusion, an essay is just a group of paragraphs. The introduction and the conclusion work together to make the topic and main ideas of the essay clear to the reader.

The introduction

What is an introduction?

The first paragraph of an essay, as you learned in Unit 8, is called the introduction. The introduction …

- is usually five to ten sentences.
- catches the reader's interest.
- gives the general topic of the essay.
- gives background information about the topic.
- states the main point (the thesis statement) of the essay.

The introduction is often organized by giving the most general ideas first and then leading to the most specific idea, which is the thesis statement, like this:

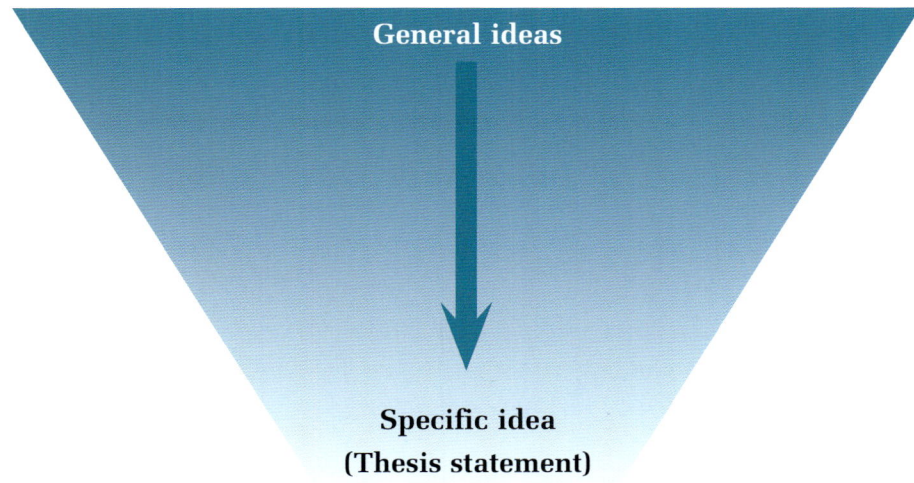

10 Writing Essays

1 Read the introduction to the essay in Unit 8, exercise 1 on page 271. Complete this diagram.

General ideas:

English as a world language today is the result of events that happened a long time ago.

....

....

Specific idea (Thesis statement):

....

....

How to write a strong introduction

A strong introduction …

- introduces the topic clearly.
- gives several sentences of information about the topic.
- states the thesis (the main idea) of the essay.

Any of the following will make an introduction weak:

- It doesn't give enough information about the topic or gives too much information about it.
- It talks about too many different topics.
- It does not state a clear thesis.

2 Read and discuss the following introductions with a partner. Mark the strong introductions with a check (✓). Mark the weak introductions with an ✗. What could the writers do to make the weak introductions strong?

a. ☐

The rate of babies being born in Japan and Korea has greatly decreased in the last fifty years. The decrease in number has caused several social changes.

b. ☐

The number of businesses using the Internet for selling products has increased greatly in recent years. Shoppers, too, are using the Internet in greater numbers to buy all types of products, such as books, cameras, and clothing. Although e-business has become popular, there are certain risks involved in Internet shopping that are a concern for both businesses and consumers.

c.

Stargazing—looking at the stars—is something everyone should try. I love it. When looking at the night sky, most people observe that the moon, planets, and stars move from the east side of the sky to the west over a period of several hours. In fact, this movement is actually the movement of the Earth rotating on its axis. In addition, as the Earth revolves around the sun throughout the year, different stars are visible at different times.

d.

The origins of Irish music can be traced back nearly 2,000 years to the time when the Celts arrived in Ireland. Music thrived under the rule of the Chieftans, but later declined during the British colonisation of Ireland. However, during the Great Famine of the 1840s, thousands of Irish people emigrated to North America in search of a better life, taking their music with them. Irish music soon became established in American cities with a high proportion of Irish immigrants, such as Chicago and Boston. These cities are popular tourist destinations with many interesting sights. However, Irish music really became well known to a wider audience in the 1970s, when musicians experimented with more modern arrangements of traditional songs and fusion with rock, world music and jazz. Jazz originated in the American South in the early twentieth century. Now, in the twenty-first century, Irish music is more popular and successful than ever.

e.

Adjusting to another culture's food can be a challenge for many travelers. The geography of a country can greatly affect the typical foods that are eaten by its people.

10 Writing Essays

Types of information

◌ **How to make an introduction interesting**

To make an introductory paragraph interesting for the reader, you can include …

- interesting facts or statistics.
- a personal story or example.
- an interesting quotation.

3 Read the three introductions in Unit 8, exercise 3 on page 272 again. What types of information does each introductory paragraph contain?

4 Look at the introduction of the essay you wrote for Unit 9, exercise 6 on page 284. With a partner, rewrite the introduction, making changes to improve it.

The conclusion

◌ **The importance of a conclusion**

The conclusion is the final paragraph of the essay. A good concluding paragraph …

- summarizes the main points of the essay.
- restates the thesis (using different words).
- makes a final comment about the essay's main idea.
- may emphasize an action that you would like the reader to take.

Don't introduce new ideas in a conclusion. A conclusion only restates or gives further commentary on ideas discussed in the essay.

5 **Look at the essay in Unit 8, exercise 1 on page 271 again. Answer these questions.**

a. Does the conclusion use any of the four techniques described above? Which ones?

....

....

b. Which sentence in the conclusion restates the thesis (from the introduction)?

....

....

6 Match each of these introduction thesis statements with its rewritten version for a conclusion.

a. ...... A lack of adequate sleep can have several negative effects on a person's health and daily life.

b. ...... Traveling is a valuable learning experience for people, especially children and young adults.

c. ...... Learning to play a musical instrument is very beneficial for children.

d. ...... Creating and owning a business offers more advantages than working as an employee in a company.

e. ...... More houses should be adapted to use solar energy because it is clean and renewable.

f. ...... The Internet can be very useful for research, but it also contains a lot of incorrect information.

1. Young people can learn many things by traveling to other countries.

2. Despite the challenges, being an entrepreneur can offer more benefits than other types of employment.

3. Sleep deprivation can result in many harmful effects on the body including chronic tiredness, being unable to think clearly or remember things well, feeling depressed, and getting sick more easily due to a weakened immune system; clearly, getting enough sleep is an essential part of a healthy lifestyle.

4. The Internet gives access to a huge amount of knowledge, but users shouldn't believe everything they read there.

5. When children are exposed to music and are taught to play instruments such as the piano or violin, there are many positive effects.

6. The sun gives a constant, free supply of clean energy, which more homes should take advantage of.

10 Writing Essays

7 Read paragraph a in Unit 8, exercise 3 on page 272 again. Choose the best concluding paragraph, below.

a.

> Thanks to this publicity, the majority of people are now aware of what makes a good diet and they understand the related health benefits. Yet many still lack confidence in their ability to achieve healthy eating in their daily lives. The message to get across, especially to families and children, is that a healthy diet does not need to be expensive or difficult. Food that is bought freshly and prepared simply can be just as cheap and quick as a microwave dinner, and is certainly more delicious.

b.

> Clearly, it is difficult to say that there is one type of British food. Every part of the country has its own special dishes based on the produce and tastes of that region. From the Ancient Britons and the Roman, Saxon and Viking invasions to present-day immigrants, the cuisine of the UK continues to change with its changing population.

c.

> People who have come from other countries to live in the UK have brought their own traditions and customs with them and added them to British culture. It is possible to find restaurants from all different ethnic backgrounds, especially in larger cities around the country. Immigrants may also maintain their traditions by building places to practice their religion, such as mosques, temples, and churches. By continuing to follow some of their customs and beliefs, immigrants can remain in touch with their past while also living a new life in a new country.

8 Look at the conclusion of the essay you wrote for Unit 9, exercise 6 on page 284. With a partner, rewrite the conclusion, making changes to improve it.

Writing Essays

10

Review

9 Complete the crossword puzzle.

A strong introduction catches the reader's [1.] i___. It can do this by including interesting [2.] f___, a personal [3.] s___, or an interesting [4.] q___. It also gives the general [5.] t___ of the essay, several sentences of [6.] i___ about the topic, and states the [7.] t___.

A conclusion [8.] s___ the main points of the essay. It also [9.] r___ the thesis, makes a final [10.] c___ about the essay's main idea, and it may emphasize an [11.] a___ for the reader to take.

10 Write an introduction and conclusion for the outline you created for Unit 9, exercise 8 on page 284. Then exchange these with a partner. Make comments on your partner's paragraphs using the information you learned in this unit about writing good introductions and conclusions.

11 Unity and Coherence

In this unit, you will learn ...
- the importance of unity in essay writing.
- how to edit an essay for unity.
- the importance of coherence in essay writing.
- methods of creating coherence.

⊃ **Writing effective essays**

You've already learned that an essay shoulc be organized into an introduction, a body, and a conclusion. The next step is to make sure that all three parts of the essay work together to explain your topic clearly.

Unity in writing

⊃ **What is unity?**

Unity in writing is the connection of all ideas to a single topic. In an essay, all ideas should relate to the thesis statement, and the supporting ideas in a body paragraph should relate to the topic sentence.

1 Read the essay on page 293 about Chinese medicine. Then do these tasks.
   a. Underline the thesis statement with two lines.

   b. Underline each topic sentence with one line.

   c. List the supporting ideas in each body paragraph on a separate piece of paper.

   d. After you have finished, review the topic sentences and supporting ideas. With a partner, discuss how the topic sentences relate to the thesis statement and how the supporting sentences relate to the topic sentences. Is the essay unified?

Next Time, Try Chinese Medicine

The last time I had a cold, a friend suggested that instead of taking the usual cold medicines, I visit the traditional Chinese doctor in our city. Although I knew nothing about Chinese medicine, I decided to try it. When I walked in to the Chinese doctor's office, I was amazed. It was not at all like my usual doctor's. There were shelves up to the ceiling full of glass containers filled with hundreds of different dried plants and other things I could not identify. Could this really be a doctor's office? It seemed very strange to me. When I met the doctor, he explained that Chinese medicine is thousands of years old. The plants in the jars in his office were herbs. These herbs could be mixed together to make medicines. He explained the philosophy of Chinese medicine. The philosophy of traditional Chinese medicine is not the same as the philosophy of modern medicine, but it is useful for curing many health problems.

Modern medicine focuses on illness. If a patient with a cough visits a modern doctor, then the doctor will give the patient a medicine to stop the cough. If the patient also has a fever, the doctor may give a different medicine to stop the fever. For every person with a cough, the doctor will probably recommend the same cough medicine. The philosophy of modern medicine is to stop problems like coughing and fever as quickly as possible. Western doctors usually see illness as an enemy. They use medicines like weapons to fight diseases.

Chinese medicine, in contrast, has a different philosophy. Instead of focusing on a patient's health problems, Chinese medicine tries to make the patient's whole body well again. Specifically, doctors of Chinese medicine believe that inside people, there are two types of energy. The first type of energy, called "yin," is quiet and passive. The other type of energy, called "yang," is active. When these two energies are in equal balance, a person is healthy. When there is an imbalance—too much yin, for example—a person becomes unhealthy. A doctor of Chinese medicine doesn't try to stop a person's cough by giving a cough medicine. Instead, the doctor gives a mixture of herbs that will restore balance in the patient's body. As a result, when the body is in balance, the cough will stop naturally.

The Chinese doctor's herbs seemed strange to me at first, but they made me feel better. My cold wasn't cured instantly, but I felt healthy again after a few days. For a very serious health problem, I would probably visit a modern hospital, but the next time I catch a cold, I am going back to the Chinese doctor. Chinese medicine definitely works for some health problems.

11 Writing Essays

Editing an essay for unity

⊃ Keeping unity in an essay

One way to keep unity in an essay is to edit the outline for ideas that are not relevant to the thesis statement or topic sentences, as you learned in Unit 9. Likewise, after you have written the essay, it is helpful to review the text and look for ideas that do not relate to the thesis or the topic sentences.

2 Read this thesis statement and body paragraphs. The writer has begun to cross out sentences that do not belong. There is still one large piece of the text that should be removed because it isn't relevant to the thesis. Can you find it? Compare your answer with a partner. Then look at the edited version in exercise 6 on page 299.

Thesis statement: Sign language, the language used by many deaf people, has a 500-year history.

The first sign language for deaf people was developed in Europe in the 1500s. In Spain, a man named Pedro de Ponce was the first person to teach deaf children using sign language. Another Spaniard, Juan Pablo de Bonet, was the first person to write a book on teaching sign language to deaf people. ~~Most of his students were from rich families.~~ Another important teacher who influenced the development of sign language was a Frenchman named Abbé de L'Epée. L'Epée understood that deaf people could communicate without speech. He started to learn the signs used by a group of deaf people in Paris. Using these signs, he developed a more complete French sign language. ~~L'Epée also taught religion classes.~~ Another Frenchman, Louis Braille, also lived during this time. He invented a system of reading and writing for blind people, using raised bumps that can be felt with the fingers. In Germany, a man named Samuel Heinicke was another important teacher of the deaf during this time. However, he did not use sign language for instruction. Instead, he preferred to teach the deaf to understand other people by looking carefully at other people's mouths when they spoke. This is called lip or speech reading.

Speech reading became a popular way of teaching the deaf in the United States in the mid-1800s. Alexander Graham Bell, who invented the telephone, was one of the strongest supporters of teaching deaf people to do speech reading. Bell became interested in deafness and teaching deaf people. With his interest in science and the production of sound, he focused on ways of helping the deaf

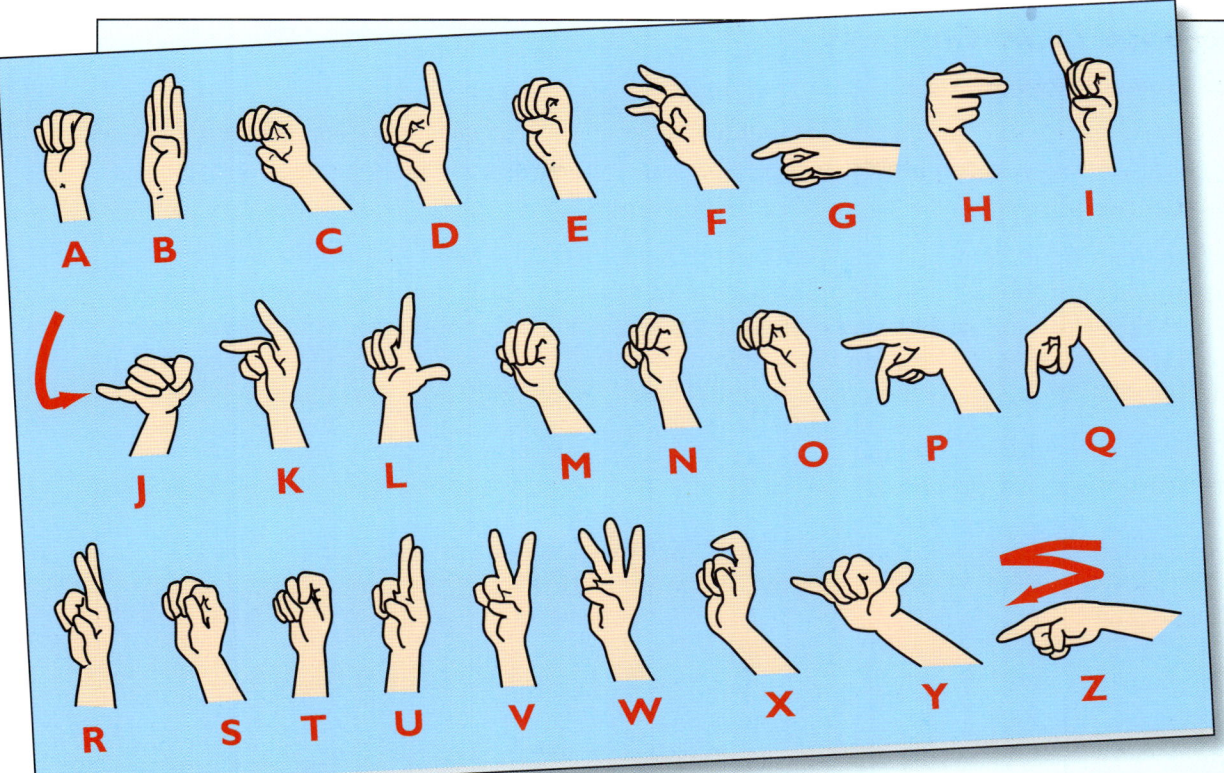

Sign language for deaf people (people who cannot hear)

communicate with listening tools and speech reading. He eventually opened a training school for teachers of the deaf.

~~Not much is known about the use of sign language among deaf people in the United States before the 1800's.~~ The early 1800s were an important period in the development of American Sign Language. In 1815, a man named Thomas Gallaudet became interested in teaching deaf people. He traveled to Europe to study ways of communicating with deaf people. He was twenty-seven years old at this time, and he studied at a school for deaf students in Paris for several months. In 1817, Gallaudet returned to the United States, and he brought with him Laurent Clerc, a deaf sign language teacher from Paris. Gallaudet started the first school for the deaf, and Clerc became the first sign language teacher in the U.S. ~~The school, called American School for the Deaf, still exists in Hartford, Connecticut.~~ American Sign Language developed from the mixture of signs used by deaf Americans and French Sign Language. Today, it is used by more than 500,000 deaf people in the United States and Canada. ~~About twenty million people in the United States have hearing problems, and about two million of these are deaf.~~

Writing Essays

Coherence in writing

⊃ **What is coherence?**

Coherence is related to unity. Ideas that are arranged in a clear and logical way are coherent. When a text is unified and coherent, the reader can easily understand the main points.

As you learned in Unit 9, creating an outline helps make a well-organized essay. When organizing your ideas, think about what type of organization is the best for your topic or essay type. Here are some examples of types of writing and good ways to organize them.

Type of writing	Type of organization
Chronology (historical events, personal narratives, processes)	Order by time or order of events / steps
Description	Order by position, size, and shape of things
Classification	Group ideas and explain them in a logical order
Comparison / contrast	Organize in point-by-point or block style
Argumentation / persuasion and cause / effect	Order from least important to most important

3 Look again at the essay in exercise 1 on page 293. What type of organizational pattern does the essay use? How do you know? What about the text in exercise 2 on pages 294 and 295?

Cohesive devices

⊃ **What is a cohesive device?**

Cohesive devices are words and phrases that connect sentences and paragraphs together, creating a smooth flow of ideas. In this unit, we'll look at connectors, pronoun references, and repetition of key ideas.

Connectors

Pronoun references

Repetition of key ideas

Writing Essays 11

Connectors

As you've learned in previous units, there are many connecting words and phrases in English that are used to connect sentences together or relate ideas to one another. Here are several types of writing and some common connectors that are used with them.

Chronology	Comparison	Contrast	Additional information	Examples	Cause and effect	Concluding ideas
before after next since first, second while when	likewise compared to similarly as … as and	however on the other hand but yet in spite of in contrast although instead	and also in addition in fact furthermore moreover Another … is/was	for example in general generally for instance specifically in particular	therefore so thus as a result since because	in conclusion in summary finally therefore to conclude to summarize

4 Use connectors from the list above, or others that you know, to connect these sentences taken from the essay about Chinese medicine on page 293. When you have finished, compare your answers with the essay.

1. .... of focusing on a patient's health problems, Chinese medicine tries to make the patient's whole body well again. 2. .... , doctors of Chinese medicine believe that inside people, there are two types of energy. The first type of energy, called "yin," is quiet and passive. The other type of energy, called "yang," is active. … When there is an imbalance—too much yin, 3. .... —a person becomes unhealthy. A doctor of Chinese medicine doesn't try to stop a person's cough by giving a cough medicine. 4. .... , the doctor gives a mixture of herbs that will restore balance in the patient's body. 5. .... , when the body is in balance, the cough will stop naturally.

Pronoun reference

Two sentences can be connected by the use of a pronoun. A pronoun (*he, she, it, they,* etc.) takes the place of a noun (a person, place, thing, or idea) or a noun phrase (several words that refer to a person, place, thing, or idea). Look at the following example taken from the essay on sign language:

American Sign Language *developed from the mixture of signs used by deaf Americans and French Sign Language. Today,* **it** *is used by more than 500,000 deaf people in the United States and Canada.*

The pronoun *it* refers back to the subject, *American Sign Language,* and connects the two sentences together.

UNITY AND COHERENCE 297

Writing Essays

5 For each of the *italicized* pronouns in this passage, identify the noun or noun phrase to which it refers. Write your answers on the lines below the text.

Montreal, one of Canada's largest cities, is a popular tourist destination for several reasons. First, the city has a beautiful location. ^{a.}*It* sits on an island in the middle of the St. Lawrence River. In addition, Montreal is both modern and historic. There are many luxury hotels, ^{b.}*it* has a clean and efficient subway system, and visitors can find a wide variety of shops and restaurants, especially downtown. The oldest area of the town, the Vieux Montreal, is very beautiful because many of ^{c.}*its* oldest buildings were protected as areas of the city were rebuilt or developed. The most interesting thing about Montreal may be ^{d.}*its* French quality. Approximately two-thirds of the people living in or near Montreal are of French origin, and ^{e.}*they* speak French as well as English. In addition to the strong French influence, there are large groups of people from Germany, Greece, Italy, Hungary, the West Indies, and China living ^{f.}*there*. All of ^{g.}*this* makes Montreal a great place to visit.

a. it = ...
b. it = ...
c. its = ...
d. its = ...
e. they = ...
f. there = ...
g. this = ...

⊃ Repetition of key nouns or ideas

Another way to connect ideas in an essay is by repeating important words and phrases. This will help the reader remember the main ideas in the text.

*Modern **medicine** focuses on illness. If a patient with a <u>cough</u> visits a modern doctor, then the doctor will give the patient a **medicine** to stop the <u>cough</u>. If the patient also has a fever, the doctor may give a different **medicine** to stop the fever. For every person with a <u>cough</u>, the doctor will probably recommend the same <u>cough</u> **medicine**. The philosophy of modern **medicine** is to stop problems like <u>coughing</u> and fever as quickly as possible.*

6 Read these revised paragraphs from the essay on sign language. Underline examples of connector use, pronoun reference, and repetition of key words. Then compare your answers with a partner.

Thesis statement: Sign language, the language used by many deaf people, has a five-hundred-year history.

The first sign language for deaf people was developed in Europe in the 1500s. Three men in particular contributed a lot to the development of sign language. In Spain, a man named Pedro de Ponce was the first person to teach deaf children using sign language. In addition, another Spaniard, Juan Pablo de Bonet, wrote the first book on teaching sign language to deaf people, at about the same time. Another important teacher who influenced the development of sign language was a Frenchman named Abbé de L'Epée. L'Epée understood that deaf people could communicate without speech. He started to learn the signs used by a group of deaf people in Paris. Using these signs, he developed a more complete French sign language.

The early 1800s were an important period in the development of American Sign Language. In 1815, a man named Thomas Gallaudet became interested in teaching deaf people, so he traveled to Europe to study ways of communicating with deaf people. He was twenty-seven years old at this time, and he studied at a school for deaf students in Paris for several months. After that, Gallaudet returned to the United States, and he brought with him Laurent Clerc, a deaf sign language teacher from Paris. As a result of his experience in Europe, Gallaudet started the first school for the deaf, and Clerc became the first sign language teacher in the U.S. American Sign Language developed from the mixture of signs used by deaf Americans and French Sign Language. Today, it is used by more than 500,000 deaf people in the United States and Canada.

Writing Essays

7 This paragraph needs more connection. Revise it. Then share your version with other classmates.

Ho Chi Minh City, in Vietnam, is a fascinating destination for travelers to Southeast Asia. It is located on the Mekong River. It was once an important trading center for the French in Southeast Asia. The influence of French culture can still be felt. Many people, especially the older generations, learned French in school and still can speak it very well. Some cafés serve French-style bread and pastries in Ho Chi Minh City. Expensive hotels and restaurants serve French food. Many of the buildings in the city are built in French style. The Vietnamese and the French fought. The French eventually left the country. There are museums and monuments documenting the country's long—and often bloody—history. If you are looking for a unique city to visit in Southeast Asia, Ho Chi Minh City is an attractive choice.

8 Write an outline for an essay on one of the following topics or on a topic of your choice.

  a. health and medicine in your country
  b. an important problem in your country
  c. the importance of technology in society

9 Edit your outline for unity and coherence, then write the essay.

10 Exchange the essay you wrote in exercise 9 above with a partner. Look for the use of the cohesive devices you have learned about in this unit.

Writing Essays

Review

11 These pairs of sentences need to be joined together to form English proverbs. Choose the best connecting word or phrase to connect each pair. Compare your answers with a partner, and then discuss the possible meaning of each proverb.

a. Don't count your chickens ………… they hatch.

   1. before   **2.** so   **3.** because

b. ………… life gives you lemons, make lemonade.

   1. Before   **2.** When   **3.** Because

c. Time flies ………… you're having fun.

   1. after   **2.** although   **3.** when

d. You can lead a horse to water, ………… you can't make it drink.

   1. and   **2.** but   **3.** or

e. Laugh, ………… the world laughs with you. Cry, ………… you cry alone.

   1. and, but   **2.** and, and   **3.** but, but

f. You don't know what water is worth ………… your well is dry.

   1. because   **2.** after   **3.** until

g. ………… the storm comes a calm.

   1. after   **2.** Because   **3.** Since

h. Don't speak of my debts ………… you intend to pay them.

   1. however   **2.** unless   **3.** moreover

12 Think of one or two proverbs in your language and translate them into English. Share yours with the class. Then choose one of the proverbs and write a paragraph explaining its meaning.

UNITY AND COHERENCE 301

12 Essays For Examinations

In this unit, you will learn …
- common instructions for essay tests.
- techniques for writing timed essays and managing time.

⟳ **Essay tests**

You may be asked to write essays for tests in your classes, or on entrance examinations for colleges and universities in English-speaking countries. You will have to write essays if you take the TOEFL (Test of English as a Foreign Language), the MELAB (Michigan English Language Assessment Battery), Cambridge Assessment (University of Cambridge International and ESOL Examinations), or the IELTS (International English Language Testing System). These essays are written at one sitting, in a limited amount of time.

Timed essays

1 You probably already have some experience and ideas that will be useful to you when you write timed essays. Discuss the following questions with a partner or group.

  a. Have you ever written timed essays in your own language? Describe the situation(s).
  b. Have you ever written timed essays in English? Describe the situation(s).
  c. In what situations will you write timed essays in English in the future?
  d. What are some ways that writing a timed essay is different from writing an essay without a time limit? Make a list. Then look at your list and say which aspects might be challenging for you.
  e. Do you know any good techniques for writing timed essays? Share them with your partner or group.

Instructions for timed essays

⊃ How to write good timed essays

- Check to see how many questions you must answer. Some exams may say *Choose three of the following five topics*. You will not receive a higher score if you write more than three essays—your instructor will probably just grade the first three.
- Check how many points the essay is worth. On a 100-point test, an essay worth twenty points should be longer and more detailed than one worth five points. Spend more time on the longer essays.
- Pay close attention to the instructions for each individual essay question. Be especially careful with questions that have several parts. It is helpful to underline or circle key instructions so that you do not leave anything out.

Example:

In your opinion, what is the <u>Key difference</u> between <u>Chinese medicine</u> and <u>Western medicine</u>? <u>Illustrate</u> this difference with <u>one example</u>.

- Use some of your time for planning (gathering and organizing ideas) and for proofreading your finished essay.
- Always write in complete sentences and pay careful attention to grammar and spelling. Don't experiment with structures or words you are not confident about using correctly.
- Write neatly. Instructors may give lower grades to essays they cannot read easily.

⊃ Common instructions on essay tests

compare / contrast
As you learned in Unit 6, compare / contrast paragraphs talk about similarities and differences. You can write one paragraph to compare and another to contrast, or compare and contrast a different idea related to your topic in each paragraph.

discuss
This broad term invites you to describe different ideas about a topic. Organize your discussion around a central thesis statement.

explain, show how
These instructions ask you to show cause and effect. You may also find instructions like these for a problem / solution essay, as discussed in Unit 7.

show, describe, use examples
Make sure that you provide specific details to support your points, as you practiced in Unit 3.

which
This word asks you to make a choice. Often a question with *which* will also ask you to defend your choice, for example, *Which solution would you recommend, and why?* Make sure that you clearly indicate your choice in your answer. Don't try to write about each possibility.

2 Underline the most important part of the instructions in these essay questions.

12 Writing Essays

Discuss your answers with a partner or group. Talk about what kinds of information you would include in your answer.

a. Compare and contrast public and private high school education in your country.

b. Think of a story you have read which has also been made into a movie. Describe the differences between the two versions.

c. Show how the rise in popularity of communication by cell phone has changed the ways in which young people communicate.

d. Discuss three results of the Norman conquest of Great Britain in 1066. Which do you feel was the most important?

e. Which environmental problem is the most significant in your community? Explain how your community can solve this problem.

Answering directly

Essay test short cuts

Time is limited, so it is a good idea to take certain "short cuts" on essay tests. Most importantly, you should write a very short introduction—just one or two sentences is OK—which includes your thesis statement. Do not include the background information you might normally include in an essay. Make sure that your thesis statement directly answers the question. Your answer should show that you know the information that the test asks about. Extra information or any information that is not related to your topic will not help your grade. Your conclusion should also be brief.

3 Underline the key words of this essay question.

Which effect of the California gold rush do you think had the biggest impact on the character of San Francisco today?

4 Check (✓) the introductions that answer the question in exercise 3 above directly. Write an ✗ by the ones that contain unnecessary information or do not directly address the question. Discuss your answers with a partner.

a. ☐

> San Francisco is a fascinating city with a very special character. Each year, thousands of tourists from the United States and other countries visit San Francisco to enjoy its unique style. Many important events contributed to the character of San Francisco, including the California gold rush, the earthquake of 1906, immigration from Mexico, and the rise of the computer industry. But the gold rush was the most important of these events.

b. ☐

> The effect of the California gold rush that had the biggest impact on the character of San Francisco today was the damage done by the mining to the rivers and surrounding land.

c. ☐

> Experts agree that the California gold rush had an impact on the state of California. In particular, San Francisco was affected by the gold rush. For example, many people came to San Francisco hoping to get rich during the late 1880s. It was a very exciting time.

d. ☐

> The California gold rush affected the character of San Francisco in many ways: the population increased, the crime rate rose, land prices went up, rivers were damaged, and people seeking adventure chose San Francisco as their destination.

e. ☐

> The character of San Francisco as an adventurous city, a place that attracts risk-takers and thrill-seekers, is the most important effect of the California gold rush of the 1880s.

Managing your time

⊃ Write a five-minute outline

Before you write a test essay, write a quick outline. This is the easiest way to be sure that your answer includes all the necessary information and that you don't waste your time with unnecessary information. With practice, you should be able to write a brief outline in no more than five minutes, including the thesis statement and main ideas. Before you write anything else, write your outline at the top of the page. If you run out of time to finish your essay, your instructor will still be able to see your main ideas, and will know that you had a problem with time and not with the content.

Topic: *In college, would you rather live alone, with your family, or with a roommate? Give reasons to support your answer.*

Sample outline 1:

> I. I would rather live with my family to save money.
> II. No rent
> III. Save money on food
> IV. Don't have to pay for utilities
>   A. Electricity
>   B. Water
>   C. Phone
> V. Conclusion: If I save on my living expenses, I will have enough money to pay for tuition and books.

Writing Essays

Sample outline 2:

> I. Living alone is the best way for me to learn independence while I am in college.
> II. Will learn to take care of myself
>   A. Cook my own food
>   B. Take care of housework and laundry
> III. Will learn to budget my money
> IV. Conclusion: College is a time not only to study, but to learn to be an independent adult. Living alone will help me learn how to handle this responsibility.

5 Write a five-minute outline for each of these topics. Write a thesis statement, two or more main ideas, and a conclusion. When you have finished, compare your outlines in groups or with the whole class.

  a. Some people like to organize their own trips, and others like to travel on a professionally organized tour. Which do you prefer, and why?
  b. Your community is considering building a new shopping mall in the center of town. Do you support or oppose this plan? Give specific reasons in your answer.
  c. Discuss why music is an important part of people's lives.
  d. What do you feel will be the most popular career choices for young people in your country in the next five years? Explain your answer with examples.
  e. Compare and contrast sending text messages and talking on the phone. Which do you prefer, and why?

◯ **Write your topic sentences first**

Some students like to first write the topic sentence for each main point on the answer sheet, leaving space to go back and fill in the details. If you choose this method, you can add information and examples to each paragraph until you finish or your time runs out. If you run out of time, you may leave out some details, but you won't leave out any main points.

> Living alone is the best way for me to learn independence while I am in college.
>
> One of the main benefits of living alone will be that I will learn to take care of myself by cooking my own food and doing my own housework and laundry.
>
> Another benefit of living alone will be that I will learn to budget my money.
>
> College is a time not only to study, but to learn to be an independent adult. Living alone will help me learn how to handle this responsibility.

6 For one of the five-minute outlines you wrote for exercise 5 on page 306, write a topic sentence for each main point.

Checking your work

◯ **Check your work**

After you finish your essay, or at least five minutes before your time is up, take some time to check your work. Read the essay from beginning to end. Although you cannot read your essay out loud (unless you are alone), try to "hear" what it would sound like in your head.

- Did you answer all parts of the question?
- Is your essay unified? Cross out any unrelated ideas.
- Are words spelled correctly and written neatly?
- Do your sentences sound clear? If you are not sure if your grammar is correct, try to say your ideas another way.
- Did you erase or cross out any mistakes or stray marks?

7 You have already spent five minutes writing an outline for the topics in exercise 5 on page 306. Now choose one of those topics and spend another twenty minutes writing the essay. Then take five minutes to check your work. Then share your essay with a partner or small group.

12 Writing Essays

Review

8 Work in groups of four. Divide into pairs. Pair A, look at the essay on American and British English in Unit 8, exercise 1 on page 271. Pair B, look at the essay on Chinese medicine in Unit 11, exercise 1 on page 292. Do the following:

- **a.** In pairs, write two or three essay questions about the information presented. Give your essay questions to the other pair.
- **b.** Individually, choose one of the questions the other pair wrote for you and write an answer based on the information given in the essay. You may use your textbook. Write a thirty-minute essay in this way: First, write a five-minute outline. Then, write your essay for twenty minutes. Finally, spend five minutes checking your work.
- **c.** Rejoin your group of four. Take turns reading your essays aloud. After one person reads the essay, the other group members should identify the thesis statement and main ideas. Tell the writer something you liked about the essay.

Additional Materials

Sample essay: brainstorming	**310**
Sample essay: first draft	**311**
Sample essay: second draft	**313**
Punctuation	**315**
Sample information letter	**317**
Sample statement of purpose	**318**
Sample résumé	**319**

Photocopiable Materials

Peer feedback—paragraph	**320**
Peer feedback—essay	**321**

Sample essay: brainstorming

Assignment: Write an argument essay of 2–3 pages. First, choose a topic and brainstorm some ideas. Then, organize your ideas into an outline. After you have checked your outline carefully, write the first draft of your essay. Exchange drafts with a classmate, and give and receive peer feedback. Using those comments to guide you, prepare a final draft.

Remember: all final papers must be typed and double-spaced! Please turn in your brainstorming, outline, and first draft together with your final draft.

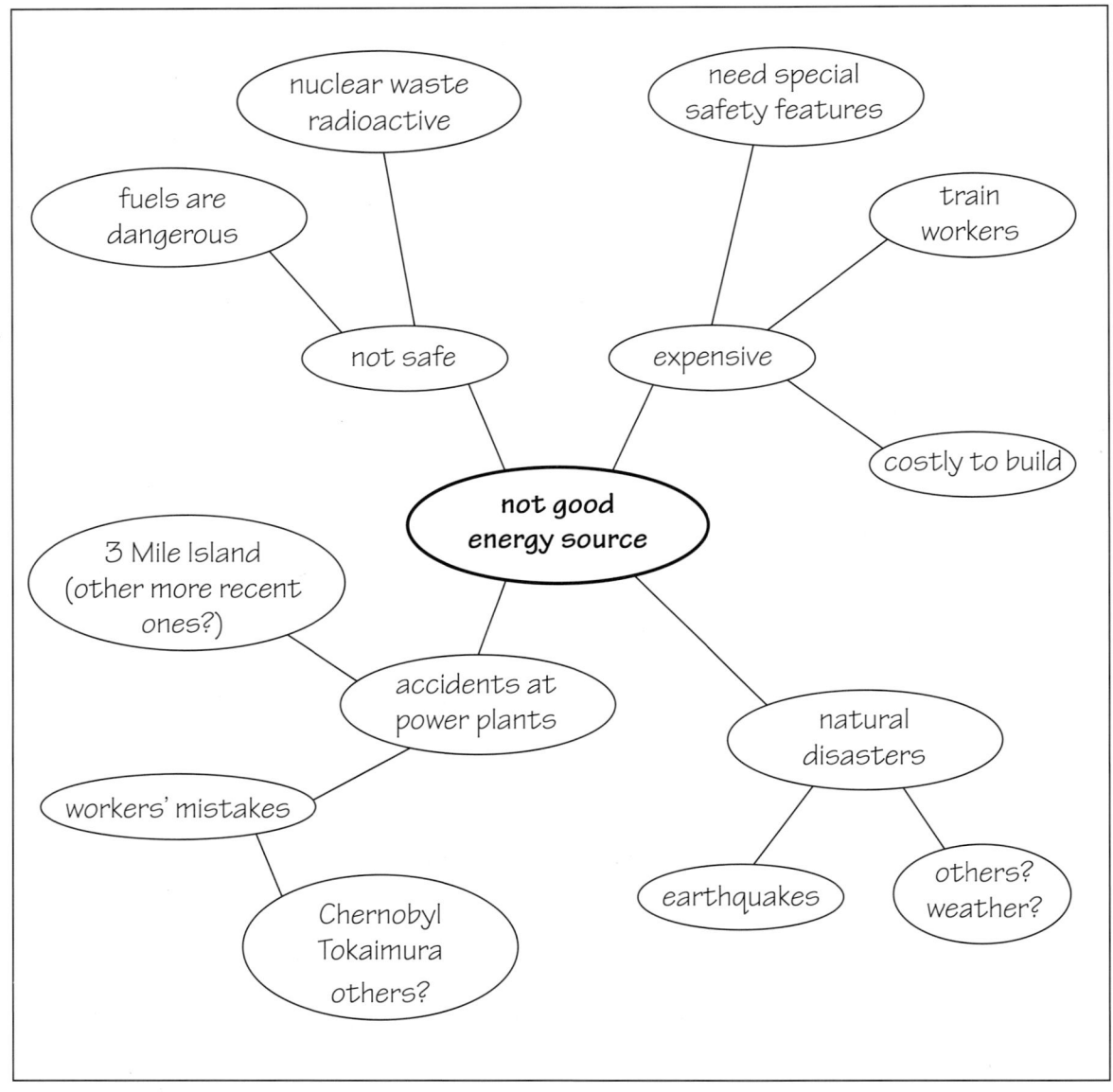

↻ The outline for this sample essay appears on page 279.

310 ADDITIONAL MATERIALS

Sample essay: first draft

○ The comments on the essay were written by one of the writer's classmates.

Don't Support Nuclear Energy!

Can you add some kind of introduction before giving your thesis statement?

Even though it can provide the world with a source of electricity, nuclear power is not a good energy source because it is too expensive, the materials used in

Good thesis statement — very clear

the power plants are not safe, and there is a great possibility of accidents.

Can you add a topic sentence to this paragraph?

First of all, nuclear fuel is expensive. It must be taken out of the ground and transported great distances. As fuels are used up, they will become even more expensive, just as oil and gas have become more expensive. In addition, nuclear

Can you explain this idea a little more?

power plants are expensive to build and to operate. It is expensive to train workers.

Needs transition *You have used "expensive" 5 times in the paragraph ...*

Nuclear materials are not safe. When uranium is taken out of the ground, radioactive gas is released. This is not safe for the miners. Uranium itself is also not

Why is uranium not safe?

safe. Being around uranium is not safe for workers.

Needs transition

Nuclear waste is also dangerous. It is very radioactive, and it is difficult to dispose of it or even to store it safely. *This is a very short paragraph ...*

Nice transition

Most significantly, there is always a possibility of nuclear accidents. The power plants themselves can fail when they get old or if they are not built correctly.

Nice specific example

The machinery can malfunction, too. In 1979, problems at the Three Mile Island nuclear power plant in the United States resulted in radioactive materials escaping into the nearby community. More recently, equipment failures were responsible for

Can you explain what happened at these places?

accidents in power plants in Darlington, Canada (1992) and Sellafield, England (2005).

Can you add a transition?

Workers at nuclear power plants can make mistakes. Perhaps the most famous of these incidents occurred at Chernobyl (in the former U.S.S.R.) in 1986. Radioactivity from the Chernobyl accident was recorded as far away as Eastern

Good detail

Europe, Scandinavia, and even Japan. Human error was responsible for power plant

Are these the only mistakes that have happened?

accidents in Tokaimura, Japan (1999) and Asco, Spain (2007–2008). There is no way we can guarantee that workers will not make mistakes again in the future.

Even natural disasters can affect nuclear power plants. A big storm in the

Can you give some comment about this?

Pacific Ocean in 1982 washed nuclear waste out into the ocean. Earthquakes are a threat, too. In 2011, a strong earthquake damaged several nuclear reactors in Fukushima, Japan.

It is true that oil and gas cannot supply all of the world's energy needs

Good restatement of thesis

much longer. However, we cannot replace them with an energy source that is too expensive and is dangerous from the time the fuels are taken out of the ground and even after the plant is running.

I think you need some kind of concluding sentence. What do you recommend instead of nuclear power?

Good essay! You have a lot of information and specific examples. Your arguments are very clear. Your organization is good, too.

Sample essay: second draft

Carol Chan
Academic Writing
Argument Essay, Second Draft
October 15, 2010

Don't Support Nuclear Energy!

These days, it seems like everyone is worried about how the world will meet its energy demands when we have run out of oil and natural gas. Scientists and researchers are investigating such power sources as solar energy, wind energy, and even energy from hot rocks beneath the earth's surface. However, there is one energy source that I believe should not be developed any further. In fact, I believe that we should stop using it as soon as possible. Even though it can provide the world with a source of electricity, nuclear power is not a good energy source because it is too expensive, the materials used in the power plants are not safe, and there is a great possibility of accidents.

Nuclear power is not an economical energy source. First of all, nuclear fuel is expensive. It must be taken out of the ground and transported great distances. As fuels are used up, they will become even more expensive, just as oil and gas have. In addition, nuclear power plants cost a lot of money to build and to operate because of the great care that must be taken with safety. Because the people who work in nuclear power plants must be highly trained specialists, salaries for workers are also high.

In addition to being expensive, nuclear materials are not safe. When uranium is taken out of the ground, radioactive gas is released. This is not safe for the miners. Uranium itself also is not safe because of its high radioactivity. Because of this, people who work with nuclear fuels are at risk of cancer. As nuclear power plants run, they create nuclear waste, which also is dangerous. It is very radioactive, and it is difficult to dispose of or even to store safely. No town wants nuclear waste buried nearby, and for good reason.

Most significantly, there is always a possibility of nuclear accidents. The power plants themselves can fail when they get old or if they are not built correctly. The machinery can malfunction, too. In 1979, problems at the Three Mile Island nuclear power plant in the United States resulted in radioactive materials escaping into the nearby community. More recently, equipment failures were responsible for accidents in power plants in Darlington, Canada, in 1992, and Sellafield, England, in 2005. Both of these accidents led to leaks of radioactive material.

It is not just buildings and equipment which can fail, but people, too. Workers at nuclear power plants can make mistakes. Perhaps the most famous of these incidents occurred at Chernobyl, in the former U.S.S.R., in 1986. Radioactivity from the Chernobyl accident was recorded as far away as Eastern Europe, Scandinavia, and even Japan. Human error has been responsible for numerous power plant accidents. Some recent well-known examples include Tokaimura, Japan, in 1999, where untrained, unqualified workers prepared some fuel incorrectly, and Asco, Spain, where a radioactive leak that started in 2007 was not reported until 2008. There is no way we can guarantee that workers will not make mistakes again in the future.

Even natural disasters can affect nuclear power plants. A big storm in the Pacific Ocean in 1981 washed nuclear waste from Mururoa out into the ocean. In 2011, a strong earthquake damaged several nuclear reactors in Fukushima, Japan. It is impossible for people to predict or to prevent events like this. Different types of severe weather or natural disasters can strike almost anywhere in the world and they can cause disastrous nuclear accidents.

It is true that oil and gas cannot supply all of the world's energy needs much longer. However, we must not replace them with another non-renewable energy source that is expensive and dangerous, from the time the fuels are taken out of the ground to even after the plant is running. Instead, we must develop cheaper and, most importantly, safer types of energy to power our world.

Punctuation

Here are some common rules for using punctuation in your writing. Of course, this is not a complete list. If you have further questions, check a grammar book or ask your teacher.

Capitalization

Always capitalize:

- the first word of every sentence.
- days of the week (*Tuesday*) and months of the year (*April*).
- the first letter (only) of the names of people and places (*Bangkok*, *Ayaka Seo*).
- the main words of a title, but not articles (*a*, *an*, *the*) or prepositions (words like *to*, *of*, *for*) or conjunctions (*and*, *but*), unless they are the first word in the title:
  The Three Things I Do in the Morning

Period (.)

A period comes at the end of a statement:

> An electronic dictionary is more convenient than a paper one.

If the sentence ends with an abbreviation, don't use more than one period:

> RIGHT: My mother just finished her Ph.D.
> WRONG: My mother just finished her Ph.D..

Comma (,)

Use a comma to separate a series of three or more items:

> I take a dictionary, a notebook, and some paper to class every day.

Use a comma before words like *and, but, or, so,* and *yet* to separate two parts of a sentence that each have a subject and a verb.

> She needed some work experience, *so* she got a part-time job.
> He did not study at all, *but* he still got an 87 on the test.

Use a comma after an introductory word or expression, such as *However, Therefore*, and *In conclusion*:

> However, the high price of electric cars means that most people cannot afford one.

Quotation marks (" ")

Use quotation marks when you handwrite the title of a book or movie:

> "Hamlet" was written by Shakespeare.

When you use a word processor, you should use italics instead:

> *Hamlet* was written by Shakespeare.

Use quotation marks to show the exact words someone spoke or wrote:

> The professor announced, "We're going to have an exam next week."
> Shakespeare wrote, "All the world's a stage."

Do not use quotation marks if you're reporting what another person said:

> The professor said that we should study hard this week.

Note: *That*, as used in the sentence above, usually indicates that the remark is not a direct quotation.

Punctuation when using quotation marks

If you are using expressions like *he said* or *the girl remarked* after the quotation, then use a comma and not a period at the end of the quoted sentence:

"We're going to have an exam next week," announced the professor.

Use a period if the quoted sentence comes at the end:

The professor announced, "We're going to have an exam next week."

Notice how a comma is used after *announced*, above, to introduce the quotation.

Periods and commas are placed inside quotation marks. Exclamation points and question marks may come inside or outside, depending on whether they are part of the quotation or part of the surrounding sentence:

"Do you know who wrote *Hamlet*?" asked the teacher.

Do you know who said "All the world's a stage"?

Quotation marks and capitalization

Capitalize the first letter of the word that begins a quotation. However, if an expression like *she said* interrupts the quotation and divides the sentence, then do not capitalize the first word of the part that finishes the quotation:

"Next week," said the professor, "we are going to have an exam."

The comma after *week* separates the quotation from the test of the sentence.

Use a capital letter only if the second part is a new, complete sentence:

"We'll have an exam next week," explained the teacher. "It will take thirty minutes."

Advice for academic writing

The following are not usually used in academic writing, although they are fine in informal situations, such as letters to your friends.

- Parentheses that give information which is not part of your main sentence:

    Cell phones are useful (and besides, I think they look great).

    If your idea is important, it should be in a sentence of its own. If it is not important, it should not be in your paper.

- The abbreviation *etc.* to continue a list. Instead, use a phrase like *such as* in your sentence:

    Students in my university come from countries such as China, India, and Australia.

- Exclamation points (!). Instead, write strong sentences with plenty of details to show your reader your feelings:

    Angel Falls is one of the most spectacular natural wonders you will ever see.

- An ellipsis (…) at the end of a sentence, to show that the sentence is not finished:

    The professor said that I should study hard, so …

    Instead, finish your sentence:

    The professor said that I should study, so I should not go to the party tonight.

Sample information letter

10-6-14-105 Sakura-cho ←——————— *Sender's address*
Setagaya-ku
Tokyo, Japan 332-3322
E-mail: sakura@ttt.ne.jp

February 15, 2011 ←——————— *Date the letter was written*

Admissions Office ←——————— *Receiver's address*
Central Michigan University
Mt. Pleasant, MI 48859
U.S.A.

To Whom It May Concern: ←——————— *Greeting*

I am writing to express an interest in the Intensive English Program at your university, which I learned of while searching on the Internet. ←——————— *Introduction*

I would appreciate any information you could provide about your program. I am interested in studying English for one semester, so I would like to know more about the courses you offer, the number of hours of study per week, and the tuition cost.

In addition, it would be helpful if you could provide information about housing. I am interested in learning as much as I can about the culture, so if it is possible, I would like to live with a family. ⎯⎯ *Body*

Thank you in advance for your time and help. I look forward to receiving more information about your program. ←——————— *Conclusion*

Sincerely, ←——————— *Closing*

Shinichi Usuda ←——————— *Signature*

Shinichi Usuda ←——————— *Sender's name*

Sample statement of purpose

What is a statement of purpose?

When you apply to a college or university in the United States for an undergraduate or graduate degree, you are often asked to write a one-page statement of purpose. This is a short essay that tells the university why you are applying, and also why you would be a good addition to their program. The essay below is from a Taiwanese student wishing to enter a Master's Degree (M.A.) program in Teaching English as a Second Language at Western Arizona University in the United States.

> I have been interested in English since I was twelve, when my family took a trip to Australia. I thought then how useful and exciting it would be to talk to the people I met. It was not only the Australians who spoke English, but also other tourists we met who had traveled there from all over the world. Whether they were from Germany, Indonesia, or Brazil, their common language was English, and I wanted to share that language with them.
>
> I worked hard at my English studies in junior high school and high school. I was a member of our school's English Conversation Club, and in my last year I was secretary of the club. I also took part in the national English Speech Contest for three years.
>
> In college, I majored in English literature. I also took English conversation lessons at a private school two evenings a week. In addition, I made friends with some of the international students at my college, and we always spoke together in English. During my last two years at college, I took a part-time job tutoring elementary and junior high school students in English grammar and conversation.
>
> Because of my long interest in English and my experience teaching English, I am sure that I would like to become an ESL teacher. I have chosen to study in the United States so that I can also learn about the culture of an English-speaking country. I have heard about Western Arizona University from other graduates, and I am impressed with the classes offered there and the quality of instruction. I think I would be a valuable addition to your ESL program because I could share my own experiences with learning English. I look forward to the opportunity to further my own knowledge of English and of American culture, and to meeting the challenges of both learning and teaching with the other students in your program.

Sample résumé

TITIRAT JINAPHAN
225 Soi Pracharak 33
Phachachuen Road
Don Muang
Bangkok, Thailand 10210
Tel. (662) 954-8081
E-mail: tj26@bangkok.com

WORK OBJECTIVE

To obtain a job working in management and marketing for an international company.

EDUCATION

CENTRAL MICHIGAN UNIVERSITY, Mt. Pleasant, Michigan, U.S.A., May 2011
Master of Science in Administration
Concentration: General Administration (Business Management and Marketing)
Activities: World Connection Program (matches international students and American students for language and cultural exchanges), Family Friendship Program (introduction to American lifestyle and culture)

THAMMASAT UNIVERSITY, Bangkok, Thailand, February 2008
Bachelor of Law (J.D. equivalent)
Activities: Law Students' Organization, Soccer Team

OTHER CERTIFICATES

CENTRAL MICHIGAN UNIVERSITY, Mt. Pleasant, Michigan, U.S.A., December 2010
SAP R/3 Enterprise Software Certificate (integrated enterprise software applications)

ENGLISH LANGUAGE INSTITUTE, Mt. Pleasant, Michigan, U.S.A., May 2009
Certificate from the English Language Program for International Students at Central Michigan University

WORK EXPERIENCE

CENTRAL MICHIGAN UNIVERSITY, Mt. Pleasant, Michigan, U.S.A., September 2010–May 2011
Computer Lab Assistant
- Assisted in maintaining lab equipment.
- Responsible for answering questions for the Computer Help Desk.
- Provided assistance to students using the lab.

SAPAKORN, Nakhonsawan, Thailand (Corporate Farming Business), April 2004–May 2008
Personal Assistant to the Owners / Sales Representative
- Responsible for sales and delivery of farming materials and supplies to farmers.
- Conducted banking and financial transactions, including payroll distribution.
- Coordinated and supervised staff of ten in janitorial and materials management.
- Developed and analyzed marketing strategies for the sales of agricultural products.
- Arranged and executed the purchase of inventory essential to business.

ADDITIONAL SKILLS

Languages: Thai (native), English (fluent, both written and oral).
Computer: Lexis-Nexis, Westlaw, Microsoft Office, SPSS, SAP Enterprise Software, Internet Applications.

Peer feedback – paragraph

Writer's name: ....

Reader's name: ....

Assignment: ....

1. What is the topic of the paragraph? What is the main idea?

2. Does the paragraph have a topic sentence? If so, write it here:

3. Does each sentence support the topic sentence? If not, which sentence or sentences do not belong?

4. Does the paragraph have a concluding sentence? If so, does it restate the topic sentence or sum up the information?

5. Are there any places where the writer could add more details? Do you have any questions for the writer?

6. What are some good things about this paragraph?

Peer feedback – essay

Writer's name: ....

Reader's name: ....

Assignment: ....

1. What is the topic of the essay? What is the main idea?

2. Read the introduction. Is it interesting? Does it give some background information? Does it include a thesis statement? If so, write it here:

3. Does each body paragraph support the thesis statement? Write the topic sentence of each body paragraph here:

4. Are there any places where the writer could add more details? Do you have any questions for the writer?

5. Is there a conclusion to the essay? Does it restate the thesis or sum up the information or flow logically from the ideas in the essay? Does it contain any new points?

6. What are some good things about this essay?

Notes

Notes

Notes

Notes

Notes

Next step…

Have you seen the fourth title in the successful Macmillan Writing Series?

Writing Research Papers is a new title in the Macmillan Writing Series. It introduces students to academic writing and shows them how to research an academic essay, cite references and put a paper together.

To order your copy go to:

http://www.macmillanenglish.com/products/macmillan-writing-series-writing-research-papers/

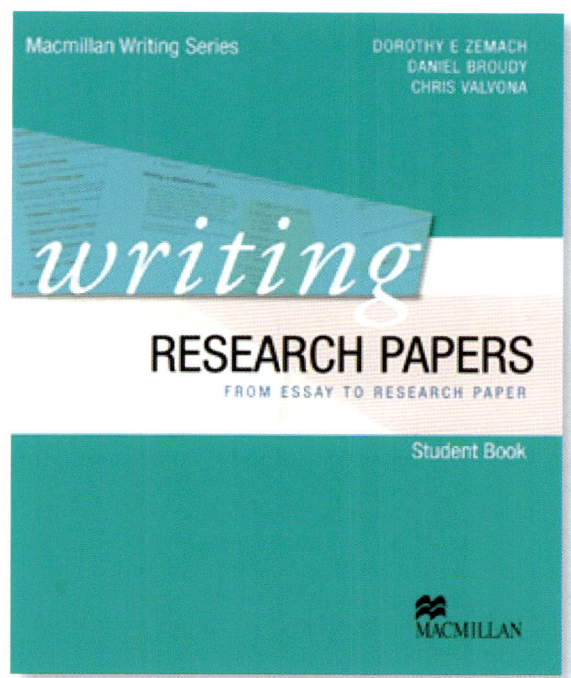

Macmillan Education
4 Crinan Street
London N1 9XW
A division of Macmillan Publishers Limited
Companies and representatives throughout the world

ISBN 978-1-786-32328-6

Text © Dorothy E Zemach, Carlos Islam & Lisa A. Ghulldu 2016

Design and illustration © Macmillan Publishers Limited 2016

The authors have asserted their rights to be identified as the authors of this work in accordance with the Copyright, Designs and Patents Act 1988.

First published 2016

All rights reserved; no part of this publication may be reproduced, stored in a retrieval system, transmitted in any form, or by any means, electronic, mechanical, photocopying, recording, or otherwise, without the prior written permission of the publishers.

Note to Teachers
Photocopies may be made, for classroom use, of pages 202-209 and 320-321 without the prior written permission of Macmillan Publishers Limited. However, please note that the copyright law, which does not normally permit multiple copying of published material, applies to the rest of this book.

Designed by xen and by Amanda Easter Design Ltd
Page make-up by xen
Illustrated by Jackson Graham, John Graham, Sophie Grillet, Ciaran Hughes, Will Mitchell, Start Perry, Val Saunders and Vicky Woodgate
Cover design by xen based on a design by Jackie Hill at 320 Design
Cover illustration/photograph by xen

The authors and publishers would like to thank the following for permission to reproduce their photographs:
Alamy/David Ball/Alamy Stock Photo p24(l), Alamy/Blaine Harrington III/Alamy Stock Photo p77(ml), Alamy/INTERFOTO/Alamy Stock Photo p282, Alamy/Michael Klinec Alamy Stock Photo p298, Alamy/Frans Lanting Studio/Alamy Stock Photo p39(bl), Alamy/SAV/Alamy Stock Photo p82, Alamy/Iain Masterton/Alamy Stock Photo p54(b), Alamy/Jack Sullivan/Alamy Stock Photo p280; **Bananastock** p9(br), pp13, 83, 116, 165, 231; **Brand X** pp135, 94, 239(r); **Corbis** pp27(l), 42, 74, 76(m), 139(tr), 225, 242(bl), 289(tm), Corbis/Corbis/Jack Hollingsworth p306, Corbis/Denis Scott p39(tl); **Creatas** p70; **DigitalStock**/Corbis pp24(r), 62 (bl), DigitalStock p272; **DigitalVision** pp41(l), 46, 62(ml), 139(br); **Getty Images** pp9(bm), 77 (bg), 80, 124, 127(l, m), 130, 169, 242(t), 257(b), 265, 289, Getty Images/Walter Bibikow/AWL Images p300, Getty Images/Getty Images Entertainment 10(br), Getty Images/Emmanuel Faure/The Imagebank p54(m), Getty Images/iStockphoto/Oleksiy Mark p255, Getty Images/Jason LaVeris/FilmMagic p10(bl), Getty Images/Manuel Queimadelos Alonso p141, Getty Images/Frank Siteman/age fotostock p54(t), Getty Images/Juan Carlos Vindas/Moment Open p39(br); **Image Source** pp9(bl), 27(r), 32, 42(m), 42(b), 57, 62(mr), 127(r), 139(tl, bl), 164, 228, 229, 247, 252, 257(t), 274, 289(br); **Macmillan Publishers Ltd** p27(m), 79, p289(bm); **Photoalto** p279; **Photodisc** pp20, 26, 41(r), 42(t), 62(tl, tr), 75, 76(l, r), 77(l), 97, 123, 154, 172, 242(br), 244, Photodisc/Getty Images pp34, 240-241, 246; **REX/Shutterstock**/Walt Disney/Everett p89, REX/Shutterstock/ImageBROKER p144, REX/Shutterstock/Moviestore Collection p251, REX/Shutterstock/James Emmerson/Robert Harding p290; Shutterstock/Africa Studio p81, Shutterstock/ChameleonsEye p77(br), Shutterstock/Thanthima Lim p77(mr), Shutterstock/wavebreakmedia p155; Stockdisc p146; Superstock/Juniors pp39(tr), 239(l).
These materials may contain links for third party websites. We have no control over, and are not responsible for, the contents of such third party websites. Please use care when accessing them.

Printed and bound in Thailand

2020 2019 2018 2017 2016
10 9 8 7 6 5 4 3 2 1

writing SKILLS

TOWARDS ACADEMIC WRITING

The Macmillan Writing Series is a four-level course that systematically develops learners' writing from the basics of sentence construction through to writing academic research papers. The books take a process approach that helps students:

- generate and organize their ideas
- draft, review, and revise their written work
- become confident and accomplished writers

This practical course takes students of all levels through the writing process: brainstorming, organizising ideas, drafting and revising, and publishing. Students at the lower levels focus on accuracy in forming sentences, organising paragraphs, and including appropriate language. At the upper levels, students focus on different academic genres, developing their ideas in a variety of ways, and incorporating outside information to support their original ideas.

Dorothy E. Zemach

Macmillan Writing Skills brings together three titles of the Macmillan Writing Series into one volume. *Writing Sentences* and *Writing Paragraphs* retain the focus on general writing skills, while at the higher level in *Writing Essays* the focus is specifically on academic writing.

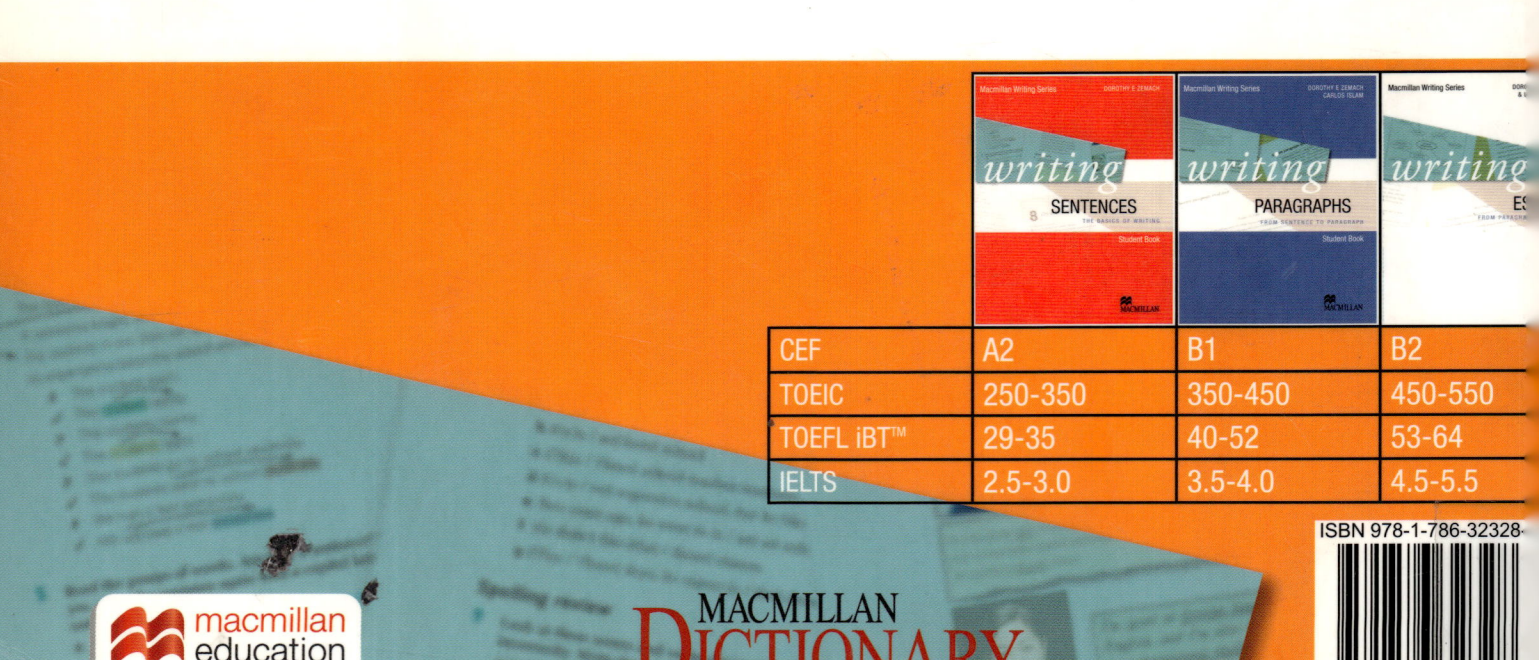

CEF	A2	B1	B2
TOEIC	250-350	350-450	450-550
TOEFL iBT™	29-35	40-52	53-64
IELTS	2.5-3.0	3.5-4.0	4.5-5.5

ISBN 978-1-786-32328

macmillan education
www.macmillanenglish.com

MACMILLAN **Dictionary**